THE HISTORY OF IMAGE GATHERING

An oral history that recounts the evolution of the art and technology of capturing real life images for TV News and "reality type" show production from 1954-2015

I0493490

Robin E. Hirsch

Brickwall Publishing
Westlake Village, California

For information contact: brickwallpub@gmail.com

Cover designed by Janna Bock
Edited by Diana Gonzalez

DEDICATION AND THANKS

This book is dedicated to Larry Greene and Randy Fairburn, two incredible image gatherers who paid the ultimate price while doing the work that they loved. RIP brothers our story has now been told.

Special thanks and acknowledgement to all of those in my image gathering family who assisted me in the writing of this history. They provided their personal stories and permission to use their pictures which are included in this book.

Table of Contents

evolved to where it was practical to take video cameras out into the field. It also takes describes how the image gatherers put down their film gear, picked up video cameras, and made the many necessary adjustments that came with this new technology both in shooting and editing. Also included are some really good stories of the trials and tribulations of faced by our stalwart image gatherers as they wrestled with this thing called videotape.

PART IV
ENG and Network News Coverage

Part IV takes a look at how electronic image gathering revolutionized network news coverage. Included are some amazing stories of how the early pioneers, with their "can-do" attitude, came up with some incredible solutions to logistical problems. It also describes how the TV networks inspired the growth of the world of freelance camera men and women, and made successful entrepreneurs out of those willing to take the plunge.

PART V
Image Gathering Goes Prime Time

Part V examines how these TV News magazine shows morphed into something bigger that ultimately led the image gatherers and their video cameras from news coverage to prime time television production. It discusses some of the shows that led the way and how the image gatherers adapted their skills to new image gathering opportunities and challenges.

PART VI
Betacam

Part VI discusses the impact of Betacam format videotape on image gathering and how it broke down the final barriers to all-electronic prime time shows shot on location. It describes how Betacam took videotape from the limited world of taped segments, to a production tool that met network standards for an entire show. It also takes a look at how this new format helped fill the time slots of the growing Cable TV timeslots. Finally, Part VI describes how mini-technology arrived and inspired even more applications that ultimately created even more new opportunities and challenges for the image gatherers

PART VII
Technology's Next Steps

Part VII discusses new cameras, new formats and beyond. Once technology made the leap from the manual world of film to the electronic world of videotape, the rules of the game changed. Electronic media did not have any restrictions. It could go as far as research would take it, which essentially is as far as human imagination can travel. However, as Part VII concludes, with all this technology the challenge of creating truthful images has never been greater. How will the next generation handle this new found power?

PROLOGUE

Before we get started…
What is an image gatherer?

I am an image gatherer. For thirty-nine years I peered through the lens of my camera, pressed a button, and rolled on life as it moved past my eye. Oh, the sights I have seen in my viewfinder. I have recorded every imaginable facet of the human condition and in doing so, gathered an incredible array of real life images.

I have recorded images of war, race riots, plane crashes, and devastation caused by the forces of nature. Of course there were also the sexy hot babes wiggling and jiggling, murderers in prison pleading their innocence, tattooed jocks with muscles rippling, millionaires and billionaires, people in emotional crisis, Hollywood's finest, and everything in between. My gathered images have been seen by millions of people, on the evening news, TV magazine shows, reality shows, and documentaries.

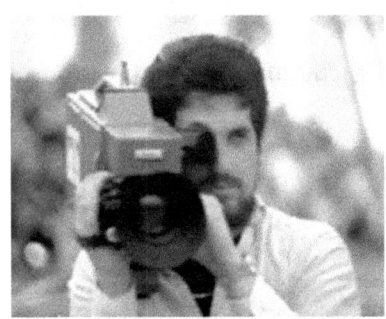

As an image gatherer my task each day was to take my camera and tell the story of a person, place, or event. The people I shot were not actors. They said what they said, walked where they walked, and did what they did. My challenge was to artfully gather their images without controlling their actions. Care still had to be given to proper exposure, composition, and lighting, but the images were always gathered, not directed. This has always been the case in my profession which actually dates back to over forty thousand years ago when our prehistoric ancestors painted images on the walls of their caves. Basically, they did the same thing that I did. It is only the technology that has changed.

The unique aspect of my career was the fact that in my thirty-nine years in the industry, I have witnessed more profound technological change in a shorter time period than has ever been experienced in the entire human image gathering experience. I began my career shooting 16mm film, moved on to videotape and electronic cameras, and finally ended up shooting discs and recording hi-def digitally onto drives. I have shot with close to twenty different types of cameras and five different recording formats. Each format came with advantages and disadvantages that challenged me, and my generation to make major adjustments on the fly. It was an interesting and exciting four decades.

The *History of Image Gathering* is the story of my generation's incredible image gathering journey as told through the thoughts and words of those who were there to see it. I want to give future generations a first hand account of how the modern image gathering business got started, grew, and progressed. This is my generation's account of how we used to do it, how the technological breakthroughs evolved, and how they were folded into the artful side of image gathering.

This is the story of my image gathering generation.

Robin E. Hirsch
2015

In the beginning…

Image gathering began about forty thousand years ago, when our prehistoric ancestors began to draw pictures on the walls of their caves. They were reflecting a basic human instinct to gather the images of their life and times. Over the years many civilizations came and went that all displayed this same tendency leaving behind a legacy of images depicting great events from their histories.

Twenty-five hundred years ago, the game began to change when a Chinese philosopher/scientists named Mo-Ti described a unique optical event that occurs when light passes through a tiny pinhole in the wall of a darkened room and casts an inverted image of the outside on the opposite wall of the room. Mo-Ti called this darkened room the "collecting place". Today, we know it as a pin hole camera. At any rate, this was the beginning of a steady march forward to where we are today.

What follows is an historical timeline that follows the development of image gathering from Mo-Ti's collecting place up to the 1950's which is when my generation began to gather images. That's where our oral history will pick up the story.

Image Gathering Historical Timeline: 1590-1954

Over the next two thousand years following Mo-Ti many scientific thinkers, from Aristotle to Leonardo da Vinci, observed this same phenomenon and wrote about it extensively. They were intrigued, but they really could not figure out what was going on or what to do with it. This all changed in the late 1500's. Technology had evolved by then that could be used to further the investigation. Scientists of the day began to make inroads in explaining exactly what was going on and how it could all be used to create real life images.

1590's: An Italian scholar named Giambattista della Porta places a glass lens over the pinhole and notes that when the image is projected through the lens into that darkened chamber it becomes significantly sharper, though still inverted. This is later corrected by projecting the image into a mirror.

1604: German scholar Johannes Kepler names this pin hole device "camera obscura" which is Latin for darkened chamber. The obscura part is eventually dropped leaving us with the name camera.

1826: French inventor Nicephore Niepce focuses the image from a camera obscura onto an 8x10 pewter plate coated with a substance called bitumen of Judea. He exposes the plate for eight hours. When he washes away the unburned bitumen Niepce is left with the world's first photograph. A British scientist named Sir John F.W. Herschel, coins the term photography, which is Greek for "drawn by light."

1839: French inventor Louis Daguerre improves the process by using a silver plated copper plate to create a photograph he called a daguerreotype. Its main drawback though is that it can only produce a single picture.

1840's: The daguerreotype process is made faster and easier leading to the development of a new profession, portrait photographer. A young man named Matthew Brady opens up a shop in Washington DC. He is credited with the first photograph of a sitting president when he photographs James K Polk.

1851: British sculptor Frederick Scott Archer develops a wet place or collodion process that creates a translucent negative image that can be duplicated in photographic prints. Thee translucent images can be used to print multiple copies of a single image.

1861: With the outbreak of the Civil War, Washington DC photographer Matthew Brady gains permission from President Lincoln to chronicle the conflict with photographs. Brady and his staff of photographers gather thousands of images from the battlefields. His effort earns Brady the title "Father of Photojournalism." Brady said, "My greatest aim has been to advance the art of photography and to make it what I think I have, a great and truthful medium of history."

1870's: Gaspard-Felix "Nadar" Tournachon goes up in a hot air balloon in Paris to shoot the first aerial photograph. Julia Margaret Cameron is among the first women to enter the field as a portrait photographer.

1878: Photographer Eadweard Muybridge uses twelve cameras with trip wires to record a running horse. When played back in his Zoopraxiscope the images blend together in a motion picture. It is available to view on YouTube.

1880: The Daily Graphic, a New York City newspaper, publishes the first newspaper photograph.

1883: George Eastman invents the film roll and the first consumer camera he calls the Kodak. There is no great meaning to the name, he just liked the way it sounded.

1888: French inventor Louis Le Prince shoots the first moving picture with a single lens camera that he invented. Called the Roundhay Garden Scene, the movie is shot on a gelatin based paper film made by Kodak. It is available to view on YouTube.

1891-1896: Movie cameras and projection systems begin to emerge culminating in Thomas Edison's Vitascope. Moments of life caught on film called "actuality films" and "scenics" are presented to the paying public in theaters theaters.

1903: Edison presents *The Great Train Robbery*, the first plot driven motion picture. Written and directed by Edwin S. Porter, the film is shot on a budget of $150. You can check it out on YouTube.

1908: The Pathe brothers introduce newsreels, which begin to appear prior to the feature films in movie theaters. These are short films that present news, sports, and human-interest stories from all over the world. They are a precursor to TV News stories. They take photo journalism into the realm of motion pictures and represent the beginning of the marriage of factual story telling to moving images. A narrator is later added with the advent of sound.

1913: A German company called Leica produces a small, single lens reflex camera that shoots 35mm stills. It is very light and easily transported and opens up the world to photography.

1914: Photojournalism magazines like National Geographic begin to emerge culminating with Life magazine in the 1930's.

1927: Philo Farnsworth files for a patent for a camera tube he calls a "television system". The national radio networks grab onto the concept and develop TV networks.

1928-1954: Over the next several decades, TV grows rapidly and virtually takes over the entertainment and information business. It becomes the place to be for image gatherers who had never before been able to gain such wide distribution for their filmed images. Millions of people around the world watch TV every day on TV sets that looked something like this old Admiral. Though the TV's were small and certainly crude by today's standards it all seemed miraculous to the viewing public..

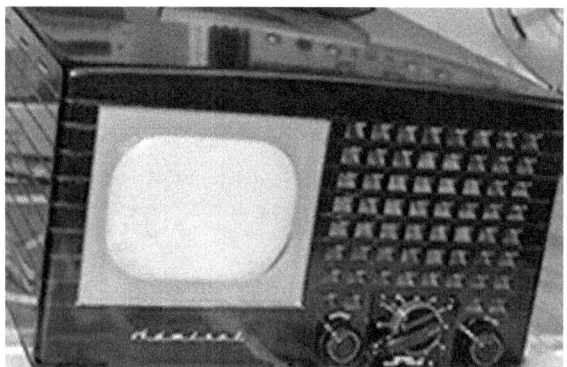

PART I
The Early Days of TV News Image Gathering

INTRODUCTION

My career as an image gatherer began in 1973. That was the year I graduated college and got a job as a cameraman for television station WTVJ in Miami, Florida. During my tenure there, I was fortunate to have had the opportunity to work with several of the early TV News image gathering pioneers that started their careers in the 1950's and early 1960's. They were the staff veterans when I was a raw rookie. They loved to tell their tales and I loved to listen.

When I first began to write this history, those old veterans were the first resource I called upon. Many had passed on, but fortunately some were still around and able to contribute their memories and photos to this history. I also contacted several of my more current image gathering colleagues who were happy to do the same. I bundled them all up along with my personal experiences and labeled them Recollections. They are included throughout this history as they complement the more factual descriptions I have provided on these pages.

Part I will take a look at the early years of TV News image gathering. It will take us from the 1950's up to 1970. It will include a discussion of the who, what, when, and where of those early days. Part I will also include a description of how TV News image gathering organized itself, created specific job descriptions, and took the high road to insure honesty and integrity in the process.

The year is 1954 and this is how TV News image gathering was done back then.

PART I
Chapter One
Early TV News Image Gathering

By 1954 the public had learned that it was one thing to read about poverty, war, or natural disasters in the newspaper, but seeing images on TV was an altogether different experience that brought the story to life and into homes across America. "We interrupt this program" soon became a part of TV's lexicon and a reason for entire families to race into their "TV room" to see what was going on.

On the technical side, all TV News images were gathered on 16mm film which was manufactured by the Eastman Kodak Company, or as it was better known, Kodak. There were basically two main film camera equipment manufacturing companies named Auricon and Frezzolini that had each developed 16mm film single system sound cameras.

The cameras shot the film and recorded audio on a mag stripe embedded in the film. These cameras became the go-to TV News image gathering tools. Adapted from their 35mm cousins, they were big, heavy, and unwieldy with big, heavy, and unwieldy batteries to match. They were a far cry from the light, easy to grab and run film cameras that were to come later.

In the archival photo on the next page you can see the effort it took just to move the Auricon Pro 600 around. This cameraman was covering government news in the state capital. Since they had to move from office to office, the cameraman was better off building his camera and tripod on some type of a warehouse dolly. Since it took so much time to put it all together, it was easier to roll it to where you needed it than to take it apart, pack it up, and put it back together again in another office.

Since necessity is the mother of invention, camera crews were especially pressed to come up with creative solutions like you see in the picture to get these big cameras where they needed to be in the timely manner that news demands. In this case the camera was rolled around on a warehouse dolly. Hey, don't laugh it worked pretty well all things considered. It was certainly a better solution than take it all a part and putting it all back together again ten times per day.

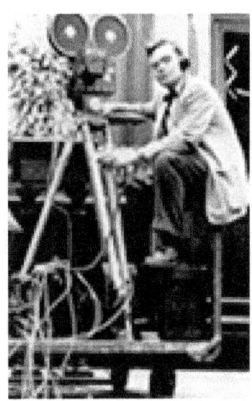

Fortunately, there was a smaller, easier to use camera manufactured by a company called Bell & Howell that could be used for breaking news TV News coverage, The Filmo as it was called was the go-to choice for image gathering that did not require audio, which was pretty much anything that was not an interview, or a reporter standup. Small, light, and easy to operate, Bell & Howell had first rolled out its Filmo, in the 1920's. Back then they were a popular tool for newsreels and later, during World War II, the they became the standard motion picture camera for shooting combat footage for the military. Many an armed forces camera crew stormed the beaches with Filmo in hand.

When TV News came along in the 1950's, Filmos fit in perfectly. Their ability to gather on the fly images made them indispensable. They were too small to use a zoom lens, but they had three different lenses mounted on a turret so all you had to do was rotate that turret to change lenses from wide to tight to telephoto. It took mere seconds to make the change.

In addition, the camera was powered by a wind up spring, so there were no batteries to drag around. The Bell & Howell Filmo could go anywhere and do anything. As you can see in the archival photo below, you could even shoot it while wearing sunglasses. Yes, really. Since you were looking through a range finder not the actual lens, if you were outside and your iris was stopped down you could still easily see what you were shooting even with sunglasses on.

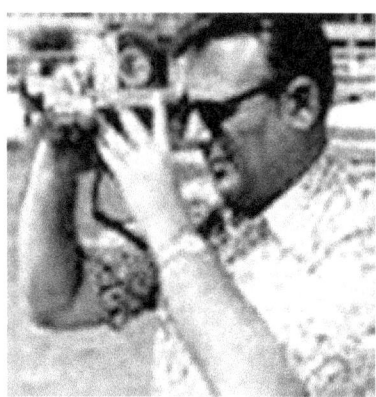

Whichever camera you used, shooting 16mm news film was not for the faint hearted. It was a manual process that required a depth of knowledge and great attention to detail to consistently master. It all started with the loading of the camera. This had to be done in a very precise manner, especially for the sound cameras which first required that the film was loaded into magazines. Then it had to be carefully hand threaded through a series of rollers and sprockets.

Film exposure was also set manually. You relied on a light meter to determine exposure, then manually set the iris ring to the correct F-stop. Color temperature was at best an educated guess, but a critically important one. All film was color balanced to either daylight or tungsten light. Filters were needed to color correct. If you misjudged this, your film could be a horrible shade of blue or orange. All of these factors had to be calmly calculated as you walked backwards shooting a bad guy who didn't want his picture taken. This was news not a Hollywood film set so every facet of shooting news film had to be instinctual.

Then there was a weight issue. Lightweight metal alloys did not exist so all the film gear of this era was very heavy. You had to be physically strong enough to throw a big, bulky sound camera on one shoulder and a heavy wooden tripod on the other, and race across a field to set up for an interview. You also had to be mentally tough enough to be able to pay close attention to all the details of shooting 16mm film while staying oblivious to danger and emotionless amidst other people's pain and suffering.

There really never has been a way to learn how to shoot TV News in a classroom, not even close. With 16mm film it was even more so. Experience alone sharpened your skills as you learned mainly by doing. This was something many college grads armed with their journalism degrees were about to find out as they tumbled out of their college journalism programs during this time period. TV News was a hot job market.

In the 1950's however, most TV News departments stuck a camera in your hand first and told you to go shoot your stories. Moat college grads had all taken classes, and "shot film", although they soon learned that doing it in the real world of TV News was a very different story.

First up to tell his story is a friend of mine named Gordon Stevens. Yes, that is Gordon in the picture below shooting with longtime WTVJ anchorman Ralph Renick, and yes back then cameramen wore coats and ties even in Miami's heat and humidity.

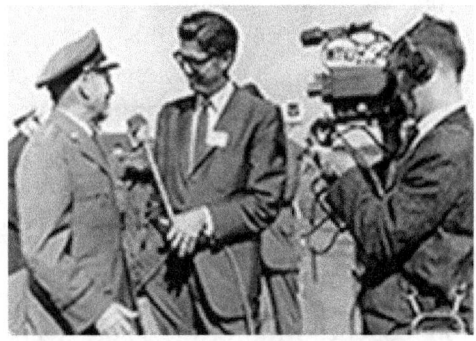

When I first met Gordon in the early 1970's he was working as an anchorman and a reporter at WTVJ in Miami, Florida, Gordon's tale is the classic story of the journalism major who graduates college and is happy to get a job, any job, just to break into the business. I figured this was a great place to start with the first of our oral history recollections. As you will see from Gordon's story, when you were trying to break into the TV News business you said yes first, then figured out how you were going to pull it off. You kind of hoped you would get the hang of things before you got fired.

Recollections
Gordon Stevens-TV Photo Journalist

I came to WTVJ in Miami, Florida right out of Indiana University in June 1961. I was a Journalism Major in college. I had had some rudimentary training in shooting film in school, but in all honesty, I lacked the technical knowledge and discipline required of good photographers. None of this mattered to the News Director. Back then, everybody started out with a camera on their shoulder no matter what your ultimate goal was. I also was not alone. There were several of us in the same boat, but what we lacked in experience we made up for with enthusiasm. Unfortunately, news stories were lost along the way because the film footage I shot was out of focus, over or under exposed, or fluttering because of a lost loop in the camera. In the case of sound on film recording, well there were some additional problems involved in producing a useable sound track. Ok, well here are some true stories.

One day I was sent out in a helicopter to shoot a boat fire in Biscayne Bay. The station had bought 100-foot rolls of film that had double sprockets. Those are the perforations in the edges of film that guide it through the camera's rollers. In the rush of getting shots and changing spools in my trusty Bell & Howell, I managed to run the same roll through the camera twice. See with double perforated film, you could not tell if a reel had been shot or not. There was no upside down. The result was very interesting. The burning boat image was at the top and bottom of the frames. I did the same thing another time when shooting coaches film for the Sports Department. Guess I didn't learn. You were not supposed to make the same mistake twice.

Then there was the time I shot two hundred feet of out-of-focus film of President Kennedy speaking at the Fontainbleau Hotel in Miami Beach. The speech took place in the Grand Ballroom and the Secret Service made us set up cameras in a projection booth at the rear of the room, more than one hundred feet from the stage. Sounds simple? Never, here's what happened.

The only lens I could use from that far away to get a useable image was a fixed focus telephoto lens. It was the only way to get the shot. This would have been fine if I had just been another 10-feet from the stage. I was just a little too close. Fixed focus lenses had a minimal focal distance, and the one I was using needed a few more feet. Needless to say there was no way the Secret Service was about to let me move my camera. Well, I shot it anyway, and of course all the footage came out soft. Not really my fault, at least in my opinion, though the news director differed with that thought just a little bit.

There were many other difficulties in film shooting by non-expert cameramen like me. There was plenty of ruined footage caused by forgetting to insert or remove color correction filters, bad lighting, shaky images caused by hand holding a camera while using a long lens, and the list goes on and on. The good news for me was that I managed to hang in there long enough for the station to finally get smart. They started hiring full time cameramen as in guys who really wanted that job. I steered my career towards reporting and anchoring, a much better choice for me.

Chapter One (continued)
Early TV News Image Gathering

As Gordon described, shooting film was complicated with disaster only a forgotten filter away. Mistakes were an inevitable part of the process, but the only way you learned was by making them, so mistakes were part of the learning process. The best you could hope for was not to make the same mistake twice.

Experience was in pretty short supply. Since there were not that many people that had had experience shooting news film, TV News stations relied on a small group of old pros to anchor down their camera departments. Some were holdovers from the newsreel days, but many of these guys had been military cameramen that shot combat footage during World War II. They were the ones who jumped out of landing craft and shot that amazing footage we watch in war documentaries. Looking for jobs after their military service, TV News was a natural next step.

When I first started my career, I had the opportunity to work side by side with one of those old vets, it was a memorable experience. The man's name was Woody Deford. Here are my recollections about Woody.

Recollections
Meet Woody Deford

Woody Deford came to image gathering from the military. He had been a combat photographer for the Coast Guard during World War II. When he was discharged after the war, he found his way to WTVJ in Miami. Woody passed many years ago and he was not around to provide me with first-hand stories. Fortunately, he was a great storyteller. I have many personal memories of Woody Deford, an image gathering legend and I am sure he wouldn't have minded sharing them.

As was mentioned, Woody learned to shoot film with bullets flying around him during World War II. He was one of those guys who rolled on shore with the troops in the South Pacific armed with his Graflex Speed Graphic still camera, a 16mm Bell & Howell Filmo movie camera, and not much else. His assignment was to shoot combat film for the military, as in land on the beaches with the assault troops. I guess you got pretty good at learning how to think on your feet and keep your head down.

By the time I caught up with Woody, he had become one of the many ageless vets that anchored down TV News camera departments at TV stations all over the country. Woody had many tales of his military image gathering exploits during the war. He told us that he learned not to be too quick and volunteer to go with the first wave when they were landing troops on the beach. A guy with a camera was an easy target. Those "eager beavers didn't last very long," Woody used to tell us.

It's so hard to imagine jumping out of a landing craft armed with only a camera as bullets were flying around you, but those guys did it and gathered some amazing footage.

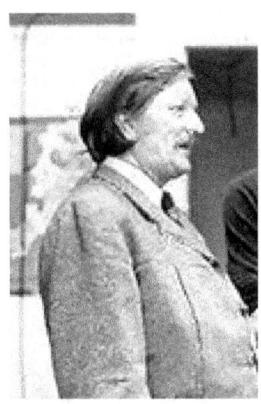

When the war ended, Woody found work as a local TV News cameraman in Miami, Florida at WTVJ. After all, he had already been "fire" tested and so was very well prepared for a news job. Over the next two decades, Woody became a fixture on the Miami news scene. Everybody knew Woody, from politicians to the cops on the street. In fact, anybody who worked in Miami during the 1950's-1970's possesses an image of Woody. I can still see him dressed in his rumpled grey suit, covering a city commission meeting looking much as he does in the old photo I found in a pile of shots from those good old days. The only thing missing from this photo is the big, fat cigar Woody always had stuffed into his cheek.

I can still picture Woody standing by his Auricon 16mm film camera that is perched on an old wooden tripod. His eye is pressed against the viewfinder and he is chewing on that old cigar as his camera rolls. Woody was hysterically funny to hang around with in the news room, but out in the field he was all business.

Of course stories about Woody abound, like the time he was sent to Cuba to cover Castro's revolution with a Bell & Howell

Filmo and six hundred feet of film. Of course Woody came back with the story because, as Woody told us "I had plenty of film. I wasn't shooting *Gone with the Wind*!!!" Or the time he walked out on an interview with the Mayor because the guy was late and it was now time for Woody's lunch break.

Of course, Woody never saw the need to go "portable" and put the sound camera on his shoulder. He'd tell the reporters that the Bell & Howell Filmo was good enough and if they wanted to do an interview, bring the guy over to him so he could do it the right way and shoot it on his tripod. Even the young hot shot reporters were too intimidated by Woody to question him.

Even into his sixties Woody pulled the same shift as the rest of the camera staff. He inspired all with his dedication to his craft and kept us laughing with his ribald ditties and stories that described his innumerable adventures. What I remember most of all though is the fact that Woody possessed a passion for image gathering that was obvious and infectious to us all. Yes, he kept us all laughing in the newsroom, but Woody was deadly serious when it came time to go to work.

Sadly, Woody died of a heart attack in the late 1970's. He was found at home, sitting in a chair with his press ID in his hand. A new cameraman was hired by WTVJ, but Woody was never replaced. He is, was, and always will be a legend to all who were lucky enough to know him and work in his shadow.

Recollections
Meet Bernie Nudelman

Another military veteran I had the privilege to know and work with was an image gatherer named Bernie Nudelman. Bernie was a giant of a man both in ability and in height. Bernie began his career as an image gatherer in the Air Force. A Staff Sergeant, Bernie filmed both training and combat films and actually lost an eye filming a combat mission during the Korean War. Bernie retired from the military and was hired by WTVJ as a news cameraman. He later went on to work for CBS News where he established himself as one of the best. Bernie covered stories all over the world. He was in Cuba during Castro's revolution, see picture below, and stayed in Cuba for the inauguration of Fidel Castro. Bernie covered everything from space launches at Cape Canaveral, to presidential elections, and on and on. If it was happening anywhere in Florida, the Caribbean, or Central America, Bernie was there with his camera on his shoulder shooting it. He was a legendary character that we all looked up to in more ways than one.

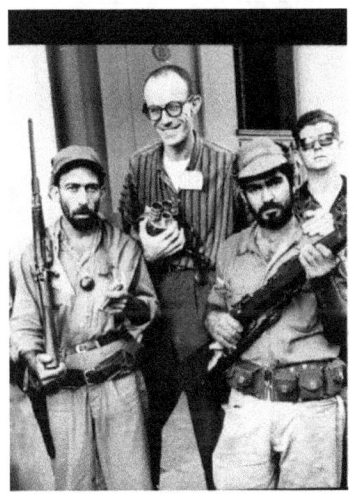

Standing six-foot-six, Bernie towered over all of us.

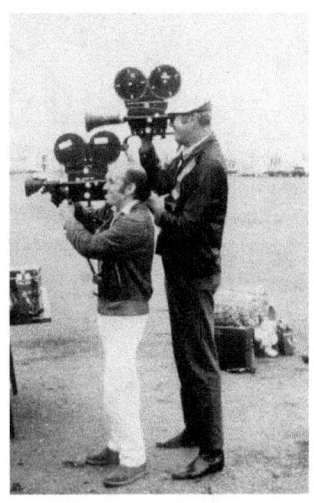

Height is a great advantage for a news cameraman when you get in those multiple camera "gang bang" situations. However even with his height, it still wasn't a good idea to get in his way.

I remember when I made that mistake. A whole bunch of us were backpedaling down the street as the defendant in a trial was walking to his car. I inadvertently drifted in front of Bernie. I felt this iron grip grab my shoulder and move me over a couple of feet to the left. It wasn't mean spirited at all, it was just Bernie telling me that I was in the wrong place and that he would see to it that I was put into the right place.

Bernie passed away in 2016 after a long life that was full of great adventures and great images gathered. His legacy along with all of his generation lived on in our minds and in our work, because they showed all of us who followed how to work as cameramen and gather our images with honesty and integrity.

PART I
Chapter Two
The "One-Man Band"

Back in the day, a hybrid type of image gatherer evolved. This was a do-it-all position, an image gatherer who shot, wrote, and edited news stories, plus did voiceovers and on-camera standups. These reporter/image gatherers were called "One-Man Bands." They were oftentimes used in smaller TV markets that were more more budget conscious, since a "One-Man Band" gave you two jobs for the price of one.

Larry Henrichs is a long time friend and fellow image gatherer that I originally worked with at WTVJ in Miami. In his illustrious career Larry has been a cameraman, editor, reporter, producer, and news director. It all began for Larry though in 1967 as a "One-Man Band." Here is his first hand account of what life was like for that hybrid position back in the day.

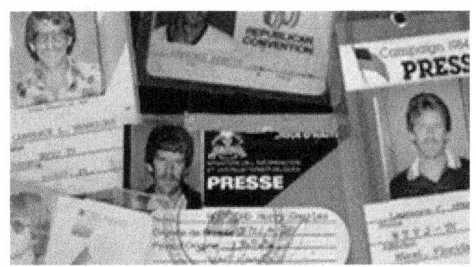

Recollections
Larry Henrichs: The First Selfie

Yes, in 1967, I was a "One-Man Band at WPTV in West Palm Beach, Florida. Each day I'd get my assignments and off I'd go with my drag-behind-me-everywhere wheeled luggage cart that held my sound camera, lights, and sound mixer for the camera, and my big, heavy wooden tripod. In all, the equipment weighed in at about 150 pounds, which actually outweighed me by five pounds, back in the day. I also had my handy reporter's notebook that weighed about six ounces, plus of course my trusty reporter's pen.

Most news stories were easy enough to cover by myself. I'd show up, get my shots and the facts, and shoot whatever interviews I needed to get. All I had to do was set up the headshot, roll the camera, and stand next to it while working a stick mike back and forth. Like I said, that was the easy stuff. Then there were the more challenging assignments like press conferences and speeches. Getting the sound bites were easy. I sat behind my sound camera and rolled on the salient points and got what I needed for my story. Then it was time for the cutaways for voice over b-roll or shots to cover sound edits. The scenes of seated listeners in the audience and reversal shots of the speaker were simple to get, but if I wanted to get on camera for those "reporter involvement" shots, well that was a bit challenging. Like any TV reporter, I wanted my face on camera, but who would shoot this part? I was, after all, quite alone with my dump truck of equipment.

What I came to find through forced invention was if I held my 10-pound Bell & Howell "silent" camera at arm's length, used the widest angle lens I could muster, and aimed it in the general direction of my own face, I could usually get a three second shot of me looking on as though I was actually interacting with the speaker. I even got to the point where I could nod in some strange sense of understanding with what was being said. Today they would call it a "selfie". Whatever, it provided the "cut away" editing shot I would need later on and, sometimes more importantly, it got my mug on the air. It also strengthened my right arm.

Another challenge I faced was shooting a reporter stand up out in the field. The light stand was my solution. Since the stand's height could be raised or lowered with a simple thumb set screw that controlled telescoping rods inside one another, it was the perfect tool. I would set up the light stand to just beyond my height then mark the height of my eyes and the top of my head on the rod with a pencil scribe. I could now use the light stand as my set up tool positioning it where I wanted to be in relation to a background I chose. I'd set it up, then jump back behind the camera and frame my shot. I carefully focused the camera on the head and eye area now marked on the stand, set the sound level for my voice, took a light reading, and set the exposure on the iris. Finally, I'd roll the camera, run into place, shove the light stand out of the way, takes its place and do my standup. It worked perfectly every time.

Such was the life of a "one-man band" way back when in the 1960's. Today they are called multi-media journalists, but to me "one-man band" fits much better.

PART I
Chapter Three
The Early Days of Sports Image Gathering

Sports events had been broadcast on TV live since the late 1930's, but back then if you missed it, well you missed it. There was nowhere to go to watch highlights. When local TV News shows came along in the late 1940's they included a sports block that featured filmed sports highlights. Even though these were limited at best by schedule and broadcast deadlines, just imagine what it must have been like for the viewer to finally get to see the winning touchdown run or ninth inning home run on the evening news show during the sports' block.

Once again, none of this had ever been done before so a whole new set of procedures had to be created by the sport's guys. Shooting sports came with a different set of challenges than shooting TV News. Beyond the technical side of camera work that required a good deal of agility to follow the action and stay out of the way, you had to do a lot of guessing. There was no way you were going to shoot an entire game on film. The film and processing cost would have been prohibitive. Instead, the cameramen covering sports had to develop a sense of what was going on and push the roll button at the right moment.

The other issue came down to time and deadlines. Filming the highlights and airing the highlights were two different things. Depending on when the game ended, you still had to get the film back to the station, develop it in the lab, then edit it and get it on the air. This process could take as long as forty-five minutes to one hour, depending on whether or not there were bumps in the road. Oftentimes, there was a very limited window between the end of the game and the six or eleven o'clock news.

For our recollections from the early days of sports coverage we turn to the true source, a man named Bernie Rosen. He can be seen below in the archival picture with boxing legend Muhammad Ali. Bernie is one of the original TV Sports Guys

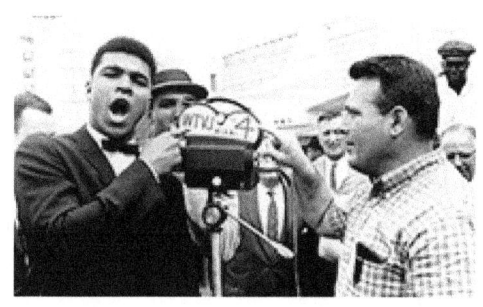

Bernie worked his entire career at WTVJ in Miami, Fl., that's from 1949 thru 2014. During this extended period Bernie set the bar high and ultimately became a TV sports information legend. His career spanned over sixty years during which Bernie blazed many trails in the TV Sports Information business. More importantly though, Bernie set a high standard for honesty and integrity that touched the lives and careers of many sport's journalists and image gatherers. Today, the name Bernie Rosen clearly stands as one of the founding fathers of TV Sports image gathering and a true legend among his peers.

In the beginning, and it was literally the beginning, way back when, Bernie flew by the seat of his pants. Sometimes he relied on skill and ingenuity and sometimes he relied on luck. Bernie was kind enough to share some stories from those early days.

Recollections
Bernie Rosen: The Sports Guy

Sports coverage began very modestly at WTVJ. When the station went on the air, on March 21, 1949, a man named Jack Cummings was hired by station owner Mitchell Wolfson to become the first Sports Director. He was the first and at the time the only employee of the sports department.

As my luck would have it, I was also working at WTVJ as a cameraman and a studio director in the production department. Jack knew that I had a big interest in sports so he gave me a chance to do some sports stories. In those days, desire was the only resume you needed to get the job.

Initially the sports' segment during the 6pm evening news was six minutes long. On weekends the segment stretched to around 10 minutes. It had its own sponsor, the name of which appeared on a placard that sat on the desk in front of the sports anchor. We also did the occasional live interview in the studio, but we still had to fit it in our allotted time slot.

We shot our sports' stories with black and white one hundred-foot film loads. They were only about two and a half minutes long, so you really had to pay attention where you were in the film roll so you didn't run out in the middle of something important.

Getting around town to cover stories was another challenge. Initially the Sports Department did not have its own car to ride around in. I didn't own a car at that time, so I took buses to various destinations to cover stories. Sometimes, if I got lucky, a sales department employee was heading my way and would to drop me off. That took care of getting there, but often, I had to take a bus back.

When I got to my assignment I usually had to shoot the camera, conduct the interviews, and cover the stories all by myself. We shot interviews on an old hand me down Auricon sound camera that came from the news department similar to the one you can see me shooting in the picture below.

Believe it or not we had to use those same one hundred-foot film loads to shoot our all of our interviews. This meant that I often would have to stop in the middle of the interview to reload the camera. This was a process that took at least a couple of minutes and definitely impacted the flow.

I also had to consider how I was going to edit the piece. This meant that I had to figure out some cut away shots. Since I was not considered on camera talent, I had to figure something else out. My solution was pretty simple I usually ended up moving the camera to get a second angle for editing purposes. This way I could cut back and forth as if I had two cameras. I just needed to find a cut point, but that is another story for another day.

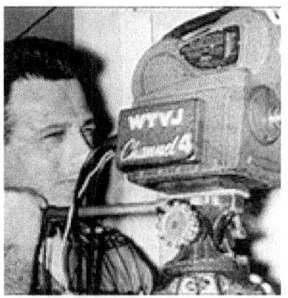

Interviews were often done "one-man band" style, which meant I shot, did audio, and yelled out the questions from the side of the camera. Eventually the station hired another sports employee, but it really did not matter. Regardless of your job description, we were a very small department so everybody in the sports department had to know how to shoot a story, including the sports' anchor.

Back then there was no such thing as network or satellite feeds so it was very challenging to get game highlights on the air if the game was outside of South Florida. For example, the University of Florida Gators were very popular in Miami, but to get their football highlights back from Gainesville was pretty tough. We had to shoot the game ourselves, then find a flight back that would get us back to Miami in time to get the highlights on the air for the 11 o'clock news. To do this we became the pioneers of what was considered groundbreaking same day out of town coverage.

I remember there was one game that had a late start so I couldn't stay for the whole thing, because I would get back too late. I only shot eighty feet of film, about two minutes' worth, and got nine points being scored. I flew back to Miami and got back in time to get thirty seconds of highlights on the sports segment. It turned out to be all of Florida's points in a 9-0 victory. Just like we planned it.

Oh those good old days.

PART I
Chapter Four
The Rules of the Game

In addition to the "how-to" aspect of TV News/Sports image gathering, the early pioneers were also faced with the challenge of creating a level of trust with the viewing public. The images they gathered had to be real beyond a shadow of doubt. Therein lay the challenge because back in the 1950's and 1960's TV News image gathering was so new that there were not a lot of rules governing how news was covered and images gathered. If you wanted to shoot something somewhere, well nobody asked permission. You just grabbed your camera and plowed forward. Without doubt there had to be a temptation among some to cheat a little bit to puff up their piece.

Fortunately, for the future credibility and integrity of image gathering, the people working in TV News in those early days saw the importance of self-policing. They developed a set of internal rules and regulations for covering news stories and strictly adhered to them. Every event had its protocols, lines you respectfully didn't cross.

Nobody really told anyone what to do, but nevertheless, everyone knew how to behave. Competition among TV News operations was fierce, but respectful. You didn't dare cross the line because self-policing brought with it serious internal repercussions for those who transgressed.

Essentially, staging news images, or breaching the code of conduct got you fired. So as the world of TV News image gathering moved forward through the 1950's, and into the 1960's, TV News and Documentary image gatherers made sure that their work was real and uncompromised. This was a very big challenge because people react to cameras whenever they see them. One can easily get people to do stuff for them with the promise of "putting them on TV". Had TV News image gathering gone this route, it would have quickly lost the trust of the pubic.

Fortunately, those in charge understood all this. As mentioned, dishonesty in image gathering was grounds for immediate dismissal. The TV News image gatherers learned early on the importance of not letting their presence affect the event in any way. They had to be as invisible as possible so as not to influence what was happening. "You must not stage the news" was the number one rule for image gatherers. They were instructed to record the event as it was happening as if they were "a fly on the wall".

All involved realized that once an image aired, it could not be put back in the camera. As we used to say, you can't put the genie back in the bottle. How you went about gathering that image was a very important part of the process. You had to be honest, and the image had to be real. Without that TV News would have no credibility, something it could not long exist without. It is news not entertainment and everybody had to understand the difference. This was a lesson that all image gatherers had to learn.

Recollections
Shut Your Mouth: Tales of an Old Pro

For news cameramen, it's so tempting to tell people what to do or say. They don't know the rules and will pretty much do whatever you ask them to do. Stand here, walk there, look over there simple stuff like that. I mean, you need to get your shots and get out of there right? So a few suggestions can move things along. After all, who's going to know?

When I began my career, this was especially true. News crews were not omnipresent like they are today. When I pulled my camera out of the news car a crowd gathered around. They all pleaded with me to put them on TV. Kids would start posing, adults would wave, and flirty girls would, well, I was a young cameraman, right out of college. As the new guy on the staff, I used to work by myself a lot covering the more nonessential type of stories. I got into the habit of telling people to walk over here, sit down there, please do that again, you know a little directing so I could get the shots I needed quickly and easily.

As I gained experience I moved up the ladder and started going out on assignments with reporters. My bad habits came with me. The first time I gave a subject some directions, I got a very stern lecture from the reporter about keeping my mouth shut and not directing the action. I was told that news has no place for staged or directed images. I believe that there was mention of going to Hollywood if I wanted to do that or something like that. He was pretty harsh, but not as harsh as the news director who told me if I did it again, I'd be out of there.

Ok, point taken. I learned to shut up. I realized the importance of maintaining integrity in the film I shot. I was there to cover a news story, not create one. Cheating is unacceptable. We cannot afford to lose the trust of the viewing public. If they do not trust our images, our images have no value. The public trusted us and we in turn had to respond with honesty in our work. This was as true back then as it is today. Honesty in image gathering is a policy that must be adhered to. It is one that I did my best to pass on to the next generation.

PART I
Chapter Five
The Image Gathering Instruction Book

With technology and technique coalescing, TV News image gathering procedures began to solidify, but there was still one more challenge that needed to be addressed. Essentially anyone can learn how to point and shoot a camera while following the rules. However, not everyone knows how to use a camera to tell a story in a real time news situation when there is no prewritten script, no director, and no production team. In today's world of image gathering there is pretty much a form that everyone can follow, but back the early days, everyone was still trying to figure it all out.

When you're an image gatherer covering a news story all you have is a camera on your shoulder and a basic plan based on experience. The experience part is key since in these early days nobody had very much. It was a pretty big challenge for the early TV image gatherers. As pioneers they were charged with the task of blazing the trail. They had to figure out how to tell a news story in less than sixty seconds by by shooting it on film.

The newsreels were the first place TV News looked for guidance, because newsreels were essentially TV News before there was TV News. They were the first to use the concept of telling a story with narration locked to filmed images. This provided a basic framework to follow, though there was still plenty of figuring out to do.

For starters, all your images had to fit into a TV set not a move theater screen. Keep in mind here that we are not talking about the huge, crystal clear TV monitors like we have today. Therefore, while TV News image gatherers could base their work on newsreel procedures, they still had to create their own basic shot list.

Ultimately, when you were shooting a news story you had to know how to think on your feet while quickly and efficiently working your way down a basic shot list. You had to have wide establishing shots so the viewer would know where they were. You had to have the tight shots to show emotion and detail. You needed cut away shots so you could string together action sequences. When someone started to cry, you learned to zoom in tight to get those tears falling. In a breaking news situation, you had to cover what was happening, but you still had to keep in mind how it was all going to cut together and fit inside of a one-minute long news story. Thus the TV News shot list was born.

The TV News shot list just made sense, and was adopted in news organizations all over the world. Big markets, small markets, and everything in between, if you watched the news you saw that the same game plan in effect. Wide shot, tight shot, cut away became an established way of doing things and is as valid today as it was back then and the basic backbone of TV News image gathering. It stuck around because it works so well.

Recollections
Learning the System

As a rookie cameraman I realized that getting the job and learning the job were two different things. This is especially true when you're going out to shoot news stories. The problem is that there weren't any instruction books about how to do it. I had taken some production classes in college, and had shot film so I understood exposure, framing, and I knew how the camera worked, but telling a story with my camera for TV News was a different matter.

I'll always remember the first time I covered a building fire. I got all sorts of action shots of firemen, hoses, and tight shots of flames. I felt really good about myself as I waited for the film to come out of the lab. It was last minute, rush-rush so the chief editor grabbed the film and started quickly and confidently ripping out the shots he wanted. I watched, admiring his coolness under pressure as he whizzed through the film. Finally, after about three minutes he turned to me and in a very exasperated voice asked, "Where's the burning building?"

I wilted under the heat of his gaze. I stammered something, about the action footage of all the firemen, realizing all the time that he was not happy, and that I had messed up. Finally, in his best sarcastic tone he said, "Next time, let's start with an establishing shot of the burning building before you begin to create your magnum opus. This isn't Hollywood." Hmmm, there was that Hollywood line again, but the point was well taken.

One of the old cameraman pros witnessed this dialogue. He pulled me aside later and said "wide shot, tight shot, cutaways, then go get creative." Anyway, I got it. If it's a story about a building fire, first and foremost, I've got to shoot the burning building. I have to establish what's going on in order to tell the story. I can get creative later on, but I better be sure I got the basic stuff first.

PART I
Chapter Six
Here Comes the Next Generation…

Meanwhile, as TV News image gathering was getting organized my generation of image gatherers were running around middle school and high school taking pictures with our Canon or Nikon 35mm still cameras. Many of us had dark rooms in the basements of our parents' home. The lucky ones got their hands on one of the 8mm consumer movie cameras that were now on the market and started shooting their own movies and documentaries.

Cameras like the Cine Kodak 8, which had been introduced in 1932 as a consumer motion picture camera were very popular. Easy to use, the Cine 8 actually shot 16mm film with a double set of sprockets down the middle. When the camera exposed the film, the first time, you had just exposed one half of the film roll. You flipped over the cartridge rolled through the roll again and exposed the other half. After you processed the film, the lab cut the film in half so you ended up with two separate rolls of film shot on 8mm film. As you can see in the archival picture below, it was small and very basic in its design.

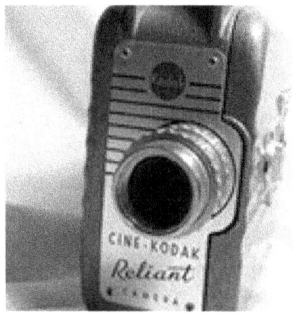

The Cine Kodak 8 quickly became a very popular choice for filming family events like vacations, weddings, births and really everything in between. Of course, every family had a kid who became the designated cameraman. Sooner or later, that kid would go from birthday parties and various family events, to shooting their own movies or documentaries with their friends.

Many future image gatherers started out with a Kodak Cine 8 camera in their hands and it was a great place to start. It was a basic easy to use camera, but after a while, what would often happen was that same kid would get the itch to do something more. They'd buy some 8mm editing equipment and start shooting movies with their friends.

One of those high school kids with a dream is a good friend of mine named Tom Feldman. Today, Tom is a gaffer/lighting director currently based in the Los Angeles production community. Back in 1967 he was a high school student in New York who got the bug. Tom shared his recollections.

Recollections
The Documentary Dream

When I was a kid growing up in New York, I became interested in still photography. I was that guy in high school who always had a camera around my neck taking pictures for the school paper and yearbook and printing them in my darkroom. It wasn't long until I took the next step shooting movies with the family Cine 8. Then I got ambitious.

In the summer of 1967 a couple of photography friends and I decided to shoot a documentary. We each contributed $1000 dollars to the project and came up with a subject. Granted we had no idea what we were doing, but at that age that is not enough to stop you.

One of my partners knew a guy named George who lived in Medusa, NY. He was a colorful old character full of life and wisdom, and to a group of eighteen year olds, was the perfect subject for a documentary. For this project the Cine 8 would not suffice.

We decided to shoot it on 16mm film even though none of us had any experience with this format. We had learned the basics of composition and exposure, and were young enough to assume we could figure it all out. We decided on an Arri-BL. After all it was the standard documentary camera in 1967 and the only 16mm camera that we had ever heard of anyway. There's a picture of it below. Pretty impressive piece of equipment and it shot beautiful images.

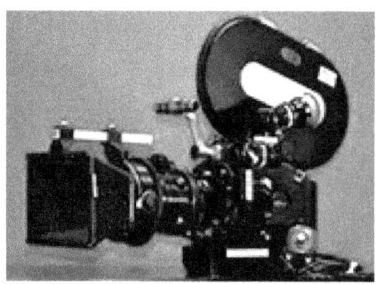

We found a film equipment rental house in New York City that would rent us a camera. I was chosen to go down to pick it up. Fortunately, the guy in the rental house was nice enough to show me how to load the film magazines and thread the camera. Unfortunately, that was about all the instruction we got, the rest was up to figure out.

I brought the gear home, and we loaded it all up, along with a light kit, some audio gear, and accessories. Our transportation was my friend's mother's station wagon and off we went. We spent two weeks in upper state New York shooting with George on black and white film.

For me, from the very first time I looked through the viewfinder of that Arri, I was hooked. Ever since that day it has always been a magical experience to see the world through a camera lens. Looking through the viewfinder and sensing the precision of the optics, well, when it's right, I feel it in my entire body. Today, almost fifty years later, I still love the challenge of figuring out how to perfectly record the image I see.

Anyway, as rookies in this new world of 16mm film production, we faced a lot of challenges. The biggest one being that we had no idea what we were doing. We shot for two weeks, but we had no idea what we had, or even if we had anything for that matter. A local newspaper came out and did a story about us, which included a picture of the boys, the Arri, and me.

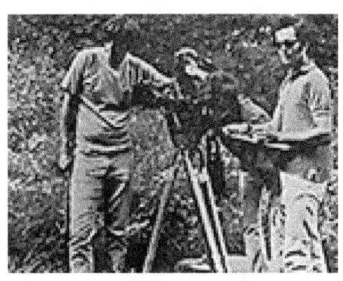

We didn't worry about things like a hair in the gate because we didn't even know what that was. All we had to clean the camera was a tool that looked like a chicken baster, a tube with a big plastic bulb on the end. You squeezed the bulb and air shot out the other end. We religiously used this device to blow out the camera without any real sense as to what could happen if we didn't do it.

Anyway, we got back home and processed the film. Luckily for us, there were no major problems so we moved on to editing. We didn't own any editing equipment so we had to find an editing house that provided a fully equipped edit bay. We didn't have much money left, just enough to rent what we needed for one week.

The edit room we found was in a building that rented out cell-like space for projects like ours. It was a small room with a concrete floor, a table to put the editing equipment on, and a barrel to hang the shots. We paid for a work print, which you had to have. No way you were going to cut on the original.

We rented a 16mm projector, watched our dailies, and made our edit plan. Oh, and in order to get it done in one week we edited twenty-four hours a day for seven straight days. We took turns sleeping on the concrete floor and cutting the film, because we had to get it done. We could not afford another week.

We finished exhausted but proud. We entered it in some local film festivals, then we graduated high school and all went our separate ways. My way led me eventually to Hollywood and a career in documentaries and TV/Motion Picture production. I still remember that documentary, though. Many years have passed, but every time I look through a camera lens, I get to experience that same thrill I got in 1967.

PART I
Chapter Seven
The Early Days: Conclusion

By the late 1960's, the next generation of image gatherers were graduating college with solid film production training and a whole lot of desire. They joined the ranks of the original old pros that were beginning to retire.

On the technological side, film gear was solid and reliable while game plans had been worked out as to how to gather the images necessary to tell the news stories of the day while maintaining integrity and honesty.

All of this came together at just the right point in time. The mid to late 1960's and early 1970's were one of the most tumultuous periods in American history. Ultimately, it had the same impact on TV News image gathering that the Civil War had had on photojournalism.

Image gatherers were on hand when the police turned fire hoses and dogs onto Civil Rights protestors, and the public was stunned. Martin Luther King's famous "I have a dream." speech was broadcast live on television, and the public was mesmerized. Kennedy's assassination, his funeral, and the live murder of Lee Harvey Oswald glued millions to their TV sets. Images of the Vietnam War and American body bags on airport tarmacs turned an entire nation against that war. TV News image gatherers were there to record all this and more.

Meanwhile, the public had realized that a million written words cannot compete with the emotions that are charged when you view real life images gathered by TV News and documentary crews. Simply put, motion pictures give viewers a "you are there" type of experience that you cannot find in a newspaper. These images, coupled with the voice over information became the public's primary means of staying informed, but there was more to it than that.

The public also loved getting it all encapsulated in a brief TV News broadcast rather than taking the time to pour through the pages of a newspaper. As a result, as 1970 rolled around, watching the evening news became a mandatory event as viewers devoured the millions of images gathered each day all over the world.

PART II
The State of Image Gathering in 1970

INTRODUCTION

By 1970, the image gathering TV News process was in the hands of the aforementioned new generation of cameraman who were graduating in droves from college after majoring in TV and Motion Picture Production. TV News provided a fantastic training ground for these younger cameramen. Regardless of their ultimate personal aspirations, film is a medium where you only learn how to shoot it by shooting it. Where else could someone shoot film all day on someone else's dime? TV News put a loaded camera in your hands everyday and said go out and shoot.

Also by 1970, sound camera bodies and batteries were much lighter and easier to work with. As a result, the sound cameras came off the tripods and onto the shoulders of the cameramen. A camera with a zoom lens is a very powerful image gathering tool, especially in a breaking news situation. TV News stories also benefited with the use of natural sound which did so much to add another sensory level for the viewing public.

Here's an archival photo of a news crew at work in the 1950's.

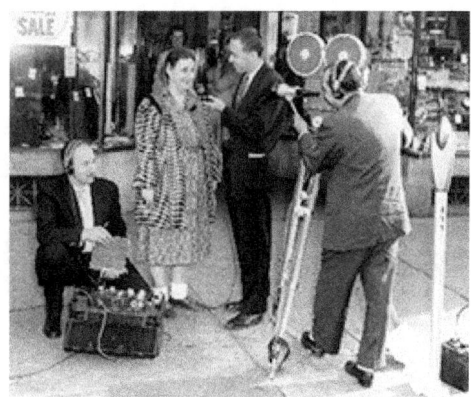

Here is how it looked in the 1970's. Clearly in twenty years much had changed.

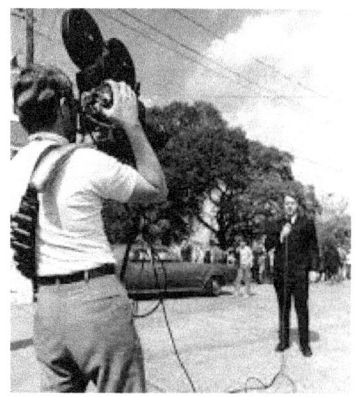

Part II describes how the image gatherers shot and edited TV News stories on film in the 1970's. This era is generally considered the golden age of news film. We'll take a look at both the technology and the know-how that was used back then all through the eyes of the guys who were there in the trenches with film cameras in hand.

PART II
Chapter One
The Image Gathering Team Is Formed

The picture below illustrates a very typical news team in the 1970's. That's then WTVJ-Miami cameraman Larry Green working with reporter Darryle Pollack. They are interviewing Watergate figure Howard Hunt whom they have just grabbed coming out of an evening event. No those are not Mickey Mouse ears sticking out of Larry's head. That's the film magazine and that belt hanging on his shoulder is a battery belt that powers the sun gun, more on all that later.

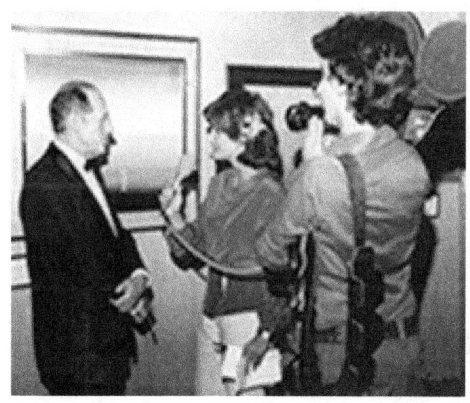

By the way, a quick aside. Larry was another one of the great ones I had the pleasure of working with. He was a very funny and manic kind of guy, but when it came time to work Larry was all business. He loved shooting news. His career took him out to KCBS in Los Angeles where he worked for many years. Tragically, he lost his life while on assignment in the Persian Gulf. Larry was truly one of a kind.

Other than the film camera this configuration has not changed all that much over the years, however, there was one important detail that was very different back then. There was still a dress code for cameramen, though coats and ties were no longer required. TV News image gatherers wore slacks and shirts. Sneakers were allowed but absolutely no jeans or shorts, even in the summer. There was a strong sense that you were a representative of the TV station when you were out in the community. You also never knew from day to day where you might end up, so you dressed neatly and stayed well groomed. You didn't want to show up at a city commission meeting looking like a bum.

Anyway, the workday for the news crews generally started at nine in the morning though there was always an early crew and a late crew. You came in and grabbed your film camera, lights, tripod, batteries, and raw film stock and loaded it all into your assigned news car. Back then cars had big enough trunks to fit an entire TV News style camera package. The camera rode in the trunk in a reinforced black camera case that was form fitted. Each cameraman had his own film camera that he was responsible for maintaining. Nobody else used your gear.

Speaking of cameras, not everybody used the same model. News departments had tight budgets so even though they might buy a new camera, they did not throw the old one away. As long as it worked, it stayed in circulation. As a result, there were still some older heavy "boat anchors" out there that the new guys had to use. It was always very funny when a new guy showed up to work and saw the gear that he was stuck with.

Ultimately, through attrition, you'd work your way up the chain and inherit better gear when the guys ahead of you left the station to go onto other markets. This actually happened quite often. Most of the camera guys were still in their twenties, so there was a lot of movement on the job front. Everybody had a dream job. Some wanted a network positions, others looked for bigger markets with higher pay, while others preferred mid markets just to be close to family and friends. Three to four years was fairly typical for cameramen to stay at one station.

Anyway, the cameramen usually hung out in the film equipment room until summoned by a reporter or producer. This was their space. Everybody had their own locker where they kept their gear and personal stuff. You kept your locker locked up over night. Nobody was going to steal anything, but there could be a temptation that if someone needed to borrow something, and your locker was open, well in a pinch it'd be gone. When you came in the next morning there'd be a note, but then you'd be screwed for your day. Locking it up was a better solution. Each locker also had a plug which allowed you to charge your batteries over night.

As a cameraman you were always ready to roll. Everything was set, your camera was loaded, batteries charged, and you had enough film stock with you no matter where you might end up during the day. The reporter would follow you out to the back parking lot where the news cars were parked. Each car had an assigned number that corresponded to its two-way radio number. When you had to call into base, you used that number. The cameraman usually drove, so the reporter was free to communicate with the assignment desk over the two-way radio in the car.

When you got to your location, you'd jump out, and grab your camera gear, while the reporter went off with their note pad. You knew what you had to do and how you had to do it. You'd take your light readings and start shooting the story, while the reporter collected the facts and figured out whom they needed to interview. At least this was the game plan. Back in 1970 there were still a few reporters who had come up through the ranks shooting film. They would occasionally offer their opinions on how to do things, or at least they would try.

Of course not every story you covered was breaking news. Back in the 1970's, when you were covering an assignment that required more of a setup interview, or a city government meeting, you'd load your gear on some kind of cart and roll it all inside to where you were shooting. You had your camera, extra film magazine and film stock, audio gear, tripod, light kit, and electrical cables. It was quite a load.

Keep in mind, in most markets, the cameraman worked without an audio guy or camera assistant. They relied on the reporters to lend a hand physically. as well as communicating the necessary information as to what was going on and what was the essence of the story you were on.

Speaking of the cameraman/reporter relationship, by 1970 a much clearer work delineation had evolved. Everyone had their own job to do. Mutual respect and trust were vital elements in the success of a team's news coverage on a given day. The cameraman shot the film, and the reporter gathered the facts.

Like any other human relationship, sometimes it didn't work and sometimes it did. Back in the film days you had enough to worry regarding exposure, composition, and color temperature. When you found someone you enjoyed working with, you encouraged the relationship. It made for a much nicer day.

Recollections
The Symbiotic Relationship

When I was employed at WTVJ in Miami, I worked with a reporter named Ike Seamans who ultimately went on to a distinguished career at NBC News. Ike was the consummate reporter. He had a keen sense of where the story was going given in virtually any news situation. We would show up and he'd gather his facts while I went about my image gathering. Ike shared this picture from a feature story we did at the Super Bowl in Miami many years ago.

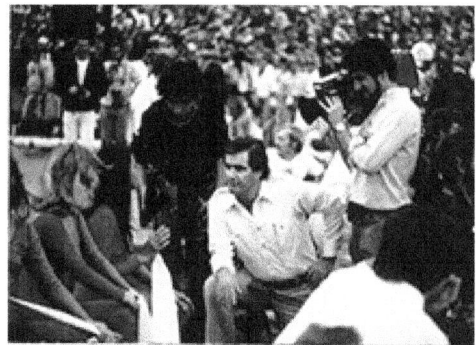

We had many adventures together covering all sorts of stories from plane crashes to features stories about miniature railroads, but our routine was always the same. When we were done, I'd tell him what I had and he always did his best to include my best images. He even took the time to review my footage before he wrote his script to make sure I hadn't forgotten to tell him about any shots.

That was the symbiotic nature of our teamwork. Ike knew I would get the images he needed to tell the story and I knew he would use the best of those images. Ike also always had my back. He knew where I was at all times, and made sure I didn't miss anything. Likewise, if I was able to worm my way into the action, Ike was right there to grab the mike and do his thing.

Many years ago, during a Papal visit in Santo Domingo, we were covering the Pope's arrival at the airport. They had deplaned and the Pope was rolling in what we called the Pope-mobile. I found an opening in the crowd and made my move. I ended up standing directly in front of the pope with my camera rolling. Ike of course was right there beside me. Without missing a beat, he grabbed the mike and fired a quick question. To our utter amazement the Pope answered him. Of course his security people pounced on us, grabbed Ike's arm and pulled away the microphone as I wrestled with a guy who was trying to pull my camera off of my shoulder. Didn't matter, we had our shot and had gotten a rare Papal sound bite.

That's teamwork, fact-gatherers and image gatherers working as one.

PART II
Chapter Two
The New Image Gatherers

As mentioned, by the early 1970's, young college grads were flooding the ranks of TV News image gatherers. These were not journalism majors, but rather were graduates with degrees in Film and TV Production. TV News was a great place to get experience no matter your long-term goals.

Shooting film very much a hands on learning experience. Only by shooting it did you learn how to shoot it. The problem was that it was expensive and few could afford to do it on their own. TV News provided a great way to go. Where else could you go where you had the opportunity to shoot film everyday and get paid for doing it?

The good news for these grads was that there were a lot of job opportunities. TV stations were expanding their work forces as the competition for ratings heated up. Bodies were needed so many grads were hired without much experience and were broken in on low-key stories like park dedications, and rotary club luncheons. These were great opportunities for them to get a solid hold on the basics. Eventually, there'd be an opportunity where they were given a chance to show what they could do. The key was being ready and prepared for that moment.

If you screwed up, you might not get another chance for quite a while.

Recollections
The College Grad

I graduated college with a degree in film production in 1970, and started looking for a job. I loved camera work and had a crazy dream that someday I would go off and shoot wildlife documentaries. Don't ask me where that idea came from, or how I planned to make money while doing it. Really though, I just wanted to make a living with a camera in my hand.

Anyway, I had interned at a local TV station during my senior year of college, and as luck would have it, one of the camera guys left right at the time I graduated. The station had a policy of hiring a totally new, inexperienced guy on the roster. I mean, he had to know how to at least take a light reading, the rest he could pick up. Meanwhile, they could pay him peanuts while he learned his trade. If the guy had the aptitude and a really thick skin, he'd have a career. Anyway, I was offered that job and I grabbed it.

I started out doing some very low impact assignments, mostly shooting and covering minor events by myself. I was the king of ribbon cuttings. I didn't care. I was getting paid to have a camera in my hands and go out and shoot film everyday. I was in heaven. This had been my dream since I was a kid shooting movies with our super 8 family film camera.

After several months spent learning my craft, I started covering stories with the reporters. This was a whole new ballgame. The reporters had little or no patience for a rookie. They were pretty brutal in their criticism and I could not fall back on my inexperience as an excuse. I realized that I either had to learn quickly or find another line of work. I felt like I was swimming in a tank of sharks. I knew if they sensed blood, it was all over, so I sucked it up. My number one goal was to never repeat a mistake. I made plenty, but I tried to make them only once.

One of the hardboiled reporters I worked with back then used to love the phrase, "If you don't like it, you can go sell shoes at Sears." Now, I'm not putting down people who work in shoe stores, but compared to being a news cameraman, well for me, there was no comparison. I showed up everyday ready to work, determined to get better at my job. I slugged it out everyday and started gaining confidence. Then a really big story fell into my lap.

I was usually the last cameraman to get an assignment. The reporters all had their favorites, and I was not yet on anybody's list. Anyway, I was sitting back in the equipment room hanging out by myself when the assignment editor came breathlessly running in. The DEA building in Miami had just collapsed. People were trapped, and all hell was breaking lose. He gave me an "I hope you know what you are doing" skeptical look as he handed me an address on a slip of paper. I took the paper, pretended that I could handle this assignment no problem, and was out the door in a flash going over a quick check in my head that I had my gear ready to roll in my news car. Yes, it was all there, and yes I had a spare, loaded film magazine.

I jumped into my news car and my adrenaline was pumping. This was my first really big assignment and my chance to prove myself. My confidence lasted only a few seconds as I saw to my horror that the station's top reporter, the guy who used to make the "sell shoes at Sears comments", was right behind me running towards my car. Gulp, ok here we go.

He got in the car and we raced off. He barely talked to me on the way to the scene, other than a skeptical look and a terse hope you know what you're doing type of comment. Actually, it was far more profane than that. Whatever. Our station was located very close to the DEA building and we were the first news crew to arrive. People were literally stumbling out of the rubble covered in dust. We had gotten there even before the fire department rescue teams.

I grabbed my camera and started shooting while the reporter went off to find out what was going on. It was complete chaos, a fact that allowed me to run around the scene without any restrictions. I had never shot a major disaster like this so I didn't know much about what you could and couldn't do anyway. I climbed over the rubble, grabbing shots of survivors.

I couldn't believe the images I was getting. They were totally real and totally raw. There was no time to think, so I went into autopilot, calculating exposure in my head and rolling on incredible shot after incredible shot. The film burned through my camera as I shot people literally climbing down from a pile of bricks and concrete. Within minutes, fire rescue showed up along with the cops and the other TV stations. I was moved further back, but I already had gold. I had gathered some absolutely incredible images of the human tragedy of this event. We spent the rest of the morning shooting interviews and more shots of the rescue workers combing the rubble, though now from a more discreet distance. All I could think about though was the images I already had in my camera.

I remember watching the finished piece somewhat amazed at the great footage I had shot. I got all sorts of complements from the other cameramen, which really made me feel good. As I was leaving for the day the reporter I had worked with, the one who scared the crap out of me, saw me, nodded, and said something like "I guess you might actually know what you're doing after all college boy." Hey for him that was high praise. Anyway, for the first time since I had gotten the job, I felt that I could say, "I am a news cameraman." This was an amazing moment in my life that I vividly remember forty years later. I was now a member of a very exclusive club. I was an image gatherer.

PART II
Chapter Three
Camerapersons

It was also right around this time that gender equality began to find its way into TV News image gathering and women began entering the ranks of the TV News image gatherers. There was never any concerted effort to keep them out, but there was a macho attitude that women were not physically strong enough to handle the gear, or at least there were some who wanted to believe this. Of course there were soon to be plenty of women prepared to prove everybody wrong.

Fortunately, this was the 1970's, and the times were changing. Racial and gender equality were big issues and TV News departments were looked at with great scrutiny by community leaders. News Directors were told that their departments had to have a full representation of the population at large both on the air and in the field.

When it came to the camera department qualified women were the hardest to find. They had been discouraged so long that many had just given up trying. Fortunately, there were still some not everyone was easily dissuaded from trying. There were still a few hanging around.

I remember there was a young woman still-photographer from one of the local newspapers who I often saw out covering stories. She was friendly and was curious about the gear, and also how to get a job in TV. I told her who to call and she followed up, becoming the first female cameraperson at WTVJ in Miami, Florida, though we never used that term. The job title was cameraman regardless of gender.

Her name is Christina Clausen. I was fortunate to have worked with Chris and remember her for her great attitude and excellent camera work. From day one it was clear to all of us that Chris could handle the workload and then some. She's a tall woman and was never afraid to hold her ground when the circumstances required it, so it was best to stay out of her way. She was also a passionate image gatherer. Chris agreed to share some memories from her early days in the trenches.

Recollections
Gender Issues? Nope

Whenever I arrived on the scene of a news story, I was usually regarded as being another guy, mainly because of my height and also the camera hid my head from one side. Besides that, most people just saw the enormous camera and that's all they needed to know. My gender was not important, especially to the other camera crews I was shooting with. Anyway, when you're covering a breaking news story, nobody has time to worry about stuff like that.

My biggest issue was holding my ground in a crowd. On big stories, network guys especially would try to shove me around. Well they would try anyway. I just had to let everyone know that I wasn't going to be pushed around. Sharp elbows do come in handy.

A friend took this shot of me covering the Iranian Hostage Crisis folks returning to West Point just after Reagan was inaugurated. I always liked to wear bright colors so as not to get run over. This was my hot pink ski jacket. Cool, eh?

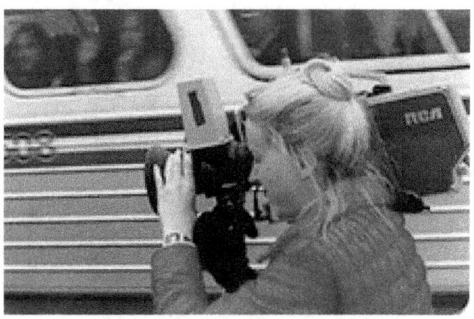

I ultimately became Chief Cameraman at WAGA in Atlanta, Georgia and again, never had any gender issues. I always found that if I treated everybody with respect I got respect back. I traveled a bit too with trips to Israel and Lebanon, covered the Olympics in Lillehammer and Atlanta and covering the Fed Pen prison riots in Atlanta.

All in all, I had a great career though I wish I had kept a diary of all the stories I covered. My advice? Keep a diary, the years go by too fast.

PART II
Chapter Four
Shooting Film: The Sound Camera

So you've seen some of the who, now let's take a look at the how. Image gathering in the 1970's was done with 16mm film. Every aspect of shooting 16mm film was manual and every step of the process demanded perfection. Any error or missed step anywhere along the way led to disaster. You had one chance to get it right. Once your film was shot and processed there were no tools for image manipulation like there are today. If the film was over exposed, under exposed, or otherwise compromised you had to live with it.

Let's start with the film itself. Kodak was the film provider and they sold their products in yellow Kodak Film boxes that looked like this archival photo. As each type of film stock was unique, Kodak also labeled all of them with specific numbers. News film was given the number 7240. The outside of the box provided information regarding the color balance of the film. This was a critical bit of information the image gatherer needed to know. News film was tungsten balanced, that is balanced for artificial studio type lights. If you shot with it outside, you needed a color correction filter.

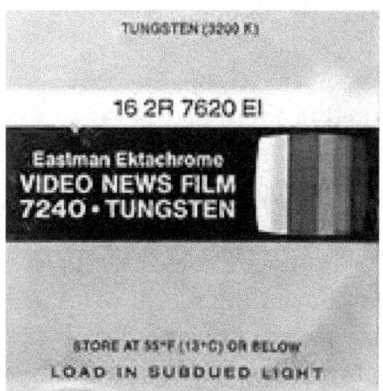

The yellow boxes contained an aluminum can with a one hundred, two hundred, or four-hundred-foot load of film inside. The can was sealed with thick white tape that was wrapped horizontally around the diameter of the can. Because redundancy was a good thing in labeling film, the same number was printed on that white tape. There was also a label on the can itself. With film you couldn't be too careful.

News film came in two types of film loads, daylight and cores. Daylight loads were wound on either one hundred or two hundred foot reels. Because the reels were made out of solid black metal they did not require a darkened environment to be loaded or unloaded into or out of the film magazine. The black metal spool protected the film from being exposed by ambient light. You just had to remember to run off about three seconds at the head and figure you were going to lose three seconds on the tail. That was as far as the light could penetrate on a daylight spool.

Cores, however, were very different. They were four hundred feet of film tightly wound around a small yellow plastic core. All the film was completely exposed, so they could only be loaded and unloaded in a changing bag or darkroom, a process described later in this history.

All TV News operations used reversal film. This was film that was processed directly to a color image without a negative. Kodak also manufactured the film with a magnetic stripe that ran along the edge of the film. The audio was recorded on this "mag stripe" in the camera.

Speaking of audio, there had to be twenty-eight frames of film between the camera lens and the audio head. If this frame count was significantly off, you were going to have picture and audio synch issues. In other words, the sound and picture would not match, and there'd be nothing you could do to fix it. This was true with everything that you did in the world of film. It had to be done right the first time. Once your film came out of the lab, there was nothing you could do to correct it. Once it was shot, it was shot. The genie could not be put back in the bottle. There were not any tools available to save the day.

To load your camera, you removed the can from the box, pulled off the tape, opened the can, pulled out the reel, and loaded the film into the camera's film magazine. Then you threaded it down through the magazine rollers, up to the take up side where you attached with a tiny piece of tape. You then screwed on the magazine doors, pulled down a short loop of film and snapped the magazine onto the camera. The loop of raw film was then hand threaded through an intricate series of sprockets and rollers like you see here in this archival photo.

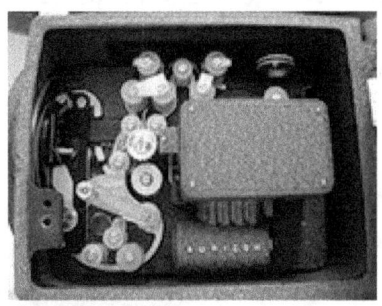

You had to leave small loops above and below the gate to keep the correct tension on the film as it passed through the gate. Now remember those twenty-eight frames between the lens and the audio head? If the loops were too big you risked being over that twenty-eight frames synch point and your sound would not be in synch with your image. If you made them too small, the film tension would be too tight and the entire gate would chatter. You'd end up with a very jumpy picture.

Of course, there was no way to physically count the frames to get it exact. That would have taken way too much time and in reality it was impossible to do anyway. It was more of an eyeball kind of thing. You knew it was right when you saw it because it just looked right.

Loading the film camera was something you got good at by loading the film camera. After you had done it hundreds of times you were really good. The only way to learn was by doing. On an average day you might go through the entire process five or six times, so it did not take very long to achieve mastery over the process. Ultimately, you could to do it with your eyes closed. This was a good thing because you never knew where you were going to be when it came time to reload your camera. You had to be able to do it quickly, as all hell could be breaking loose around you. This was after all TV News.

When you were all done the TV News sound camera looked something like the archival picture below. As you can see, it was not particularly pretty, but it was very reliable. These cameras were manufactured with news coverage in mind. They were solidly built and could easily withstand the rigors of TV News image gathering. The main thing was to stay on top of maintenance. We always said, if you take care of your camera, then your camera will take care of you.

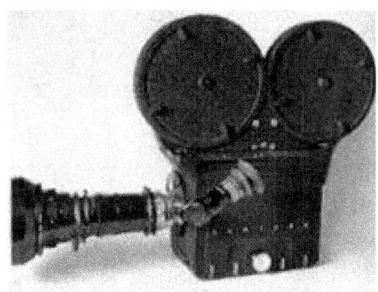

Once your camera was loaded, you had to manually zero your footage counter on the back of the camera. This was the only way to keep track of how much you had shot so you'd know when it was getting close to the time to reload. There was no worse feeling than looking back at that footage counter and realize you hadn't zeroed it. There literally was no way of knowing how much film was left in the magazine. Obviously, opening it up and looking was out of the question.

Now you were ready to start shooting, but you still needed to stay aware of any variations in the lighting conditions. You had to take light readings with a light meter, manually set exposure, and double check that you were using the proper color correction filter to compensate for the color balance of the film in relation to the color temperature of the light in the place where you were about to start shooting. Clouds were a particular favorite, but there were many other issues you had to take into consideration. You took frequent light readings with your meter and reset your exposure as needed.

When you were finished shooting or when your film load ran out, you unloaded the film from the camera's film magazine, packaged it back into a film can, and delivered it to the film lab. There it was loaded into the film processor, or the "soup" as it was called, and about forty-five minutes later, you had the one and only print of your work. The load of processed film was manually edited and hot spliced together into roughly a minute and a half news story. It was then rolled live to air during the news broadcast.

In order for the TV News image gatherers to successfully create an image, they had to have an in depth knowledge of exposure, depth of field, and color temperature. Basically, it was impossible to fake knowing how to shoot film. There were far too many variables and far too many unique situations for anybody to just pick up a film camera and start shooting. Experience was a must. The only way to get good at shooting film was to shoot film.

Recollections
The Miracle of Film

Regardless the medium I recorded on, image gathering was image gathering. I had a camera on my shoulder, I'd point it at my subject, zoom in or zoom out to compose the frame, then roll. Sounds easy right? Well in the film days the answer would be not exactly. There were several more steps in the process.

First, I had to take a light reading with my light meter, then set the exposure. Setting exposure for film was more about taking an average of the entire area you were shooting in. No environment has completely flat, even lighting, so if I could I'd take multiple readings of the entire area. Some parts of the frame would be brighter, some darker, especially if I was outside and dealing with shadows. I always had to evaluate where the middle was and set exposure accordingly. I especially had to pay closer attention if there were faces in the shot. I would always try to make them look good and let the background take care of itself. The people were always the most important element.

Then it was time to compose my shot. The viewfinder gave me a view through the actual glass of my lens. There were no electronics just precision crafted glass. I'd zoom in to focus, and I could almost feel the elements in the lens lock into place. Ready to go, I set my frame then punched the roll button on my pistol grip as the camera jumped to life. Gears turned and sprockets grabbed the film. It chattered through the rollers and slid under the pressure plate past the lens as each frame of the film was exposed to the light recording my shot.

Every time I shot film I was amazed. To me it was seemingly miraculous that you started with a chemically coated strip of plastic, ran it through the camera, dumped it into a bath of chemicals, and out came images. If I had done my job correctly these were beautiful images. If I had screwed up somewhere in the process, these were horrible images. Whatever, good or bad, they were images that I had handcrafted, that I had created.

I can still remember that tightness in my gut that I always got when my film came out of the lab. I had generally been waiting around for close to an hour. The lab would call over when the film was ready, and I'd walk across our parking lot to a metal pull down window at the back of the lab. The window had a small hinged window like a mailbox that I pulled open to reveal a metal shelf where film was dropped off and picked up. I always got a strong whiff of the film developing chemicals as I'd grab my film, and anybody else's that was there, then head back over to the newsroom.

The film was wound very tightly around a plastic yellow core, but I still had to be careful winding it onto a film reel. I'd balance the core on a finger on my left hand, tape the tail to the film reel, and with my right hand wind the film onto the reel. Once finished it was time to take a look.

A quick glance through the Moviola viewer assuaged my fears. The film had images, they were good, and nothing weird had happened. There weren't any random flashes from light leaks, my exposure had been dead on, and the color temperature was perfect. I kind of knew it already but with film seeing was the final confirmation.

At this point my stomach relaxed and I started to edit.

Part II
Chapter Five
The Cameras

As mentioned earlier, in the 1970's, a news cameraman worked with two types of cameras. There was a sound camera and a smaller, more portable silent camera. Simply stated the sound cameras recorded audio and silent cameras did not. Anyway, let's start with the sound camera.

The most popular sound cameras of the day were manufactured by one of two companies, Auricon or Frezzolini. These were called single system cameras because as we've described, they had a magnetic sound recording head inside the camera. Both the image and audio were recorded onto the film as it rolled. Thus the name single system.

There was also a double system process, but that required an external audio record deck, a clapboard to synch audio with picture, and a camera assistant to snap the clapboard with every shot. A soundman was also a necessity as the audio was recorded on a tape recorder that synched to the film camera. This was a pretty complicated setup which made double system way too complex for most TV News situations. It was used primarily in documentary and motion picture production.

Fully loaded with batteries and film, these sound cameras weighed in at around twenty pounds. When you added a battery powered camera light or sun gun, the rig started to get bulky too. Nevertheless, having natural sound as part of a story adding texture to the report, so the sound camera was the preferred way to go. It was also always nice to have audio available just in case the reporter wanted to grab a quick interview in a breaking news situation. So though they were bulky and a bit awkward to work with, we made it work. Hey it was all we had so we just did it.

Here's what it all looked like in action. That's cameraman Jim Duffy at work apparently shooting a goat. Not sure why, but we never asked those types of questions.

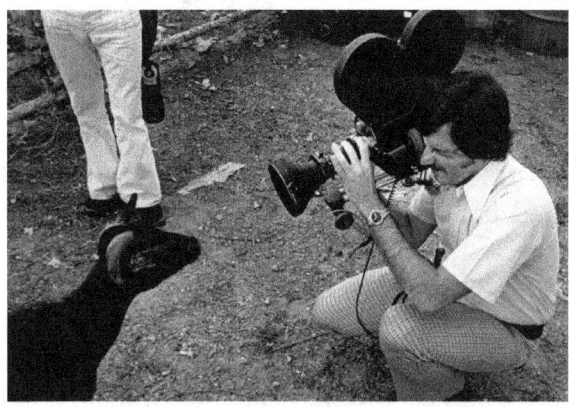

Anyway, whether shooting a goat or a quick interview with the Mayor, twenty pounds on your shoulder bone is twenty pounds on your shoulder bone. After a while, it's going to hurt. Basically, our shoulders were never intended for us to put heavy, hard, flat-bottomed metal objects on them for hours and hours on end. That spot just gets rubbed raw. The memory of that pain lingers on, even after all of these years.

Recollections
The Boat Anchor

We used to call the old sound cameras boat anchors, because they were big, heavy, and awkward to carry. Many thought they would serve better tied to a rope and holding a boat in place. They were certainly never originally designed to shoot hand held, but that is what the job demanded. After a long day of shooting with one on your shoulder, you sure felt like if you tied a rope to one, you could anchor an aircraft carrier.

Everything about those cameras was cumbersome. If I needed to mount a sound camera to my tripod, I had to lift the camera up, and had to hold it in place on top of the tripod while leaning it over at a forty-five-degree angle so I could line up the tripod's screw to the hole at the bottom of the camera. Then I had to lower it down and push the screw up into the hole. If I had lined it up properly the screw would spin nicely and I could tighten the camera in place. If they weren't lined up I had to, well, just keep trying.

Taking the camera off was much easier, well at least the unscrewing part. I still had to deal with the clean and jerk move that I needed to lift the camera off the top of the tripod which was good for bicep and triceps development, but unfortunately not my back and neck muscles.

Note here, tripods back then were a whole different story than we use today. The tripod legs of the day were wooden and very heavy. The tripod heads were made out of some kind of cast metal and did not have a ball level. In order to level a tripod, I had to spread the tripod out then finesse the legs up and down until I centered the bubble on the side of the tripod head. I always did that before mounting the camera because it was really a challenge to level the tripod with a camera screwed on to it.

As a result of all these factors using a tripod on a news story kind of slowed me down a bit. It was so much easier to just grab the camera, throw it on my shoulder and run off after the reporter. News interviews were generally not that long especially on breaking stories. In 1970 this was called "going portable" and it rapidly became a part of the overall job description. "Forget the tripod go portable" became the reporter's battle cry.

The only problem for me was that there was no easy way to put a flat-bottomed camera that weighs twenty pounds on my shoulder and shoot comfortably. After rubbing my shoulder raw a few times, I taped a small foam pad to the bottom of the camera. I had to leave one side unattached so if I needed to mount the camera onto the tripod, all I had to do was to let the foam flip back over to access the screw mount. It wasn't pretty, but it worked.

There were other options. Some guys preferred a shoulder to belly brace rig like you see in this picture of fellow cameraman Steve Von Born. As you can see in this picture the camera was screwed onto an upper bracket while the belly brace came down at a forty-five-degree angle to support the camera weight on the gut. In addition

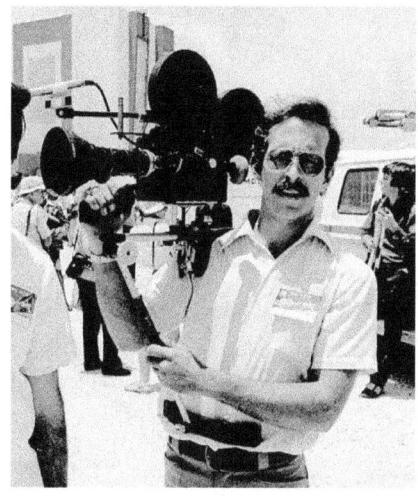

to a weight distribution advantage, this rig also gave the cameraman two free hands to work with. The only downside occurred when you wanted to put the rig down. No easy way for that to happen unless you took it all apart.

Screwing the cameras on and off of tripods and shoulder rigs was challenging to say the least. I mean, I had a heavy camera in one hand, while my other hand was holding onto the mounting screw and trying to push it up through the top plate of the tripod and line it up with the hole in the bottom of the camera. I had to get it all just right with the threads linked properly so I could tighten the screw.

In case you were wondering, yes, every once in a while the threads got stripped because of an improperly lined up screw. At that point, I was really screwed, no pun intended. The entire camera needed to go into the shop and get that hole drilled out and rethreaded.

Nevertheless, going portable became the only way to go. Remember, this was news and speed was always of the essence. It wasn't much fun to be messing with tripods and screws when you know what was hitting the fan. News wouldn't wait for us to get all of our gear set up. Slowly but surely, shooting news became a hand held exercise. Tripods were relegated to speeches, press conferences, and long interviews.

Part II
Chapter Six
Recording Audio on Film

In 1970 in the mid to small TV markets, many TV News image gatherers were also required to be sound techs. In nonunion TV stations especially, the cameraman both shot and recorded audio. Nope, no way the budget would allow for a sound guy. It was up to the image gatherer to do it all.

Trying to record audio and shoot film was very challenging. As has been described, the cameras were single system, which meant that the sound was fed to the camera through an external mixer, and recorded at the camera's record head on a mag stripe that was on the film. That part was easy, the difficult part was keeping an eye on your sound levels while shooting.

Cameras back then did not have built in sound mixers or vu meters in the eyepiece. The mixers were external and generally hung around your neck. An umbilical audio cable fed the sound camera the mixer's output. You monitored the audio by listening through headphones plugged into headphone jack on the mixer. If it sounded clean, then it was usually good. Well at least you hoped it was anyway.

Of course there was no way to do any kind of audio playback on shot film, so ultimately, you found out if your audio was clean for sure after your film was processed and you listened to it on your sound reader in the edit bay. Of course by then, if there were any issues, it was too late to do anything about it. Like everything else with film, you had to live with it. Generally speaking, if it sounded clean when you were laying it down, you were more than likely going to be in good shape. There were very few surprises after the fact.

Now dealing with issues in the field, that was fun. We basically had a couple of adaptors and a spare mic cable. That was pretty much it. Plus, we're talking 1970's technology. Plugging a light into an electrical outlet could lead to all sorts of grounding issues that audio cables loved to pick up. There was no worse feeling in the world then hearing that low end buzz in your headphones, that is if you could pick up anything subtle like that in your headphone as in singular.

Yup, little ear bud types of headphones did not yet exist. The headphone you used back then was big and bulky, completely covering your left ear. Yes, left ear. You couldn't wear a normal set of headphones because the right side of your head was up against the side of the camera. If you were wearing normal headphones that covered your left and right ear, your head would be pushed too far away from the camera body, and you couldn't see through your eyepiece.

Of course, leaving your right ear uncovered meant that you had to filter out all the ambient noise of your environment along with the sounds of the camera motor and the film going through the rollers. It's a little hard to listen to only one ear, but you did get used it. See archival picture below of one-eared headphones.

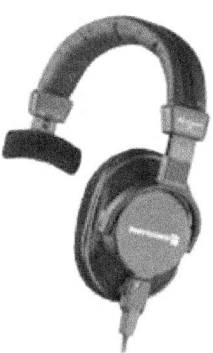

Microphones were a whole other story. In 1970 there were very few options for microphones. The stick mike, the ECM 50, was the basic means of recording audio, though there were shotguns and lapel mikes which were called lavalier microphones. These lapel mikes were not the tiny little bug sized microphones that are in use today. They were a few inches long and hung around the reporter's neck with a string. Wireless mikes existed, but were very limited.

The distance between the transmitter and receiver was miniscule compared to modern standards. They also had only one fixed wavelength. It either worked, or it didn't. If it didn't, well you had to try something else. You developed all sorts of ways to hide mike cables, like dropping them down pant legs or running them under shirts and out the back then shooting waist up. Hey, it worked.

Once you solved all the mike placement issues, you then had to deal with shooting while also mixing sound. This required a delicate balancing act. You mainly listened through the headset. If it sounded good to your ear, that was a good thing, but to be sure you still had to monitor the mixer's VU-meter. So how do you watch the vu meter on your mixer and look through the eyepiece of the camera at the same time?

Well, you can't do both, so you needed to pull your eye away from the camera's eyepiece and glance down. The problem with doing that was that you had about one second to confirm all this while holding the shot steady on the person being interviewed or making a speech. Longer than a second, well, anything could happen like the person could move and disappear from your frame which seemed to always happen the second you took your eye away from the eyepiece.

Also, if you were shooting outside you had to remember to close off your eyepiece with a little built in eyepiece diopter before you took your eye away from the it. If you didn't, you risked having daylight leak through and fog the film.

So, how did the image gatherers turned sound tech check their vu meter level? There was a way. It was not perfect, but it did work most of the time. What you would try to do to check audio was to open your left eye, which you normally kept closed so your right eye could concentrate on the viewfinder, and quickly glance down to look at your mixer. As long as the vu meter's needle was bouncing normally and not going into the red and staying there, you were pretty safe. If it wasn't you had to reach down and adjust the audio level on the mixer with your left hand. Of course this had to be done super quick because if you were looking down you weren't looking up and we have already described what always seemed to happen when you did that. Riding audio became a test of your ears and your manual dexterity.

A popular option was the listen and feel procedure. This method required you to rely on your auditory experience to monitor sound levels. If it sounded low you blindly reached down with your hand, felt for and found the audio pot, and raised the audio level until it sounded right. If it sounded hot, you lowered the audio level. At least if the camera was on a tripod you had a fighting chance.

Riding audio when going "portable" was an altogether different experience. Imagine fumbling around, trying to make audio adjustments while at the same time concentrating on your shot and making sure the exposure was holding steady, as in sun in and out of clouds.

I mean, look at this guy in the photo below. That's fellow image gatherer Jimmy Giritlian, back around 1970. He's got a camera perched on his belly brace, but the audio mixer is down near his waist. You can see how precarious it would be to reach down and adjust audio level, but once again, that's how it was done.

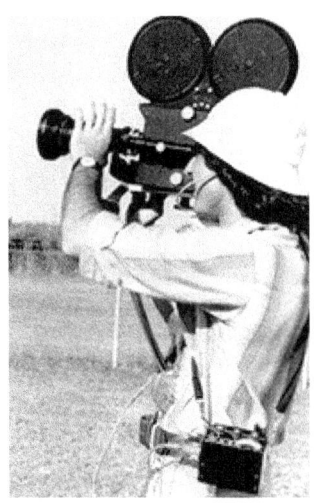

Ambient sound recording was a whole different game. When the cameraman was working "portable' and just shooting B-roll with the sound camera, the microphone that the reporter used for their interviews was placed in a shock mount on the camera to pick up the ambient or natural sound as we called it, of the area. This was a crude solution at best. Recording ambient sound so close to the camera meant that the noise of a squeaky film magazine, the grinding movement of the interior gears of the camera, or any rustling or inadvertent banging or rattling of the camera was also recorded.

The ECM-50 mike was also designed as a directional interview microphone. When used in an ambient sound situation it pretty much sucked up sound from everywhere. So why was it used? It basically came down to a "I have no other options, so this will have to work" type of situation.

Ok, so the system wasn't perfect, but remarkably, with all these challenges, the it still worked pretty well. Once again it was a simple case of doing the best we could with the technology we had at our disposal. In other words, we had no other options. We had to figure out a way to make it work.

Recollections
Cameramen Recording Audio

Graduating with a major in communications and film production, I knew a bit about cameras, but almost nothing about recording audio. "Don't let the sound meter needle get into the red" was pretty much the working formula for using a sound mixer as far as I was concerned. I had a vague notion about over modulation. Well, at least I knew what it sounded like through my headphones. I also knew that when the needle on my vu meter stayed in the red, it was bad. Other than that, besides that little bit of knowledge, I was pretty clueless.

Then there were the real challenges like a hum in the audio. When that happened my only alternative was to start frantically changing cables, microphones, checking extension cords for grounding issues. I unplugged, reconnected, and prayed a bit hoping the problem would miraculously disappear. Sometimes it did and sometimes it didn't, in which case every once in a while you just lived with it. Of course I'd get my butt chewed when I got back, but hey that was part of the game too.

Our standard issue microphone was called an ECM-50. This is the mike you see in old news pictures with wire mesh on the head. It was big, heavy, and indestructible, so much so that on more than one occasion the ECM-50 was used by a reporter as a defensive weapon. Our windscreens were big, grey, foamy looking things and we slapped our station's big, ugly, mike cube station logo on the end so everyone would know which news station we were with. This practice is still in use today. The only difference is that today cameras are usually manufactured with a camera mike attached. We plugged the mike into the camera via a thick, heavy, black XLR audio cable and let the cable hand down in a loop.

Of all the weird stuff that could negatively impact your audio, the biggest pain was the squeaky film magazine. Every once in a while, either the film reel or the take up reel in the magazine would jiggle just a tiny bit loose. No biggie except when it started to rub against the magazine door. Every time the reel turned I'd get this metal on metal sound. This resulted in a pretty loud rhythmic squeak. The only way to fix it was to open everything up and reseat the loose reel back on the spindle which you could do as long as you were shooting with daylight spools, and if there was time.

Remember. This was news was news so stopping was often out of the question as a breaking news story did not wait for technical issues. Solution? Let it go. It was kind of like a squeaky bed when "you know what" is going on. Not worth worrying about under the circumstances.

Shooting and watching my levels at the same time was another fun thing. I am not sure why, but it seemed that every time I looked down to check my vu meter, the person we were interviewing moved. When I looked back through the eyepiece, oops where'd they go? Well, you know, that's what they made b-roll for. A cut-away shot of the reporter nodding always took care of that. It happened to everyone anyway, so nobody got too upset.

I have to say though that once I got the hang of it, recording and mixing audio really wasn't all that bad. I generally only had one microphone to worry about, so I wasn't really mixing or anything thing like that. In the end, surprisingly, the system worked ninety-nine percent of the time as long as the reporter remembered to point the microphone at the person he was talking to, but that was their problem not mine.

PART II
Chapter Seven
The Silent Camera

As previously mentioned image gatherers also had access to what was called a 'silent' camera. The Bell & Howell Filmo was the mainstay of every TV News camera department throughout the world from the earliest days of TV News. It was a small, light, easy to use, and very rugged camera with three turret mounted fixed lenses. It was powered by an internal spring that was hand wound via an external hand crank. You accomplished this by holding onto a big key on the camera and rocking it up and down to wind the spring. When you hit the roll button the spring provided the power to pull the film through the camera at a constant rate. You got about a forty-second roll when it was fully wound. In all probability billions of feet of TV News film were shot with this camera.

The real beauty of the Bell & Howell Filmo was that it did not require batteries, so it was always ready. All you had to do was pick it up and point. We used to call it our "point and shoot camera". This is what the camera looked like, a very simple design.

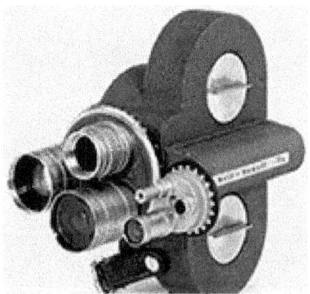

The lens configuration was usually a wide, a one-inch, and a telephoto lens. If you needed to tighten or widen your shot you spun the turret and switched lenses, pretty basic stuff. With this design, however, the cameraman did not look directly through the lens when shooting, but rather through a viewfinder called a range finder. The rangefinder had lenses that corresponded to the camera lens that you were using. It also had a distance dial that lined up the viewfinder so it corresponded to how far away your subject was from the camera. This way, you were looking through a good approximation of the actual frame.

Focusing was another challenge since you were not looking directly through the lens. The camera had a tiny side window that you could theoretically look through and focus the lens. However, it was very small and to see through it you had to lay the camera on its side and lift it up to your eye, scrunch over and try to look through the little window as you moved the focus wheel. This was virtually impossible, so instead, you made a best guess at about how far away you were from the subject and set the focus ring on the lens you were using to that distance.

Depth of field generally had you covered, at least outside. FYI depth of field is the range a shot will be in focus which is determined by your F-stop. The higher the F stop the greater your range, or depth of field. At F22 you had more or less an infinite depth of field, while wide open was much more critical.

Nothing could beat the Bell & Howell Filmo for ease of use though. It was small and relatively light so all you had to do was grab it and go. Its compact size allowed you to hold it up high or hang it down low to get all sorts of interesting angles. Since it was spring powered not battery powered it was literally ready to shoot with just the push of a button as long as you remembered to keep the spring wound.

The Filmo was also just about indestructible. They lasted for years with just a minimal amount of maintenance. Every once in a while the spring would snap, but this was a rare occurrence and not something you spent a lot of time worrying about. The neatest thing about the filmo was just how easy it was to learn how to use. All you had to do was to choose your lens, set your iris and start shooting. It was about as fool proof as it could get.

As seen in the following archival picture below, the image gatherers could operate the camera while hanging off just about anything or anywhere. That's Gordon Stevens standing on a chair getting a shot of President Kennedy. Notice also what all the other camera guys in the picture are shooting with. That's right, they all have Bell and Howell Filmos in their hands.

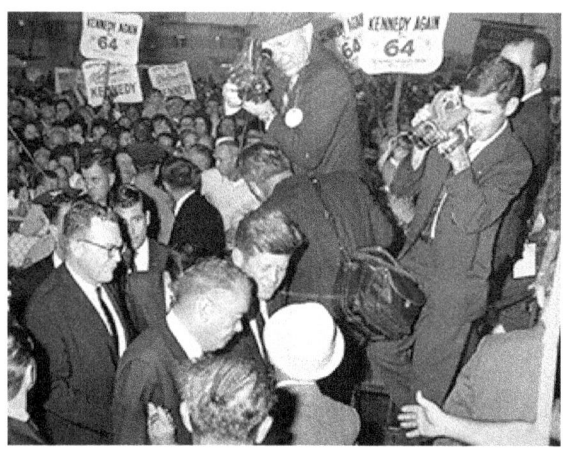

The "silent" as in "silent camera" referred to the fact that the camera could not record audio. The camera itself was anything but silent. It made a loud grinding noise when it was rolling.

One other point in Bell & Howell's favor was that the camera did not leave a flash frame between the shots so if you were really good you could edit in the camera by shooting in order, wide shot, medium shot, tight shot. while counting off the seconds in your head. This was great when you covered a late breaking story. Theoretically, if shot in sequence the film could come out of the lab ready for air. This was called editing in the camera and was a common practice on late breaking stories.

Bell & Howell Filmos were the staple of the TV News image gathering industry for many, many years. They were so easy to take around that most news stations sent their camera staff home every night with a fully loaded Bell & Howell in case a breaking story occurred during the late night hours.

Like a fireman in the firehouse, a cameraman could be out the door in minutes with his Bell & Howell in hand.

Recollections
My Bell & Howell Buddy

We carried our Bell & Howell cameras with us everywhere. Even if we went out to see a movie with a girlfriend, we were supposed to have it with us, well at least in the car. We carried them around in small brown cases with a suitcase type handle. The cases had a wooden molded interior covered in a soft corduroy type fabric. The camera had its molded spot along with a slot that fit a couple of rolls of film, and a spare take up reel. I always left my light meter inside the box in case I had to grab it in the middle of the night. It was a great little camera. I cannot remember ever having any problems with one.

The Bell & Howell was also the camera of choice for shooting out of helicopters. We used to fly around in those old bubble Bell choppers. The pilot would remove the door and strap us in and off we'd go. The camera had an adjustable film speed dial so we could shoot hi speed slow motion shots. We used this function for the chopper shots to slow down the bounces from air turbulence.

Talking about chopper shots, shooting out of a helicopter with a Bell & Howell was quite an adventure. Like I said, the pilot removed the door and strapped you in. You just had to be careful not to lean out to far. Choppers moved pretty fast and if you caught the air outside the bubble the camera would easily be yanked out of your hand by a one hundred miles an hour plus wind.

Of course, there was the time my little brown camera case got jammed behind the foot pedals of the helicopter. See the chopper had two sets of controls, one for the pilot and one for the copilot just in case. I had taken out the camera and set the case on the floor. It slid behind the pedals on my side. We were flying low over the ocean and the pilot was hovering so I could get my shot. Suddenly I noticed waves splashing alongside me, and the pilot pointing frantically at the camera case. Oooops. I quickly kicked it out and we were up and away. My fault, not the camera's. Like I said those Bell

& Howells never gave anyone any problems and that went for the cases too.

Shooting with a Bell & Howell was like doing the Foxtrot. It worked great if you followed the right steps. This was not complicated, but it was mandatory. First, crank up the spring, then I could shoot three or four shots, then crank, then shoot, then crank then shoot. I also had to remember to set and watch the footage counter. One hundred feet of film could go by pretty quickly and you didn't want to run out at the wrong time.

With all the noise the camera made it was hard to hear the sound of the film tail going through the camera. Have to admit, on more than one occasion, I didn't hear it and kept shooting on an empty reel. Yes, this was very embarrassing to try to explain to the reporter you were working with. "Ummm, I know you saw me shoot it, but errr, ummmm, the film ran out, and I didn't hear it…." Not a good career moment.

Mostly, I loved shooting with a Bell & Howell Filmo because it was my link to image gathering history. The camera was first introduced in 1923. By the time I came along they had been in use for over fifty years. Every time I picked it up a I felt a link to that history. I couldn't help thinking that the camera that had shot footage of so many major news events was now in my hands. It was my turn to take the Bell & Howell Filmo out on its next adventure.

PART II
Chapter Eight
The Light Meter

In the 1970's, besides the camera one of the image gatherer's most important tools was the light meter. You could not shoot anything without it, because it was the only way to accurately measure the light and set the exposure on a film camera. Remember, film cameras were manually operated, so exposure had to be manually set by the operator.

That is not to say it was used every time. Outside especially, a good cameraman knew from prior experience that certain light situations had certain exposure settings. Bright sun was standard, a cloudy sky might also be, but after that you better have a light meter. Over or under exposed film just did not look very good.

The light meter measured the light level of the subject you were about to shoot, whether it was the person's face, a building, or scenic landscape and translated it into an iris exposure setting that was based on the ASA of the film and the frames per second speed of the film through the camera. You did not go out with a film camera and even attempt to shoot anything without a calibrated light meter.

Properly using the light meter began with knowing the ASA of the film you were using. All film was rated according to its light sensitivity and assigned an ASA value (American Standards Association). The higher the ASA number the greater its sensitivity to light. ASA 125 was less sensitive than ASA 400 and so on. The 7240 news film that was standard throughout the industry was rated at ASA 125.

After setting the light meter for the ASA of the film stock you were using, you held the light meter into the main light source, making sure you did not inadvertently shadow it with your body. The light meter did its thing and its needle pointed to the proper exposure. It was always wise to walk around a bit and get an average reading of the area determining the range from dark to light.

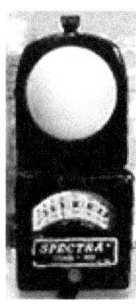

Finally, you had to calculate for the actual speed the film moved through the camera which was measured in frame per second or fps. TV News image gathering cameras ran at a constant twenty-four fps. Some cameras, like the Bell & Howell Filmo had variable speed settings to allow shooting fast or slow motion. When you shot at anything other than twenty-four fps you had to adjust the exposure accordingly in order to properly expose the film. There was always a lot to think about with exposure so it required a good deal of vigilance on behalf of the image gatherer who better be paying close attention to what was going on. Speed was important of course, but so was not making stupid mistakes.

Exposure was also dependent on what you were shooting. If it was a person's face you pretty much stuck with the reading you got from the light meter. Although even there an individual's skin color had to be taken into consideration. Darker skin required about a full stop below your light reading, so again you had to make the necessary adjustment. If it was a scenic type shot, you also adjusted according to the ratio of light to dark areas. Fortunately, the film had significant latitude so as long as you were close it worked. The closer you were to perfect though, the richer your color, so perfect was always the goal.

Using a light meter was an art form that you learned by trial and error. Film cameras did not have a monitor to evaluate color and exposure. You'd take your readings, shoot your film and hope for the best. You would critically view your results and determine the accuracy of your exposure under the specific circumstances you were shooting. Then you'd file this information in your brain for next time and apply it accordingly.

In the world of TV News, you literally had about five seconds to figure all this out. In the more exacting world of news documentaries using a light meter was way more precise. Tom Feldman from high school documentary fame, spent a number of years working on documentaries. He became well acquainted with light meter usage. Keep in mind that documentary production was a bit more involved than TV News image gathering. Translated, you got a chance to scout a location first and make a plan, rather than just showing up and shooting like news guys did. The extra time was great, but the budgets were very tight which meant you had to get it right the first time. All in all, Tom's story reveals the vital importance of the light meter when shooting film. There were no short cuts in the process.

Recollections
Using a Light Meter and More

Back in the 1970's, the first thing I would do to prep for a job was to get my light meters calibrated. Notice I said "meters", I always carried more than one. I carried a Spectra light meter and also a low light Spectra light meter, because often we were working with as low as six-foot candles. A mistake of two-foot candles meant you had twenty-five percent more or less light. That was significant, so you had to be precise.

Learning how to take a light reading was key to the whole process. The film had maybe a half stop tolerance. Any mistake bigger than that and you were looking at a reshoot. The film we used had a pretty low ASA so we needed a good amount of light to get a properly exposed image. Also, nothing was left unlit. Blacks became just mud, so even dark areas needed some light to make the image look good. This was especially true when we shot at outside at night.

We took light readings constantly as we lit. With every light we added, we had to calculate its effect on the overall scene. Film only went through the camera one time. Once it was exposed and processed it was done. We did not have the luxury we have today to tweak color or exposure in postproduction. We got what we got, and if we wanted to keep getting work, we had to be spot on. Film was an artist's medium. We had to know what we were doing in every aspect of the process. Any mistakes or miscalculations resulted in catastrophes.

With all we had to deal with, our set-ups took some time. Actually the whole process could be long and arduous. For us though, there was great satisfaction when we saw the dailies and everything looked good. Film was a handcrafted experience. When it looked good, you got a craftsman like feeling of satisfaction so the light meter for us was more like a paint brush is to an artist.

PART II
Chapter Nine
Film Exposure

As you can see from the previous recollections, image gathering on film was a very complex process. It required a depth of practical knowledge that could only be acquired through hands on experience. The deeper that level of experience, the better your chances were for a good outcome. Experience was especially important when you shot news film in the midst of a breaking news story. When that happened the degree of difficulty went up several notches so you absolutely had to know what you were doing. You had to rely on instinct.

To shoot TV News film, you had to understand exposure, color temperature, film stock, and filtration for starters. You were out there by yourself so you had to be able to think on your feet and evaluate every situation to determine how all these elements would interact in order to give you the image you were after. Each time you picked up your film camera you thought of a previous, similar situation and you'd base your game plan on what had worked before. It was vital to store all this knowledge in the image gathering database in your brain.

Of all the elements involved exposure was the most important. Over or under exposed film looked horrible, and since you shot with reversal film, there was absolutely nothing you could do about it once it came out of the lab. Setting exposure for TV News image gathering was crucial. Having said that, determining the proper exposure for news image gatherers was very different from the world of documentary production as described by Tom Feldman. News guys had light meters, but did not always have time or opportunity to use them. You couldn't exactly stop a breaking news story so you could walk around with your light meter and figure out exposure.

Here's how it worked. You showed up at the scene, got your gear together, and went to work. You tried to take some quick readings to confirm your thoughts, but you also had to have a light meter in your head. News film stock had about one stop of latitude, so you had a little flexibility. You could be a little over or a little under, but not much. You had to develop an eye that could look at a scene and judge where to set the F-stop on your camera. The light meter was more for confirmation. It would give you a starting point, but from there you were constantly tweaking.

This sounds a bit daunting, but in reality after you had been doing it for a while, it became second nature. Since you always used the same film stock, you intuitively knew the correct exposure in most situations, at least when you were outside. Bright sun was f22, light shade you'd drop to f16, deeper shade f11 and so on. You knew those values. As mentioned, you had your light meter around your neck, or on your belt so you could pull it out and take a quick look to make sure you were in the ballpark. Many was the time you'd see guys back pedaling down the street while holding the camera in their right hand and taking light readings with their left. Usually though, you found out how close you were when you viewed your film.

The biggest challenge came in those situations in which the light conditions were not consistent. Following the action outside as clouds darted across the sky blocking the sun, or even worse, the person you were shooting passed in and out of the shade.

Good luck when that happened.

Recollections
Setting Exposure

So, I was standing outside the courthouse with my camera on my shoulder along with three other camera guys from the different local TV stations and a still guy from the newspaper. We were all staring at a door in the back of the Dade County Courthouse in Miami, Florida. It was late afternoon and we were waiting to get a shot of a defendant in a big court case. This was and will always be known as a "gang bang". Translation, you, and about three or four other camera crews, plus a few still guys wait and wait and wait. Then suddenly the guy you need to shoot comes out the door and the whole camera gang has about seven seconds to get their shots. Hence the name "gang bang".

The lighting conditions at this time of day were particularly challenging. The door from the courthouse was in the sun. The sidewalk path leading from the door to the street had many twists and turns. It went into light building shade, then deeper shade, and finally back out into the bright sun. There was a difference of about three or four stops. I had shot here before, but I still took a few light readings when I first arrived. Unfortunately for me, the earth kept moving around the sun and the conditions kept changing. Oh and did I mention the big, white, puffy clouds that danced across the sky that occasionally blocked the sun wrecking havoc on my exposure?

Well, the door opens and here he comes alongside his attorney. As a group we all start shooting while walking backwards. I keep the frame wide to minimize the bounciness, leave my focal length at about ten feet, and start opening up my iris as we get into the shade. My brain begins making quick calculations; light shade is half a stop, deeper shade full stop, the deepest shade two stops. I've got one eye on the eyepiece and the other eye checking the iris ring. My third eye keeps glancing back to make sure I don't trip over something and break my neck. My elbows are also subtly jabbing in order for me to keep my position in the mob.

In the deepest shade the attorney decides to stop and answer reporters' questions. While I am still rolling I pull out my light meter, which I always kept in a case on my belt, and took a quick read. My guess was a half stop off so I made the adjustment just as a cloud rolled across the sun. I checked my meter again, opened up another half stop, then had to back off again when the sun came back out.

The interview was brief and they started walking again out of the shade and back into the sun. Everything was moving too fast for me to use the meter, so I had to make my best guess with the iris. The only way to be successful in these situations was to go on auto pilot and let my instincts guide me. There was no time to think, I just had to act.

I always viewed the footage when it came out of the lab, and then filed all the info in my brain for next time. That mental data was all I had to get me through those tough shooting situations. It came down to instinct, some luck, and experience. Viewing the film though was key to my success. To be a good student, you have to study, study, study. Everyday I shot film, I was in school. Everyday I shot film I learned something new. Everyday I shot film I had to reach back into my bag of experience and grab something out to apply to what I had to do. It was not easy, but when it worked it was magical.

PART II
Chapter Ten
Color Temperature and Lighting

Next up is color temperature. All light has a color temperature value measured in degrees Kelvin, named after physicist William Thomas, First Baron Kelvin. Lord Kelvin as he is known was instrumental in discovering and determining the color temperature of light back in the late 1800's. Now, in our daily lives nobody really thinks about the temperature of color. In the world of film however, it makes a huge difference.

All film is coated with a light sensitive chemical emulsion that is balanced for a specific color temperature. Generally speaking, film's color temperature is either rated for daylight, 5600K or incandescent light, 3200K, though there are other variations for specific uses. The bottom line is if you want your film to come out with accurate color you better be aware of its manufactured color temperature before you shoot with it.

As mentioned earlier, in the 1970's, news film was color balanced for 3200K or tungsten light, with an ASA of 125. Quick note, tungsten is the element used in movie/TV production interior light bulbs because when you run electricity through it, tungsten glows at a constant 3200K. This is very important because color photography must be matched with a consistent value in order to produce consistent results.

When shooting TV News film, you literally could go from inside to outside and vice versa. Obviously, you couldn't change film stock during news coverage so you needed a way to quickly and easily make the necessary adjustment. The answer was the color correcting filter. Because TV News film was tungsten balanced, if you were shooting outside you needed an orange color correction filter to add warmth to the more bluish daylight so the color would be right. The 85B filter was the recommended choice to color correct Kodak 7240. There were glass filters you could screw on to the front of the lens, but the quick and dirty solution used in TV News was a small plastic, orange colored gel sheet made by a company called Wratten.

Using scissors, you'd cut out a small piece of the filter gel and set it into a filter holder that slid into a slot behind the lens inside the camera. Because you had to open the camera to do this, you had to roll off a couple of feet of film or you would expose the film that was threaded in the camera. The Bell & Howell Filmo had an outside slot that you could access without exposing film.

The real trick with color correction was remembering to put the filter in or take it out as needed. There was no worse feeling in the world than shooting for several minutes then opening up the camera to change film and discovering you had accidentally left the filter in when you didn't need it or vice versa. Shooting inside with tungsten light with the filter in turned everything orange, leaving it out when you went into sunlight left the film blue. Both of these were very poor choices.

Adding the 85B filter also changed your ASA. It went from ASA 125 to ASA 80, so you had to remember to adjust your light meter to get an accurate exposure reading. For really bright, exterior conditions Wratten added neutral density to the filter, which once again lowered your ASA though it did not affect the color temperature.

Understanding color temperature was a vital part of learning to light for TV News. To begin with lighting for TV News image gathering was pretty basic when you actually had time to do it. Outside it was what it was. A white bounce card or small reflector was the most you could hope for. You did not have access to exterior lighting fixtures.

Interiors offered a different challenge. Since you were on a news story, not a movie set, you pretty much had to figure out how to make it work. Lights were often needed to get a decent exposure, but you usually found yourself adding to the existing situation and trying to match the color temperature, rather than turning everything off and starting from scratch. You were always in practical locations not on sound stages. You couldn't very well ask the office manager to turn off all the lights in an office environment. You learned how to make it work.

TV News cameramen carried small very basic light kits. Standard issue were three 600w open faced tungsten fixtures and a few pieces of color correction gel and diffusion. This was fine for a basic interview set up. Three light set ups were about all you had time for anyway. They gave you a key, a fill, and a back light for separation. The bigger lighting challenge was trying to light an entire room.

The trick was learning to blend different light sources into a workable color temperature. You had to decide if the unlit room was more daylight or more tungsten or more fluorescent. You pretty much had to go with it because you had neither the tools nor the time to start blocking off windows or unscrewing bulbs. This way your lighting added to what was there, rather than fighting against it. You used your eyes and brain to read the room and lit accordingly. Once again, you based everything on what had worked for you in a previous, similar situation.

Recollections
Reading the Room

Ok, so I'd be in a room with a window and overhead tungsten lights. I had to decide which light was dominant, the daylight or the bulbs? If I set up my own lights how much color correction would I need, half blue, quarter blue, full blue? With film all these values made a big difference in the end product. The wrong color correction would leave me with some weird looking film that could range from blue to orange, depending on how close or far I was in my assessment.

Florescent light was a whole different game. Many offices back then used big banks of florescent fixtures to light their workspace. In those days' fluorescent bulbs ran from blue to green to pink depending on the manufacturer. There was a separate filter for them, but it didn't always achieve the look I was after. It all depended on, that's right, the color temperature of the bulb itself. One trick I used was to squint my eyes and stare at the bulbs. Somehow doing that allowed you to see their color. I would choose the filter and gel my lights accordingly.

The biggest challenge shooting inside were people's faces. I mean, nobody watching TV knew what color the room was supposed to be, but they sure knew that there was no such thing as blue people, so I concentrated on the light that hit people's skin. As long as the people looked good, I could live with the background.

Whatever, with film I got what I got. However, it was vital to remember the conditions I was shooting in and results I got for the next time I was in a similar situation. That way I could make the proper adjustments to improve the outcome. I based everything I did on past experiences. It was that old data base in the brain thing. There was a good deal of trial and error, but with experience the errors became less and less. Precision was a dream, I just had to be close.

PART II
Chapter Eleven
The Sun Gun

In fast breaking situations at night or inside a building, setting up lights was out of the question. In these cases, lighting for TV News usually meant sticking a portable, battery powered light on top of your camera and off you'd go. These lights were given the name "sun-gun", not sure why, but that was the name then and that is still the name now. Shooting with a sun-gun is still done today, but it sure was different back in the film days.

Check out the archival picture below. That's a 1970's sun-gun on the camera of Gordon Stevens.

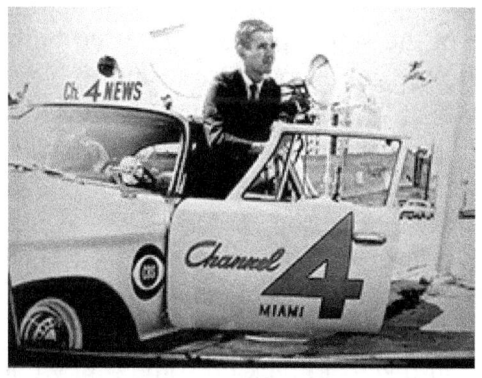

As you can see, back then the sun gun was a big, aluminum reflective lamp with a large flood light type bulb. It put out a very soft and even source of light. This huge thing was mounted to the camera by a large gator type clamp that was clamped to the camera's film magazine. It also fit on the Bell & Howell Filmo via a camera shoe mounted to the camera like you see in the picture.

A large rechargeable battery belt powered the sun gun. You could either wear it around your waist or sling it over your shoulder. Setting exposure was the big challenge. With this type of lighting you had to activate that light meter in your brain, as you could not hold the camera, turn on the sun gun and take a light meter reading.

You just had to know that at four feet away you were at a certain F-stop, and at eight feet you opened up a stop, etc.

You also had to take into account ambient light. Shooting interiors gave you one set of values, shooting outside at night was very different. It really depended on what else was going on. Darkness has a nasty habit of swallowing light so you had to adjust accordingly.

An interior shot of say an office setting with office lighting was a whole different story. Once again, there was that good old experience thing. You had to know the correct formula for each type of lighting situation when you shot film with a sun=gun. The only way to get that knowledge was by shooting in an environment and remembering what you did and how it all came out.

The bulb in the sun gun was a tungsten bulb. It could be color corrected with blue gel if you were trying to blend it into a daylight situation. However, doing this resulted in the loss of about half the punch of the light, so it had no real value outside during the day. It also meant that the on the fly exposure settings changed as well.

Sometimes you just said screw it, and blasted away with a tungsten bulb even though the ambient light had daylight spill in it. This got you a properly shot face, but as the light fell off in the background, you'd start to pick up some funky color. Again, as long as the face looked good, you could live with the background.

Whenever you shot film, there was always something to figure out and with every adjustment there was a ripple effect that altered a different value. The sun gun was no exception to this rule. Using it was definitely an acquired skill that took experience to master.

Recollections
Shooting with a Sun Gun

Image gathering on film with a sun gun was quite a challenge. To begin with, the lamp and the battery belt added quite a bit of weight for me to carry around. Since shooting with a sun gun usually meant I was also shooting hand held, the extra weight made a big difference.

The second issue was the battery belt. It weighed about twenty pounds. If I wore it around my waist it could slip down taking my pants with it. If I had it hanging off my shoulder it was also awkward, especially in a crowd. I'd swing around quickly and whack somebody in the head with it, or it could slip off my shoulder and yank the light, which was clipped to the magazine via a gator grip, off the camera.

Of course there was the time I was shooting a somber church service with my sun gun. I was being so careful to be quiet so as not to interrupt the quiet decorum. Unfortunately, my sun gun did not cooperate. The belt slipped off of my shoulder, and yanked the lamp off of the camera. Bang, crash, boom the aluminum light rattled across the stone floor. Miraculously the bulb did not shatter. I quickly picked it up and clamped it back onto the magazine, never looking up to see the glaring stares that I am sure were directed my way.

I only got one belt to use for the day. It was rechargeable, but after about twenty minutes of use, it started to die and essentially, you were screwed. Lunch break at a friendly restaurant offered a prime charging opportunity since we usually did not come back to base until the late afternoon. It took a couple of hours to recharge, but I took what I could get. A one-hour charge bought me some time.

If my sun gun died, my only other option was pushing the film. This was a processing technique where the lab altered the development time which gave us an extra stop or two. It came with some pretty nasty grain, so it was never a great option, but I did it when I had to. It also kind of messed up the lab processing schedule. If they were pushing your film, nobody else's could be run at the same time. Forty-five minutes were lost for the whole operation, and this was not always possible. Needless to say film got pushed if and only if there was not better alternative.

Shooting with a sun gun and a film camera was even more complicated when multiple crews were involved. On a big story, there might be four or more cameras shooting beside to me with their sun guns blazing. The problem was that if two more cameramen jumped in and turned on their lights, suddenly I was two-stops hot, or if two broke off and left, I was two stops dark. I had to keep one hand and one eye on my iris ring, opening it up or shutting it down as the situation dictated it. I had to ride the iris like a wild pony while relying on the light meter in my brain to make the necessary adjustments.

When I shot news film, it was vital to always pay attention to changing lighting conditions. I always kept my hand on the iris ring on the lens ready at any moment to open or close the iris.

PART II
Chapter Twelve
Handling Film

In many ways film seemed alive. It was this mysterious coated plastic stuff that rolled through the camera, and past your lens. Then after processing, it suddenly became a strip of images. Miraculous right? I suppose there is a sound technical explanation as to how all this worked, but whatever. The bottom line was if you had done your job correctly, these were beautiful images, if not they sucked. Either way there was little you could do about it once it came out of the soup.

The Kodak film we used in 1970 was called reversal film. This meant that you processed the film and got your images directly without the use of a negative. There was only one copy and no chance of making any more. Basically it came out of processing ready to edit. That was the good news. The bad news was that if anything happened to your film during or after processing, you were out of luck. There was only one copy. If it got screwed up for any reason you were done.

Since film processing was also a manual operation in a film lab, anything could and did go wrong. Entire news stories were lost due to a processing malfunction or human error in the lab.

Film was also prone to certain technical issues, but there was no way to check your work in the field. Film playback was an obvious impossibility. You could have a light leak in your camera and shoot an entire news story. The only way you found out was when the film came out of the lab and portions of it were fogged, or had weird flash frames. You could collect a speck of dirt on the pressure plate or on a roller that would scratch your film.

The only way you found out about scratches was when went to unload the camera and you opened it up, looked inside, and saw film shavings piled up. This was the telltale sign that your film would have a squiggly scratch line wriggling through the image. All issues with film were revealed after your film came out of the lab, when, of course, it was too late to do anything about them.

Loading and unloading film was also tricky. We've already described threading it properly through the camera's series of rollers, but the loading and unloading was equally precarious. Film is exposed when it comes in contact with light. When that happens through the camera lens it's magical. When it comes in contact with light outside of a camera, it's a disaster. The image is completely wiped out and all you are left with is a strip of clear plastic. An important part of the cameraman's job was to make sure the film was exposed in the right place

Ok, well guess what? This was news coverage and that meant that often you had no control about where you changed camera loads. You were out somewhere covering a news story, and your camera ran out of film. Wherever you were at that moment was where you had to change the film load. You stopped what you were doing, set the camera on the ground or in your lap, and you unloaded the exposed roll, placed it in an aluminum film can, taped it up, and loaded a fresh load. It wasn't hard, you just needed to be careful to do it properly.

Changing those two hundred-foot daylight loads was pretty easy. The solid black reels protected the film. You would just lose the last three feet or so. No big deal there, you knew it and rolled off a few feet of film before you started and before you unloaded your film.

Changing four hundred foot cores was a different story. They were the preferred choice for those situations where you knew you needed to shoot for longer periods of time and you did not want to stop and change the film, like an important speech or press conference. These cores were wound tightly around a yellow plastic disc and did not have the benefit of protection from exposure that the daylight rolls had. They were four hundred feet of raw film, and had to be loaded or unloaded in complete darkness. Film was exposed by coming into contact with light whether inside of a camera or an inadvertent moment.

If you were out in the field, obviously it was not possible to access a dark room. Under those circumstances, your only option was to unload or load your film in a changing bag. This was a large, heavy-duty black sack with two elasticized armholes to reach through to work inside of the bag, and a zipper to close it up. A changing bag was a great tool that could quickly become a nightmare if handled incorrectly.

Recollections
The Changing Bag

I used a changing bag only when I had absolutely no other options and I had to change a film core out in the middle of nowhere. Why do I say that? Let me explain. Keep in mind, I worked in hot and humid Miami, Florida so sticking your hands into a black cloth bag was not much fun. Think sweaty arms and sweaty palms, and you begin to get the idea.

Anyway, here is the process. The bag was opened and closed via a heavy zipper so the first step was to lay out the bag, find the zipper and well, open it up. I put my shot film magazine and a fresh film core inside, then zipped it up. Note here, you had to put both the new load and the shot load in the bag at the same time. Once you opened things up, there was no going back. Remember, when light hits film, it is all over for the film.

Once it was all zipped up and secure, I put my arms in the armholes then blindly removed the fresh roll from the can. Kodak wound it up super tight so it was easy to handle. I found that if I closed my eyes while I did all this I could visualize what my hands were doing inside the bag.

I laid the new roll carefully down inside the bag then opened up the magazine and gingerly removed the shot film, put it inside the now empty film can and closed it up. Then I grabbed the fresh, raw film core, fit the core adaptor inside the yellow plastic disc, dropped it onto the magazine spindle, threaded the beginning of the roll out through the magazine roller, and then, screwed back on the magazine door. I could then unzip the changing bag, take everything out, and I was good to go.

It sounds pretty simple, right? Ha-ha-ha, changing film in a changing bag was one of the most stressful events a cameraman ever faced. Where do I begin? Trying to use a black changing bag outside in ninety-degree tropical weather was interesting. The second I put my arms and hands inside, they immediately started to sweat profusely, as in soaking wet. The moisture on my hands made the film sticky and all sorts of things could happen at this point. Sticky fingers, film coating, was potentially a really bad combo. Not to mention the scariest moment of all when the plastic film core disk slipped out of the middle and all of the film turned into a big pile of spaghetti. All I could do at that point was to carry the whole mess back to the lab and let them figure it out in a darkroom. Yes, this actually happened.

Assuming I got the shot core out properly and into the can, I then had to feel around and find the fresh load. Once I found that, I located my magazine, got everything lined up, and pulled off the little piece of light blue tape Kodak used to stick the end of the film to the core so it didn't unwind by itself. By the way, that little piece of tape could be deadly if I lost track of it and it ended up in my magazine or something. It could really gum up the works if it stuck to the wrong place and was fed through the camera. Yes, it actually happened to me, once, and yes it was a big mess.

Anyway, I always pushed the film end through the magazine roller and fed about six inches through before seating the film core on the little black core adapter which was hopefully still there. If that had fallen out, well let's hope it hadn't. The six-inch tail was very important. If for any reason I lost it, I had to put the magazine back in the bag, open everything up, and push it through again. Obviously, I could not reload the camera unless I could pull the film out of the magazine. Anyway, once I had seated my new core I had screwed the door back on the magazine, and I was good to go.

All I had left to do was to remove the magazine and shot film can from the bag. I had to tape up the can with the shot film and label it as shot film. Raw film had a thick piece of white tape around the diameter of the can. For shot film we wound the tape around the top and bottom of the can so that it crossed the label. This was the universal symbol for shot film, but we also wrote on the can anyway.

Finally, last step, I took my newly loaded magazine and fed the film through to the take up side, affixed it to the take up reel, and screwed on the magazine door. If you were good at it, and nothing went wrong, you could get it all done in about three minutes. Trying to go faster was always a bad choice. It was better to take my time and do it right than risk ruining four hundred feet of a filmed news story that could not be reshot.

With all this changing bag stuff to deal with, if I could wait until I returned to the station to can my shot film, I did. This was a better choice, though it was not free from its own set of issues. Even though I was inside an air-conditioned building, changing cores was still an adventure. Our equipment room had a lock on the door, so nobody could walk in on me when I had shot film out on the counter. I just had to remember to lock the door. I also had to be very exact about where I put everything on the counter. Once I turned the lights out and started the process, I could not turn on the lights to find the magazine door, the film core, or the can. So I would very carefully prep it all before I turned off the lights.

If I did the proper preparation it was a piece of cake. The camera's take up wound the film tightly and there were few issues. However, if I was in a hurry I ended up feeling around the counter in the dark, desperately searching for where I put all the little pieces of the puzzle. Failure to prepare, is preparing to fail as the saying goes. Anyway that was the deal with film. It had to be processed in the lab, not exposed on the counter.

PART II
Chapter Thirteen
Rolling Film

Film was an expensive budget item for TV News operation so over shooting was a big no-no for cameramen and reporters alike. Management always harassed you about your film ratio. This was how much you shot on a story versus how much film you actually used when you story was edited. It was especially tricky shooting speeches and press conferences. You could not just roll on everything and figure it out in post like they do today. The reporter had to listen, have you roll at the right time, and then stop, roll again, then stop.

Also, when you started to approach the end of the film roll, you had to figure out the right time to reload the camera. You always carried a second loaded film magazine, but timing was everything. You'd signal to the reporter what was going on, and he'd know he had about a minute or less to decide. On the reporter's signal you stopped the camera, pulled off the film magazine, grabbed the second magazine, locked it onto the camera and threaded the camera. If you went super fast it still took about a minute to actually accomplish the whole task. Of course the minute you stopped to reload something really important would happen. Murphy's law always applied.

And then there were the short ends. Whatever unexposed film you had left in the camera when you were finished shooting a story was called a short end. Anything over twenty-five feet was deemed necessary to save, so you pulled it out of the camera and dropped it into a film can. You'd label the can accordingly and save it for a shoot where you just needed a few shots and a small load would work. You never threw away unused film. That was very much frowned upon by budget minded upper management to whom film was money.

There was one final important detail to this whole film loading procedure. You had to remember to reset your film counter on the back of the camera. The film counter was like the odometer in your car. You reset it at zero when you put in a fresh load. It measured the film in feet as it went through the camera. If you forgot to reset, it at zero you had absolutely no way of knowing how much film you had left in your camera. You couldn't exactly open up the magazine door and take a look inside. This would quickly become a huge problem because obviously you could not anticipate the next load change.

Of course, even if you had reset your film counter, you still did not know exactly when you were going to run out of film. Viewfinders were just eyepieces that gave you the view through the lens. There were absolutely no informational readouts posted. As you were shooting you might have an idea, but it was at best a guess-timate. Even if you reset the footage counter, you did not know exactly when you were going to run out of film. All you would hear was a tick-tick sound of the end of the film which was the sound the tail made as it was running through the rollers and sprockets. Hearing this sound at the wrong moment on a breaking news story was every image gatherer's nightmare.

Recollections
The Nightmare Comes True

We were covering a visit by then President Ronald Reagan. I had the indoor camera position to cover the press conference. Chris Clausen, whom we mentioned earlier, was the outside crew shooting local color and the arrival. She was with a reporter and he thought it would be nice to shoot a short piece about the excitement generated by a presidential visit so they'd have something different for the 11 o'clock news. They shot a bunch of color stuff, and did some short interviews. In the midst of this President Reagan pulled up in the limo, got out and started working the crowd.

Reagan was standing right in front of Chris when it happened. A man in the crowd pulled out a toy pistol and pointed it at the President. All hell broke lose as the Secret Service agents wrestled him to the ground. She was in the perfect spot to get the action. Later when the film was processed we could see it all. You saw the

President, you saw the guy, you almost saw the gun then you saw an immediate flash frame that signified the end of the film roll. That's right she ran out of film just when it all hit the fan. Everyone in the newsroom saw the footage, and everyone groaned. It was truly a nightmare realized. By the time Chris reloaded it was all over. President Reagan had been whisked away, the gunman had been cuffed and carted off to jail, and the President had moved inside. The moment was gone, but never forgotten.

Some might say, well so what, but when your life is dedicated to image gathering, these are the moments you live for. I have been retired for several years, but I still have dreams where I'm somewhere with my camera and something incredible happens and the camera won't roll. I wake up with a start, my heart pounding, and this terrible feeling of frustration and loss permeating my mind.

PART II
Chapter Fourteen
Film Editing and Getting it on the Air

Even though editing is not the same as image gathering, it is an important part of the image gathering process and certainly bears mentioning in this history. It is the point at which your gathered images are assembled into a cohesive story and the determination is made as to how successful your image gathering efforts were. A well-told story matched with well-crafted images is after all the ultimate goal

In the 1970's, after you'd gone out, shot your story, unloaded your camera, and dropped your film off at the lab, you became an image editor. There was a chief editor, but there were way too many stories for one person to cut, so the process relied on the individual cameramen to edit the news packages they had worked on with the reporters. Here's how it worked.

It took the lab about forty-five minutes to process your film. The film came out on large film cores that the chief editor would spin down, and separate into the different stories onto separate film reels. After this was done, everyone grabbed their footage, found an open edit bay and started looking at what they had shot.

Each edit bay had a small tabletop Zeiss Ikon Moviescope viewer. There were two hand cranks to roll the film back and forth through a little 3 inch by 3-inch viewer window. You ran your film through this viewer and assessed your footage. See archival photo below.

The little glass screen was illuminated with a small light bulb that projected your film's images in that little window. Over time, the window got scratched and dirty so your film looked like it was shot with a fog filter or something. Ultimately you got used to the look and even though it was not crisp and clear, you comprehended what was a good image, and what was not. At the very least it did give you an accurate reproduction of color and exposure.

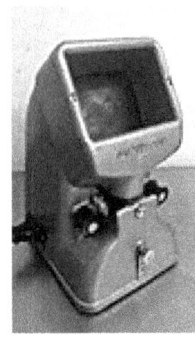

Once you had the film set up in the viewer, the reporter came in. You'd discuss your shots with them, emphasizing the best moments and hoping they'd be included in the script. You always wanted your best shots used, while the reporter had a news story to report, so there was a certain level of necessary compromise. The reporter picked out their sound bites by listening to them on a mag stripe sound reader as seen in the archival photo below. The sound reader was hooked up to a small speaker so you could monitor the audio. The speaker was just good enough so you could gauge the quality of your sound recording. Not that it mattered. As long as you could hear something, it went on the air.

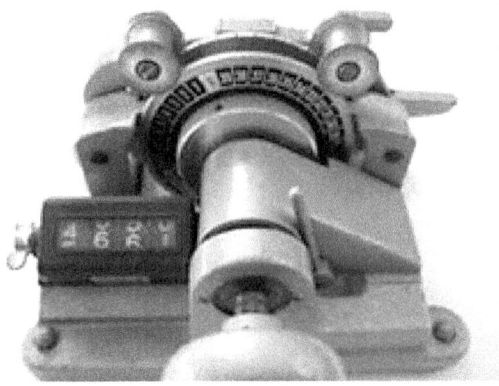

The newsroom was soon filled with the sound of the clicking and clacking of script writing. Once approved by the show producer, the reporters cut audio tracks on an audio cart machine that put pauses in the tape at the end of each block of copy. Each block was timed with a stopwatch with special notations for specific story points. This info, along with the ins and outs of the sound bites, were noted on the script and turned over to the image editors who usually had a little over an hour plus to pull the shots and hot splice it all together into a film package for the evening news.

The actual editing process was completely manual. It began by reading the script and determining which shots you needed. You were pretty familiar with the footage because you had shot it a couple of hours earlier. You'd set up the film reel on the spindles, thread it through the viewer and sound reader, and then cruise through the film tearing off your shots and finding the sound bites.

Each shot was hung in order on a pin on the film hanger perched over a canvas covered barrel. Film scratched very easily so care had to be given during handling. You had worked so hard to shoot it, the last thing you wanted to have happen was to physically mess it up in the editing process. You were, after all, working with the one and only original.

One note here, the reporters often wanted to combine two sound bites to create a shorter and more to the point statement. This was done by literally splicing together the two sound bites. The problem was that this left a jump cut where you made the edit. The solution to this problem was to take a shot of the reporter listening and put it on a separate reel for a cutaway to cover the splice. The main story was on the A-roll and these cutaways were on the B-roll. The B-roll shot would be cued up, and the news' show director was given the time cue needed to roll the B projector. He would then roll the B-roll, hit the switcher to cut to it then cut back to the A-roll at the appropriate time. You usually provided about six seconds of film to create a three second cut away shot.

The same procedure was followed with footage that illustrated what the interviewee was describing. If the sound bite was about garbage in the bay, you showed the garbage the person was talking about on the B-roll. Eventually the term B-roll became the name for all footage that was not a sound bite. It is a term that is still used today with the same definition, even though most people have no idea where it came from.

After the story's shots, sound bites, and B-roll were all pulled it was time to assemble the piece. You grabbed the first shot, and hot spliced it to what was called academy leader. This was the classic 5-4-3-2-1 count down filmstrip that you used to see all the time when you watched movies. The film was always cued by the projectionist to the "2" to give the show director a two second lead for the story. It was his job to roll it in from there.

Anyway, you'd cue the first frame to zero on the sound reader/footage counter, cut it to the length you needed, then lay it back into the hot splicer. This device was plugged into the wall and was designed to heat up to a specific temperature that would greatly speed up the gluing process without impacting the film. It literally took only a few seconds to cook your splice. The last thing you wanted was to have a splice break while your film was rolling live to air on the film projector. See archival photo below of a hot splicer.

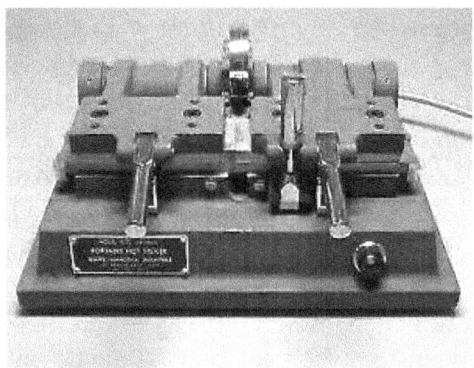

The next step was to grab the next shot, trim the edge in the splicer, scrape the emulsion off the film, gave it a brush of glue then slam the splicer down. There was a rhythm to it. You grabbed the shot, set it in the splicer, sliced away the jagged edge, scraped away the emulsion, swabbed on the glue, slammed down the splicer, locked it briefly, and glued the new shot onto the reel you were building.

One, two, three you counted in your head before you flipped up the hot splicer, checked the splice, and moved on to the next shot. Set, scrape, glue, slam, set scrape, glue, slam was the beat as you built the piece. If you have ever done it, you can probably still recall the sounds of the film edit bay mixed with the pungent odor of the glue.

When you were finished, you would roll it through the viewer and sound reader one last time to listen and to make sure you had hit the time marks with the right shots. It was critical that your edit times and the reporter's times on the script matched. If he was describing a red house at sixteen seconds, you had to show a red house at sixteen seconds. If the block of copy was timed at twenty seconds, then you had to make sure that you had twenty seconds of film to cover it.

That is basic editing 101, not much has changed there. However, in those days these pieces were not preassembled. The film went up on a reel and the reporter's narration went up on an audio cart. They only met live on the air.

All you could do was your part in the process. You wanted to be as accurate as possible according to the information you were given. After that, if someone else in the process messed up, well, it was on them not you.

Next step. When you finished assembling your story, you hand cleaned it by running in a cleaning solution soaked film wipe to get off any fingerprints or dirt. Then you handed your work to the chief editor. It was his job to compile all the stories in the correct order on two show reels, the A-roll and the B-roll.

The show reels had to be assembled exactly in the order that they would be viewed during the news broadcast. Amidst the reporters' stories were also other film stories that the anchorman was going to voice over live so the chief editor had to be spot on with his assembly. If the order on the reel was messed up, well there wasn't much you could do about it. All the show editors always did a quick double check before the film left the newsroom for the film projection room

Just a quick tribute here for the chief editor I had the honor to work with back in the 1970's and 80's. His name was Joe Martinez. Joe had seen it all and done it all. He was very cool, calm, and collected under fire never adding to the chaos, but rather providing the quiet port in the storm. I never saw Joe get flustered or upset. Even with last second beat the deadline work, his demeanor never changed. This was and is a vital attribute for any TV News editor that works under a deadline. If you lose it under pressure, it is all over, so go find something else to do with your life.

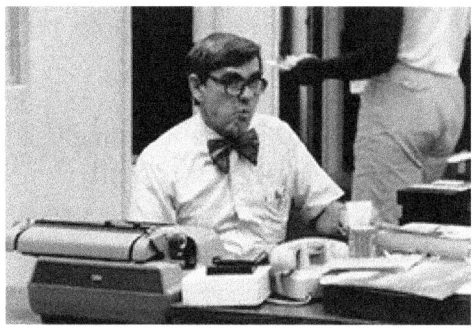

Joe was a great mentor and role model to all of us that passed through WTVJ. Joe was also known for his bow ties. This was an age where people came to work more formally dressed. Ties were mandatory for men in the office, but Joe always wore a bow tie for a very practical reason. He said that a regular tie could get caught in the hot splicer. Makes sense right? Ultimately, it was Joe's job to get the reels up to projection for the six o'clock evening broadcast. He never panicked and he never failed.

Finally, everything was ready for show time, well sort of anyway. What you had were several pieces of a puzzle that still had to be assembled. You had the film stories on reels and reporter's audio on carts. How are you going to put Humpty Dumpty together? Well, in the 1970's, this was done live to air in the TV station's control room. There was a director, an AD, a sound mixer, and a producer to oversee the process.

Here's how it worked. The film was cued up on a projector called a film chain and rolled on cue by the director. The film chain converted the film images to an electronic signal that would then be broadcast in real time to the viewers. The audio tech in the control room had the carts ready to be manually rolled at the appropriate cues. The news' show director was responsible for making it happen live to air.

In this picture, sent in by John Lutz a news' show director I worked with at WTVJ, you see him at the control board. It was his responsibility to roll the film, punch in the B-roll shots, and make sure the anchorman knew what was going on. He had the script and all the cues to look at, but an AD was at his side to call out the cue times, counting down sound ups, ends of stories, B-roll cues, and commercial breaks, for the director and the audio mixer who was riding the sound levels. As long as everybody did their job, it was a well oiled machine.

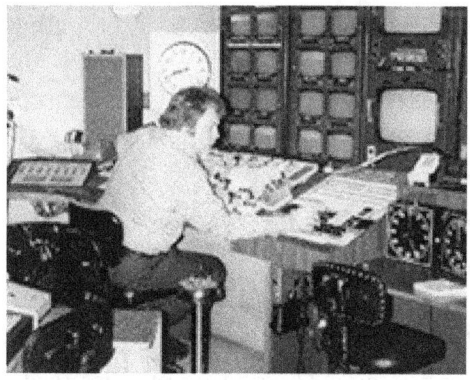

The success of this operation, however, was really on the shoulders of the image gatherers/editors. It was vital that they did their job correctly. A TV News show was and is all about the visual images of the news pieces. The cameramen were responsible to gather the images properly. They had to be spot on for color, focus, and framing. Once the images came out of the lab, they had to be cut and molded into a story.

Back in the film days, any errors in the shooting or editing process had disastrous ramifications for the news show. Each block had to be properly timed, B-roll had to accurately placed, and even those hot splices had to be solid or your piece, which often represented an entire day's work, went down the toilet. That's right, broken splices pretty much doomed your piece to oblivion. There was no fixing that. The film got yanked off the film chain, the anchorman read some back up copy, and the show moved on to the next story while you tried to become invisible if it was your story.

One final note regarding editing: with all the stress, there was a tremendous upside to editing for the image gatherers. Editing was the big payoff. It was really the only chance they had to view their shot footage on a TV screen and accurately evaluate their work. That's right, film offered no other means of viewing other than by putting it through a projector and watching on a screen, or watching it broadcast on TV. Any errors in exposure, color temperature, or composition became glaringly apparent when the piece aired. The opposite was also true. You got the chance to see how good it looked. Then there were the actual shots. Did you have enough cutaways? How did your sequences string together? Did your images paint an accurate picture of the news event you were covering? At any rate, it gave you the opportunity to learn. Editing your shot footage, and viewing it on television was like a day in grad school.

Recollections
Film Editing

Most of what I learned about shooting film, I learned from editing my own footage. The editing process forced me to look at my shots very critically and determine what worked and what didn't. Was my exposure correct? Did I properly assess color temperature? Did I have enough establishing shots? Did I get enough cutaways?

There was nothing more frustrating than to be in the middle of an edit session and realize I needed a shot or an angle and I didn't have it and I had only myself to blame. These moments stuck with me, and next time I made sure I got them. I also learned to shoot in sequence. As I shot, I clicked off a list in my head: establishing shot, follow the action, get a cut away. When I was done shooting, if I had done my job right, I already knew how it would all go together.

Editing also gave me important feedback on the technical side of shooting film. How accurately had I evaluated the lighting, exposure, and color temperature? I could think back to how I had shot it, and see the end result. Shooting film was all me. It was my brain telling my hands what to do, and my hands doing it. Evaluating how it turned out was critical to my personal growth as a cameraman. Editing was the perfect place for me to accurately assess how successful I had been. There was always so much to learn from each situation. I filed it away in the experience part of my brain in order to remember for next time.

I got a craftsman like joy editing film. It was like carving something out of a block of wood or marble except I started with a reel of shot film. I chipped away at it as I cut it and spliced it together shot by shot shaping it into a story. The big payoff of course was to see it all come together during the newscast. When it all clicked it was an indescribable feeling. Nobody else watching had any idea how hard it might have been to get that shot, or put together that sequence, but I sure did.

Back in the 1970's watching my piece on the evening news was my one and only chance to see the finished product. I did not have any means to record the show or my individual work. No matter how good it might be, it was there and gone in less than two minutes.

Good or bad, I moved on to the next day, but I was always just a little wiser.

PART II
Chapter Fifteen
Editing Film as the Clock Ticks Down

The goal of TV News has always been to be as up to date as possible. This meant that if it was remotely possible to get late breaking stories on the air, you did it. This is as true today as it was in the 1970's, but in today's word there are live options to broadcast from the field. Pieces can also be cut on laptops and sent back to the station via the Internet. In the 1970's the only recording medium was film. You had to deal with a half-hour to forty-five-minute lab processing time. Following that, the film had to be manually cut and spliced. Six o'clock in the evening was the absolute deadline. With late breaking stories you faced an ever-shrinking window of opportunity.

When there was a late breaking story, everybody scrambled. You knew the competing stations were doing the same. The first step of course was to get the film in the lab. Even if the story was ongoing, the cameraman in the field would can what he had shot so far, and someone would race the film back to the newsroom where it was taken directly to the lab. Then everyone would wait an agonizing forty-five minutes for processing.

While all this was going on, the script would oftentimes be written for the anchorman instead of taking the extra time for a reporter to write it and do a voice over. The story would be included in his read over scripts, if possible the lead story. Meanwhile, someone who could run really fast waited by the lab's pick up window. The second the film came out of the soup, he would grab it and race it over to the newsroom.

When you are facing that six o'clock deadline, every second counted. Last minute stories were cut and pasted with incredible speed. Set, scrape, glue, slam and it was done and spun onto a separate reel as the rest of the show had already been compiled. There were many nights that it went to the wire.

Recollections
Upstairs/Downstairs

Our newsroom was in a separate building of the TV Station from the control room. When the reels were done for the evening news, they were taken out the back door, across a parking lot, and up two flights of stairs to the projector room. At a brisk walk this took about a minute to accomplish. With late breaking stories, you often did not have even that much time. The second the piece was cut and spun heads out onto a reel it was handed off. Bam, I'd blast out the door and race across the parking lot.

The door to the control room building required a security card. I already had that in my hand so I was able to quickly slip it in and out, then yank open the door. I flew up the concrete stairs two at a time, then blasted through another door and entered a narrow corridor that was always lined with piles of cables and engineering stuff. As I rounded the corner to the projection room I could hear the intro music to the six o'clock evening news. The projectionist grabbed the film reel out of my hand and threaded the story into the film projector as the anchorman began reading the story intro.

The second the anchorman finished his intro, the director saw the number two on the academy leader pop up in his monitor. He hit the button and rolled the film as I leaned against the wall gasping for breath. The viewers, of course, never knew a thing as they watched the breaking news story, but man was everybody in the newsroom was jazzed. Beating the clock was a huge adrenaline rush. I felt giddy as I walked slowly back to the news where everyone was high fiving each other. We had gotten a breaking story on the air. If we were the only station to have film coverage of what had happened, we had an exclusive and that's what it was all about. We loved exclusives.

PART II
Chapter Sixteen
The Final Payoff

So you'd gone out, shot your story, edited the footage, and handed it all off to the chief editor. Now it was time to take care of your gear. The cameramen worked with the same camera package everyday and it was their responsibility to take care of it as if they owned it. That has always been a big part of an image gatherer's responsibility. It's a "you take care of it and it will take care of you" mentality. That's not to say that there were never problems, but with good maintenance you could minimize those moments.

Most importantly, film gear had to be kept spotlessly clean. A speck of dirt and you could end up with scratched film. You paid particular attention to the film gate. Any dirt there was sure to scratch your film. Your film would come out of the lab and you'd see a weird squiggly line across your images. Not good, so you made sure to blow out your camera with an air compressor whenever you could. You also constantly cleaned your lens. Just a speck of dirt on the outside element resulted in a blurry dot on all of your film. If anything got on the rear element, that blurry dot was much more focused. Anyway once all this maintenance had been completed, you stowed everything in your equipment locker and made sure your batteries wee on charge. You never went home unless your gear was ready to go for the next day.

At six o'clock you'd hear the theme music for the news show and you knew it was time to view the fruits of your labor. All the cameramen gathered around the newsroom monitor to watch the show. As we mentioned earlier, this was the image gatherers' only chance to see their finished pieces on a TV monitor. The news show was recorded on big two-inch video quad machines for legal purposes, but it was virtually impossible to get a copy of anything let alone play it back and look at it.

Sitting in the newsroom and watching your piece was your only chance to see compiled with the reporter's audio track. Even though we were all off the clock at six, every cameraman working that day sat and watched the first ten minutes of the news broadcast.

Recollections
The Classroom

Every time you picked up a film camera there was a lesson to be learned. Each situation was different, as you dealt with framing, focus, exposure, and most important, the ever changing color temperature which could deviate significantly with just a cloud rolling past the sun. The only real way to judge your success was by watching your work on the six o'clock news. Back in the 1970's we all sat for the first ten minutes of the evening news show critiquing each other's work. I watched, listened, and learned. The next day I tried to replicate the techniques and shots I liked, not just mine, but the other cameramen's too.

I was the newbie in the crowd so I had so much to learn and I really benefited from these sessions. There were no field monitors to guide me, or edit bays with big screen monitors for me to look at. Watching my work and the work of my colleagues on TV was the only way to view the footage and assess the day's work. This was also my only chance to see my finished product and get some input from guys with more experience. To me, this was the best part of the day because it was my chance to learn and grow.

Of course when my piece came up I was on the hot seat. If I had done well it was great to get good nods. If my piece looked like crap, well the guys let me know. At any rate I always look back on those days as my graduate school. I was so fortunate to have had some great guys to learn under, guys who were willing to take their time to teach me the craft. Warren Jones, Glenn Kirkpatrick, Steve von Born, Randy Fairburn, and Jimmy Giritlian were the stalwarts of the camera department who helped me lay down a solid foundation and set my career as a cameraman on its proper course.

By the way, all of those guys went on to great careers as cameramen. Sadly, though Randy was killed in a helicopter crash while covering a news story out in the Bahamas. He was truly one of the great ones, both in attitude and talent. Randy taught me so much just by example. I can still picture all of us sitting there around the big newsroom monitor watching and learning from each other. It was a unique and remarkable experience, thanks guys.

I actually still remember my first big success. There was a trucking strike going on and I was given the assignment of going out to a local truck stop to see if I could round up a group of drivers and get some reactions to what was going on. The assignment editor sent me out alone, figuring it was not crucial, and not worth wasting a reporter on the low probability that there was anything to get. This was better known as a wild goose chase. I was young and enthusiastic enough to savor the challenge of getting something good nevertheless. I had to take every chance that came my way to make a name for myself.

Anyway, I drove out and as luck would have it found some truckers having lunch and hanging around the truck stop's café. They agreed to talk to me and I got permission from the café's owner to shoot there. I gathered about five or six guys in a group around a couple of tables, facing the window so I had a great light source. I hid my microphone behind a napkin dispenser. I threw out some questions and encouraged them to talk to each other. In a few minutes I was all but forgotten.

I shot it all hand held or portable as we called it back then. I worked it for about ten minutes, listening as I shot so I could get some good sound bites. I worked the angle of the window to their faces finding positions where the lighting was just a bit more dramatic than straight on. I also grabbed listening shots, did some rack focus shots, and really worked it getting some great footage. When I was on a roll, I hated to stop. The creative juices just got me going.

When it was all done and edited the news producer really liked the story and moved it up to the top block of the show. I sat quietly as it aired on the six o'clock news. It looked even better on the TV monitor than it had looked in my little moviola viewer.

When the piece finished, well, it was my coming out party. All the guys had great things to say, and for the first time they were asking me how I had gotten some of my shots. Asking me, the newbie!!! Moments like that stay with you for the rest of your life. I can still feel the excitement now forty plus years later.

You know it's funny I have never lost the thrill of seeing my footage aired on TV. Knowing that I had captured those images and there they were broadcast in front of millions of people was always both exciting and satisfying. Nobody in the public knew who I was or really cared. I always wondered if they even knew that cameramen existed.

Whatever, none of that really mattered. I was an image gatherer and my thrill came from watching my work and judging its quality. I was my toughest critic, but I also lived by the credo, that if I had done the best that I could under the circumstances, then I was successful. After that, came all the other opinions. Regardless, the very next day the process started all over anyway. You had no time to linger on those memories, good or bad.

PART II
Chapter Seventeen
Image Gathering as a Tool for Change

So now you've heard the story of how images were gathered in the 1970's and who was out doing the gathering. It's important to take a brief pause here and take a look at the impact this era of image gathering had on the world. In so many ways, as TV News came of age in the 1970's it gained the trust of the public and cemented itself into everyday life. Emboldened by its success TV News began to look at subjects beyond the news events of the day.

The power of broadcast images was apparent to everyone involved in the business, so TV News started flexing its muscles. One of the areas that got its attention was consumer advocacy, fighting wrongs for the betterment of society. This area of interest gave TV News the aura of fighting for the little guy, as well as garnering big ratings. These types of stories were great examples of how pictures and sounds could make a big impact. Here's a great example.

In March, 1973, Bob Mayer, a reporter at WTVJ in Miami, Florida began a three-month investigation of dirty restaurants in Dade County. It was ground breaking reporting and image gathering. Titled, *Not on the Menu*, the series shadowed county health inspectors as they made their rounds inspecting local area restaurants. The impact the images had was astounding.

Recollections
Not on the Menu

Each night the public watched as Bob Mayer and the news crew followed the Dade County Health Department as they made their inspections of area restaurants. They gathered images of rodent and insect infestations, filthy kitchen appliances, and otherwise horrific and unsanitary conditions in Dade County restaurants. The public watched in horror as they were sitting down to eat dinner.

In all, Sixty-two percent of the restaurants, ranging from small fast food type places to very high-end establishments, failed the inspection. The public was outraged by these images, not only because the conditions were so bad, but also because the county inspectors lacked any enforcement power to close these eateries.

These images were so powerful that after three months of watching *Not on the Menu*, the Dade County Commission had to react. They passed an ordinance giving the County Health Department the power to close restaurants that failed inspections. *Not on the Menu* was one of the first examples of a consumer oriented investigative TV series that actually impacted local laws. Those shots of dirty restaurant kitchens inflamed the viewers more than any kind of written description ever could. The image of rat feces lying on a food prep counter was more than the public could stomach and the County Commission was compelled to act.

This type of reporting rapidly caught on and has become a staple of TV News. As the public was learning, the images gathered by TV News cameramen could make you laugh, cry, or just piss you off. Whichever one, you reacted. TV News understood this fact and ran with it.

PART II
Chapter Eighteen
Investigative Reporting

In addition to consumer protection based reporting, TV News gathering also expanded to investigative journalism which, while a noble concept, presented the image gatherers with some major challenges. TV requires images to tell stories, so how do you gather those images without tipping your hand to that which you are investigating?

Back in the good old days there weren't any tiny little cameras that could surreptitiously record images from hidden places. If you wanted a shot and didn't want anyone to know you were there, you had to get very creative at hiding the camera and the cameraman.

The most popular choice for TV News was to park a nondescript white panel van on the street somewhere near what you were trying to shoot, and hope for the best. This was of course assuming that the images for the investigation you were trying to get were accessible outside. If not there was always the barging in with cameras rolling technique.

Since there were no laws yet in place that prevented you from doing anything you wanted to do with a camera, you just did what you had to do to get your shots. Back then there was the strong belief that if you had a camera on your shoulder you were invincible, so off you'd go.

Recollections
Dateline Bimini

This all happened about thirty years ago. I was working with WTVJ news reporter Diana Gonzalez on an investigative piece detailing the smuggling of illegal immigrants from Bangladesh into South Florida through Bimini, a tiny island in the Caribbean. The immigrants would fly there, then pay to be smuggled into the United States usually by boat.

We initially did several interviews locally with immigration officials, but we needed some provocative images to properly tell this story. The best place to get them was of course on the island.

Bimini, for those that have never been there, is a tiny tourist island that is part of the Bahamas. Back then it was barely developed so a camera crew really stuck out. Undaunted we arrived on the island and heard that there was one international flight that flew in everyday that often had people from Bangladesh on board. Off we headed to meet that plane.

The Bimini airport was tiny, with no security at all so we walked out on the tarmac as the passengers debarked from the plane. Sure enough we caught up with a man who looked like he came from that part of the world. We charged forward and Diana started asking questions. He admitted that he was from Bangladesh but claimed he was just a tourist.

We of course knew better. We checked around town a bit and found out that there was a small, local hotel called The Chic Hotel that was frequented by Bangladeshis. We charged over to the hotel, walked into the lobby, and sure enough it was full of men from Bangladesh waiting, we assumed, for transport. They didn't speak English and really had no idea what we were doing. I got some great shots of the men sitting in the lobby lit in moody, shadowy window light and we left.

It never once occurred to us that we were playing with fire. This was a major human smuggling ring and looking back I am sure that those running this operation had the resources to gather us up and feed us to the sharks. We were oblivious to all of those possibilities. We never considered the danger. We were an investigative TV News crew. We were invincible, which in a way we were. Back then you could get away with stuff like that.

After the shoot we patted ourselves on the back, stowed our gear at our hotel, and went out and had a great island dinner. We flew home the next morning without incident. The piece looked great by the way. The moody images of those men in the lobby were sensational and really told the story of what was going on. Only now, years later, do I realize how foolhardy we were, but whatever. That is the nature of what we do. Sometimes, you just have to yell charge.

PART II
Chapter Nineteen
News Magazine Shows

The success of series like *Not on the Menu* and the many investigative pieces encouraged TV News to move in yet another new direction, providing even more opportunities for the image gatherers to stretch their legs. The public was clearly interested in more than just headlines. Viewers wanted some depth, but documentaries were too long and expensive to produce.

In the 1970's a new type of news program emerged that combined the headlines of news stories with the depth of documentaries. TV visionary, Don Hewitt, rolled out a show on CBS called *60 Minutes*. The show was a huge success and ushered in the era of the TV News Magazine show. With *60 Minutes,* TV News type image gathering on 16mm film truly hit its peak. The film pieces broadcast in the early days of *60 Minutes* were visually spectacular. The show was an immediate ratings hit and local TV stations were quick to follow.

Featuring the reporters instead of the anchormen, local news magazine shows offered an in depth look at important stories of the time. Whereas TV News stories were one to two minutes in length, news magazine pieces were five to seven minutes long. Image gatherers loved this longer format because it allowed them to combine the speed of news type image gathering with a highly developed level of artistry.

Many affiliates rolled out their own versions under the supervision of the Pubic Affairs department. I had the opportunity to work on such a show at WTVJ in Miami. The show was called Montage and it aired at seven o'clock in the evening on Saturday night.

The executive producer of Montage was a man named Joe Abrell. Joe was a creative and daring individual who was not afraid to push the envelope. He inspired the show's staff to do the same.

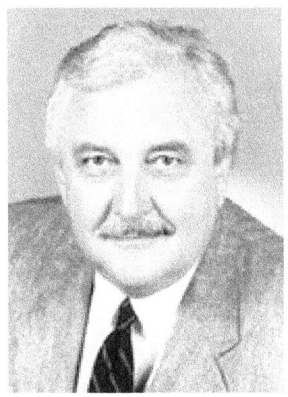

Some of the best pure documentary type of image gathering that I ever did was done on Montage. Joe turned a throwaway public service half hour weekend time slot show into must see TV. A true visionary pioneer, Joe left his mark on the careers of producers and image gatherers alike.

Recollections
Montage

After working as a news cameraman for seven years, Montage was a welcome change. Instead of the run and gun shooting that news required, the news magazine format was very different. At Montage I generally spent two to three days shooting elements for the piece. The producer/reporter would boil it all down and write the story, which was then handed back to me to edit.

Our edit sessions were long and epic. We cut together the piece using A, B, and C reels. The three reels would then be compiled on two-inch videotape in a full on control room session that allowed us to add visual effects like wipes and dissolves, as well as music and other audio effects. When it was done I had piece I could be really proud of.

The best part of Montage though was that Joe Abrell gave us full rein to cover the subjects we were passionate about and to not back away from anything controversial. Of course there was the time that we shot and aired an autopsy on a man who had drowned while high on Quaaludes and beer.

We were doing a story on the effects of mixing alcohol and drugs, and how this had led to a high incidence of drowning on South Florida beaches. Just as we were finishing up our interview with the Dade County Medical Examiner, they rolled in a drowning victim and we were invited to film the autopsy. As he sliced and diced. he showed and we filmed all the signs of alcohol and drug use.

Those images remain the most graphic I have ever shot. They included the Medical Examiner holding up the man's brain as he showed us telltale signs of his drowning. I have to admit it was tough to shoot. I hid behind my lens and distanced myself by only viewing what was happening through the camera's viewfinder. That does work by the way.

In the end we put together a great piece, well we thought it was great. I mean the images were pretty powerful and certainly drove home the point, don't mix alcohol and drugs while swimming at the beach. The only problem was that our show aired around dinner time and well the viewing public did not take too kindly to watching a doctor slice open a corpse while they chowed down on their steak and potatoes. Oh well, can't please everyone. The important part was that our point was made. Mixing beer, Quaaludes, and swimming was a lethal combination.

Of course I did many other types of stories as well. With each one I had the time to creatively develop my craft gaining skills that would serve me well throughout my career. We only learn by doing and working on a long form format was like a PhD program for me.

PART II
Chapter Twenty
Conclusion: The 1970's and the Days of Film

One final note…In the 1970's the job of a TV News image gatherer while seemingly glamorous, was physically and mentally very demanding. I've described the complexities of shooting film, so imagine what it was like out in the elements. Cold, wind, rain, snow, heat, whatever, it was your job to gather the images not worry about the weather.

On top of all that, image gatherers also faced the ever-present element of danger. This fact has not changed. Wars, riots, earthquakes, hurricanes, forest fires, and everything in between is part of the job. No matter what was going on you had to keep a clear and focused mind on what you were doing. You still had to be sure of focus, color temperature, and exposure. Try that during a hurricane or firefight. Sadly, every once in a while an image gatherer pays the ultimate price. Two colleagues and friends of mine, Randy Fairburn and Larry Greene, were tragically killed while out covering news stories. It happens, yet we persevere.

In the 1970's typical pay for a TV News cameraman was in the $200-$300 a week range for a forty-hour week depending on the size market you worked in, so clearly you weren't in it to get rich. It was also tough on your time. Beyond your working week, you were on call any day, any time, anywhere. When the call came you went. If you had to leave your family dinner, piss off your wife, or your parents and report to work because news is breaking, you did it.

So why did we do it? Simple answer. Whether its 1863 or 1973, or 2016 you become an image gatherer because you love the job. You love the excitement, you love the creativity, but most of all you love the sense that you are recording history. One hundred, or two hundred years from now, historians could be looking at your footage of an event to see what went on. They won't know who you are, but someway you are connected to that footage forever. You are dust, but your work endures through time.

Anyway, by the late 1970's, TV News was the king of media, series similar to *Not on the Menu* began popping up on TV stations all over the country. Investigative reporting gained even greater power and influence. The old adages, "seeing is believing" and "a picture is worth a thousand words" spurred TV Newsrooms across America into action.

The public especially took great pleasure in seeing guilty parties being grilled on camera by a reporter. They also loved hidden camera reports that captured illegal activity. TV News reporters and cameramen became noble crusaders exposing bad guys and lifting up the downtrodden. A TV News story about a family that lost its home in a tragic fire would often result in an outpouring of donations by the viewing public. TV and its image gatherers were making a huge impact on life around the world.

All this infused TV image gathering with a noble sense of purpose. This was ultimately projected by the newscasts and it gave the media great credibility making daily evening local and national newscasts an important part of everyone's daily routine. TV News took its place as the primary source of information for Americans. TV's images reached millions and millions of people every day. The immediacy of TV News and its short, to the point stories were perfect for busy families living the frantic pace that was starting to characterize life on planet earth.

The only thing holding back TV News image gathering was technology. As the business became more and more competitive there was a real need for news stations to be faster and faster in providing the images of the day to the public. The one thing preventing this was the medium they used, film. It had been pushed to the max, and just couldn't go any faster.

News directors wanted instantaneous results, but you had to wait almost forty-five minutes to run the film through processing. Then the film had to be edited by hand and run over to the projector before being broadcast and mixed live with a narration track through a control room. All this left way too much room for error and again taking time.

Then there were the cost issues. Shooting film was expensive. It was a one time use expenditure that had a very high waste factor. If you shot six hundred feet of film, less than ten percent of that actually aired. Nevertheless, you paid for the film and the processing by the foot, so regardless of how much you used, you paid for all that you shot and processed.

Film also came in relatively short loads, and had to be carefully hand loaded and unloaded. The loading process required a time consuming careful threading through a complicated series of rollers and sprockets. Exposing it to light at the wrong moment was disastrous and the list goes on and on.

So, as technology has always done since the first pinhole camera, it evolved to meet demand. As the 1970's passed on to the 1980's film got first nudged then shoved away by a new form of image gathering, electronic new gathering on videotape.

Recollections
One Last Nostalgic Glance

There was just something special about shooting film. The goal was image perfection, and it was only through my own skill level that this goal could be reached. I took the light reading, I set the exposure, I assessed color temperature and chose the filter, I framed and focused the shot, and then I pushed the button that rolled the film through the camera. I had a direct influence on every aspect of the quality of the final product, the image.

It was incredibly satisfying when it all came together. The fact that I had no time and nobody to help me made it challenging. The feeling I got when it all came together was indescribable. There was and is nothing so sublimely satisfying to an image gatherer to look at a great shot and know that the image was created by your hands.

Technology marched forward and left film behind as only a nostalgic memory for those of us who had the opportunity to hold a camera in our hands and listen to the sound of film rolling through the rollers and sprockets.

I will always miss that feeling of ultimate creativity that I got shooting film, but technology has no conscience. We said good bye to film and hello to electronic image gathering.

PART III
Electronic News Gathering-ENG

INTRODUCTION

Shooting TV News on videotape solved many logistical problems for TV News image gathering by adding a new dimension to news coverage capability. Since it did not require processing, videotape could be shot then immediately edited and aired. Add to that the fact that videotape production was significantly cheaper since videotapes could be used and reused so there were no film purchasing or processing costs.

The electronic cameras also gave TV News live from the field capability which allowed direct updates from the scene of breaking news stories. With all that going for it, from the day video was first introduced to the world of TV News, it was obvious to all that it was only a matter of time until videotape shoved film aside.

Part III examines the rise of electronic news gathering or ENG as it was called. It will take a look at how the technology first appeared, then evolved to where it was practical to take video cameras out into the field. It will also take a look at how the image gatherers put down their film gear, picked up video cameras, and made the many necessary adjustments that came with this new technology. Again, the recollections are mine, and those of my colleagues.

PART III
Chapter One
The Early Days of Video

Videotape recording had actually been around since the early 1950's, but its use was confined to high-end studio production. Shooting video required a sound stage type setting with a huge amount of light to shoot it, and a control room with engineering equipment and big tape decks to record it. As you can see in the archival picture below it had a big footprint even when it was just an anchorman sitting at a news desk.

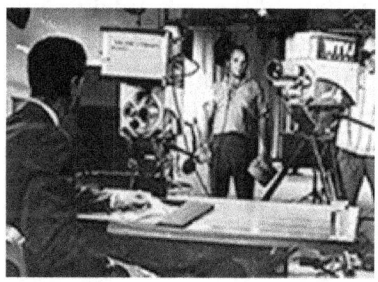

In those early days nobody even dreamt that videotape had a future in the world of TV News image gathering. That's not to say remote shoots never happened. They happened all the time. It's just that any kind of remote video shoot required lugging those huge video cameras outside, hooking them up to big, heavy coax cables, and powering everything up with a massive generator. As a result, it was pretty much relegated to live sports events or major news stories.

Because of its size, videotape production required a pretty big crew. There were cameramen, engineers, utility guys, and all types of logistical support. Generally, a day or more was needed to put it all together and tech it all out, so clearly it was not possible to shoot a breaking news story.

Basically, you had to take the entire studio with you stuffed into the trailer of a huge semi-sized diesel truck. Once you arrived on location it all had to be unloaded and set up. Then the engineers took over and matched the cameras and made sure that the decks were recording. Everything had to be perfect, as post production had limited options to save the day.

Even if you had all the gear you needed and an experienced crew, remote video shoots were like the proverbial square peg in a round hole. The fact that you were not in a studio meant you better be able to think on your feet and make adjustments on the fly. There was always a good amount of jury-rigging necessary to make it all work.

This picture from WTVJ in Miami of a live shot from the Goodyear blimp in the 1960's is a great example of what you had to do when you shot video remotes. Yes, that is a full size studio camera hanging out of the blimp and a hand held microwave dish to broadcast the signal back to land.

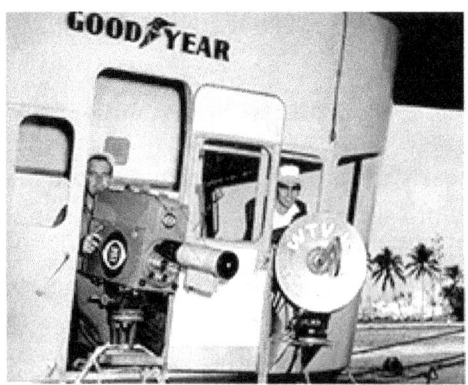

Anyway, note the rope holding up the 135mm telephoto lens. was there because the lens was so heavy that the engineers had to figure out a rig to hold it up. Since necessity is the mother of invention, they guys must have figured out a jury rig as we call it to support the lens.

The camera meanwhile was perched on a hi-hat that was screwed to a board and ratchet strapped to the base of the blimp. Another example of make it work technology. A second operator was responsible for the transmitter dish that had to be manually pointed at the receiving dish on the ground as the blimp flew around. This classic image from the early days is a great example of the fact that, when you went outside, you had to get creative to make it work.

Getting back to our history, the video camera was not the only aspect of video production that was big and bulky. The video record decks were even bigger and bulkier. They were huge machines that required their own room in a studio or production truck. The camera's output was connected via a massive umbilical cable to an engineering rack which housed all sort of scopes to insure that the electronic signal was going down properly.

All this technology meant that the engineer was a very important person. He was responsible for matching and shading the cameras. The video signal then went to the switcher, where the production team of the director and AD would choose the shots which were fed fed to the record decks. All this still goes on today of course. The big difference though was that the recording format was two-inch videotape that was called quad. That's right the tape was two inches wide so of course the record machines had to be large enough to handle that size of a format. They were huge.

The picture below shows one quad deck. If you had multiple cameras, then each camera needed its own deck. Add to that a deck to record the directors cut, and you begin to get an idea of the size of this operation. There were lots of decks, and lots of scopes and they needed lots of room.

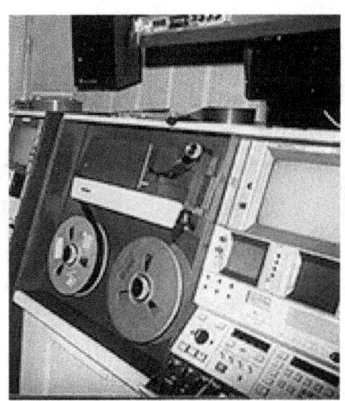

Editing video was even more complicated. Even though the recording process was electronic, there were not any computer driven control units yet that could synch up editing machines. As a result, editing was still done manually just like it had been done with film. When we say manually, we mean truly by hand. The videotape editor literally had to cut the videotape with a thin blade then manually tape it all back together. It was literally assembled shot by shot by shot just like film. The only difference was that you couldn't see images on the piece of tape. It had to be viewed electronically on a TV monitor. So how did they do it?

Larry Shulman, was a videotape image editor during this early era. He provided these pictures and a description of the incredible effort it took to edit an entire show. and the primitive tools, at least by today's standards, that they had to work with. Once again it was the case of making the best with what you had to work with. Nobody knew any different, because that's all that there was, so they editors put their heads down and made it work.

Recollections
Editing Quad in The Good Old Days

I first began editing videotape back in the late 1960's. Back then, there was no such thing as computer brain that acted as the controller of the editing process. Instead, everything was done manually. We used a microscope, a razor blade, and splicing tape to edit quad videotape.

Here is how it all worked. Looking through the magnifier that you see in the picture below, I made a careful razorblade cut on the diagonal helical scan line on the master. By the way, we edited the master, so you had to be very careful. There wasn't much you could do if you screwed it up. Anyway, then I found my next shot, cut it the same way on the source tape, then using special adhesive recording tape I taped the two shots together. This was followed by the next, then the next, and then the next. So when we said we were cutting videotape we were physically cutting videotape. It was literally done, shot by shot by shot, and painstakingly taped together.

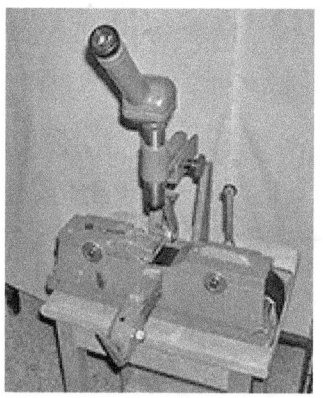

Needless to say it was a very tedious. Seriously, it could take days to edit a one-hour show. At the time though it was all that we had so we just did what we did. When that's the only way to do it, you just do it. To anyone who has spent time editing in a modern nonlinear edit bay, can you imagine using this thing to edit a show? I mean seriously.

PART III
Chapter Two
Tech Catches Up

In the late 1960's things began to change. Video camera technology took a giant leap forward and began heading in the right direction for image gathering. The main impetus for this big step came from the world of live sporting events. Up to this point, all the cameras that covered live TV sports were more or less in fixed positions mounted on pedestals.

The producers and directors of live TV sports craved more flexibility. The goal for them was the ability to go anywhere in the stadium to get the shots they needed to add visual excitement to their broadcasts. To do this they needed something smaller, something mobile that could be shot hand-held by a camera operator.

The prayers of sport's production were finally answered when a camera manufacturing company named Phillips/Norelco came out with a portable hand-held camera that they called the PCP-90 or as it was later labeled, the Minicam. With this innovation, suddenly, everything was possible.

Please note here that the word mini is a very relative term. The Minicam weighed eighteen and a half pounds and was attached to a thirty-two-pound backpack control unit via a thick umbilical cable. Yes, there was a backpack as in you wore it on your back like you were going to go out hiking. It just did not have all the creature comforts that camping packs had. Actually, the only resemblance it had to a real backpack were the two straps that fit around your shoulders. It was not manufactured with comfort in mind.

The Minicam's output could be either recorded on videotape or transmitted live, depending on the needs of the specific show. Most importantly, the Minicam could be taken out into the field with relative ease and could be shot hand held as seen in this archival picture. That's Dick Bergen shooting the Minicam for WTVJ in Miami.

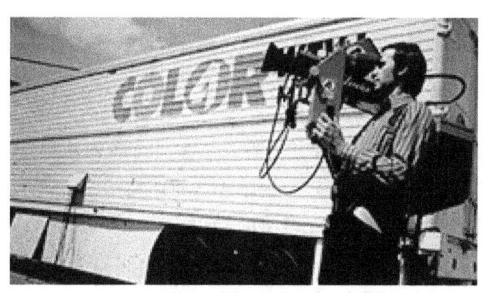

The Minicam was an immediate success in the world of Sports production. The cameras were soon everywhere, moving around sports' stadiums to get unique angles and live reaction. The directors loved them. The Minicam was like having five extra cameras to cover the game. They were so successful that word spread throughout the TV production world, so it wasn't long before the Minicam caught the eyes of producers across the hall in the news department and it couldn't have come at a better moment in time. Coincidental to the arrival of the Minicam, was a new wrinkle in local TV News. Many local affiliates had started rolling out morning news/talk TV shows. These shows were more feature-oriented and were a perfect fit for the Minicam which could be taken out into the field to shoot live human-interest type stories from anywhere in the TV station's broadcast market and dropped live into the morning show. The live thing gave an ordinary story that much more pizazz. All that was required was a Minicam, an engineer, a soundman, a cameraman, a field producer, and a Winnebago camper that had been converted into a TV production truck with a full engineering rack and a microwave signal dish to beam everything directly back to the studio. Many local markets stepped up.

In 1972 a TV station in Boston, WCVB, began broadcasting *The Good Day Show* as their daytime morning show. They decided to include in each broadcast of this feature filled show, a live field segment that they would shoot with a Minicam. Great idea right? Now how to make it happen.

The station engineers converted a Winnebago camper into a production truck, filled it with the necessary engineering equipment, and they were ready to roll. They hired a young and energetic producer named Bob Raser, to go out with the crew and produce these segments.

Bob went on to a stellar career as a producer, director, and show host. I worked with Bob on many projects in the Los Angeles area. During our many times together Bob recounted to me his adventures with the Minicam. Since field producing live feature segments for a morning TV show had never been done before, Bob and crew had to make it up as they went along. He provided these recollections.

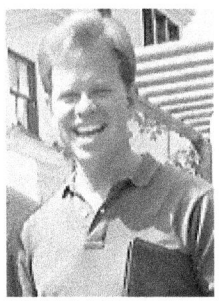

Recollections
Shooting with the Minicam

The Good Day Show was broadcast all over the New England area. Essentially it was a local version of the *Today Show*. My job was to find interesting people and places, and go-live with these feature type stories. We shot it all with the Phillips/Norelco Minicam.

To make this happen our engineers had converted a Winnebago camper into a production truck. It had a full engineering and audio rack, a microwave transmitter, and a quad videotape recorder in case we were unable to get our signal back to base and had to tape the story instead.

Our segments were all shot out on location. We drove our camper/production truck out to wherever our story was happening and transmitted a microwave signal back to downtown Boston, well hopefully anyway. Our microwave receiver was on the tallest building in town, the Prudential Tower. For those of you who have never been to Boston, this is a fifty-two story building in the heart of downtown, so at least we had a tall target to aim for.

Nevertheless, it was often quite a challenge to first find a place to park the truck in a spot where our dish was high and clear enough for its signal to find that tower back in downtown. Second on that list was that this parking spot was close enough to our shooting location so our cables from the camera could still reach the truck. About one hundred feet was the max.

As you can see from the picture below, when needed we could always borrow a forklift, trim a tree, or move a mountain, whatever we needed to do to lock in our signal and get our shot. We didn't worry too much about legalities back then. Our shot was way more important to us. As the saying goes, it is better to beg for forgiveness then ask for permission.

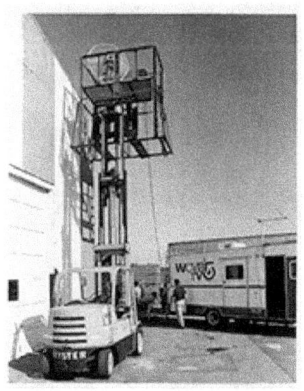

Once our signal was locked in, we hooked the Minicam up to its umbilical cable that ran back to the truck, dropped an XLR cable for audio, and we were ready to roll. As I said, back then nobody worried about shooting permits. We did what we had to do wherever we had to do it. We just let it rip. We carried chain saws, bolt cutters, and anything else we might need to get our vehicle to where it had to be and our signal back to downtown.

We were empowered by what we considered to be the inalienable right of the media to do whatever we had to do to get our shots. We rode over people's lawns, parked illegally, cut tree branches and basically did whatever it took. We even needed the occasional tow when we pushed our luck a few times and our vehicle got stuck. Anyway, once our signal was locked in, we'd prep the location, set up our guests, and go-live. That shooting part was easier than all the prep stuff. The Minicam performed flawlessly.

At the time I was just doing a job, but looking back across forty years I realize that we really were paving new highways. Nobody, I mean nobody had done what we were doing. I know they were only feature stories, but the idea of going live from the field like we were doing was unheard of in 1972. Today, this type of stuff is common place, but back then, being able to broadcast images live from anywhere within visual proximity of a fifty-two story building seemed miraculous. We were true pioneers using a new technology. The only thing was we didn't think too much about all that stuff. We were having too much fun doing it.

PART III
Chapter Three
The Next Step Forward: The Portapak

The Minicam was a major technological step forward, but the fact that it was tethered by a cable to a truck limited its range as an image gathering tool. No worries here because in the mid 1960's, Sony Corporation which at the time was a relatively small company, had rolled out a black and white portable videotape recording system that they called the Video Rover. It originally shot and recorded in black and white, but a few years later Sony fixed that when they launched a portable color video recording system they called the Portapak.

The Portapak system consisted of a video camera and a half-inch video tape recorder as seen in this archival picture. Now, color images could be recorded electronically independent of a production truck and the big quad machines. Finally, the video cameraman was untethered as shown in the Sony ad below.

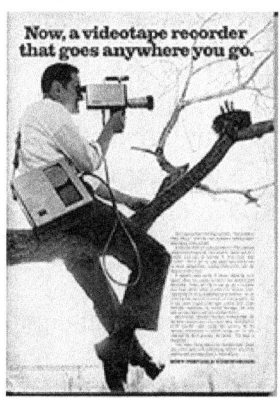

TV News image gathering was quick to take notice as a new world of possibilities opened up. Imagine if a cameraman could shoot a news story on videotape, return to the station and immediately get it on the air bypassing the tedious film processing time. News directors everywhere salivated at the possibilities that this opened up for them. In a business where being first with breaking news was and is of the utmost importance, the concept of a

Portapak was a dream, come true. It was dawn of a new age, as everybody sat back and imagined the possibilities.

Recollections
Video Untethered

The newsroom had just gotten a new Portapak to play around with as a demo from some sales rep. It seemed pretty cool, but nobody paid much attention to it. One day though we got a last minute tip that then Secretary of State Henry Kissinger was coming to town for some kind of political fundraiser. He was due to land at a small, local, executive airport in Miami, Florida around five o'clock in the afternoon. Now way to shoot it and get film back and processed to air on the six o'clock news. Then someone mentioned the Portapak. The news director said let's give it a try. With a little bit of luck, we could get an exclusive of Kissinger's arrival on the six o'clock news. Our news director like all other news directors past and present loved exclusives.

I did not have a piece to edit that night so I was given the assignment. I had messed around with the unit a little and had a basic knowledge of how it worked. So I grabbed the gear and me and a reporter sped off to the airport. I wasn't too concerned. We weren't going to be chasing the guy down the street or anything. They just wanted a tripod shot of Kissinger getting out of the plane and getting into his limo. My film camera was sitting in the trunk, just in case anyway.

We arrived, found a good vantage point about one hundred yards away. I set the camera up on a tripod and hooked up the cable to the deck. Kissinger's jet landed and I rolled. I could see the image in the camera and the tape was moving in the deck so I assumed all was well. The entire shot took less that a minute to shoot. When Kissinger drove off I broke down and we raced back to the station.

The boys in the video tape room grabbed the deck and hooked it up for playback They took a quick look and cued it up to just before Kissinger stepped out of the plane. There was no way to edit anything, so they were going with raw footage. Fortunately, my shot had been steady throughout the shot.

The anchorman introduced the story and the director hit play. There was Kissinger stepping out of the plane and getting into his limo. It was one of those great moments that the general public was never aware of. They saw Henry Kissinger walking down some airplane stairs and getting into a limo. No big deal for them. What we saw was an historic moment for TV News. It was the first time our station had aired videotape of a news event less than a half an hour after it had happened. It was basically less time than it would have taken just to get the film out of the lab, let alone edited. Pretty miraculous from our perspective back in the day.

PART III
Chapter Four
Shooting with the Portapak

Portapak quickly became a tantalizing option for TV News operations. Unfortunately, there were a few issues that limited its wide spread acceptance. Portapak, though an exciting technological breakthrough, just did not have great picture quality for broadcast TV. On top of that there were also had some serious reliability issues.

Simply put, sometimes Portapaks worked, and sometimes they didn't. This is not something a news organization can deal with on a regular basis. You've got one chance to shoot a news story so your tools have to be solid with a high probability of success.

However, all was not lost. There were still image gatherers out there who leapt at the opportunity to get into Portapak production. The high cost of film production had always made it a tough go for independent, creative image gatherers who lacked the funds to shoot film. For them it was all about finally getting a hold of a camera and recording system that they could afford.

Portapak was the game changer. It gave them an affordable means to market themselves to clients as well as to experiment with and expand their personal vision of the visual arts. Portapak allowed mid-level producers to fit into a more cost effective production position that had never existed before. By eliminating the cost of film purchase and processing, Portapak allowed them to find a price niche well below film production thereby opening up many new markets. In areas like in-house corporate videos, video depositions for legal purposes, educational applications, and the list goes on and on.

Portapak fit the budget. Portapak gave many independent producers sudden hope. It allowed them to pursue their own projects without mortgaging their homes or otherwise going into debt. Like the guy in this archival picture, they were off and shooting as electronic image gatherers.

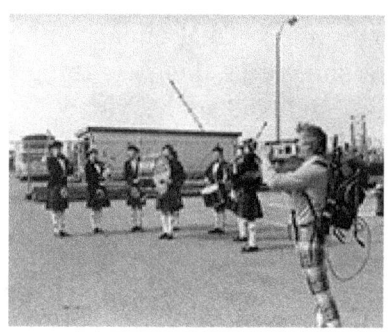

Independent entrepreneurs were quick to purchase the Portapak. One such individual was a man named Frank Beacham. Frank has worn many hats over the a long and productive career. He has worked as a cameraman, editor, producer, and writer. Frank has had much success in his career. For him, it all began the day he purchased a Portapak and hung out his shingle as a videographer, a new term that described an image gatherer that shot video. Frank shared a tale of the highs and lows of Portapak production and yes that's Frank out shooting in the rain.

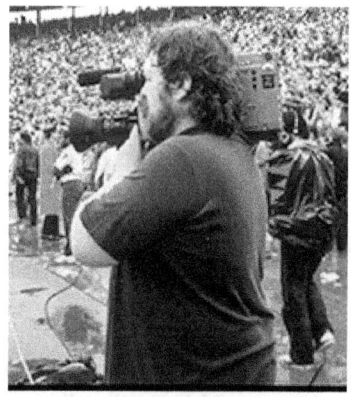

Recollections
Portapak Highs and Lows

In 1975 I first heard about the new Portapak and I had to have one. I had long been interested in getting involved in camerawork, but film had always been way out of my budget. This seemed like a great opportunity. I went to my mother and borrowed $12,000, and purchased a color Sony Portapak along with some other associated gear. I hung out a shingle as this new thing called a videographer, that's a cinematographer who shoots video.

I started my business by shooting and editing court depositions and "Day in the Life" videos for court cases. The videos were affordable to produce and worked extremely well, increasing jury rewards in cases where the recordings portrayed a particularly compelling story.

Then there were the other times when the work was totally exasperating due to technical glitches. It's hard to communicate to a generation who has grown up with reliable video technology just how unpredictable that early gear was. I'll never forget traveling to Buffalo, New York from Miami in a snowstorm to shoot a video deposition, only to arrive home with nothing on the tape. The recorder had failed and since there was no way to check the tape while on the road, we had no way of knowing. Try and explain that one to a client. The Portapak was so new we hadn't been able to come up with excuses yet.

It seemed every shoot was an adventure and we were often literally flying by the seat of our pants, but I loved every minute of it. I had always wanted to do this kind of work, and now I had the chance. My Portapak also gave me the opportunity to follow my real dream without going into serious debt. It ushered the era of Portapak documentaries, and I experimented with a few myself. I made one of the first videos of Ram Dass, a spiritual teacher and author of *Be Here Now*. Dass was known for his association with Timothy Leary and their work with psilocybin drugs at Harvard University in the early 1960s. I turned one of his rallies into a giant television studio using Portapaks.

I also did a video of the pardon and prison release of Freddie Lee Pitts and Wilbert Lee, two African-American defendants who were charged with murder in Florida. The case was known for its civil rights implications, because it involved two African-American death-row inmates who were later exonerated after it was discovered that the prosecutors had deliberately tampered with evidence. When,

Florida Governor Ruebin Askew released Pitts and Lee on September 20, 1975 I was there recording it on my Sony Portapak.

I had many adventures with my Portapak. Although there were headaches, it started me off on my ultimate career path so to it I am forever grateful, well sort of. It's hard to forget some of those oh so painful memories.

PART III
Chapter Five
Three-Quarter Inch Videotape

The Sony Portapak showed the potential that an electronic image gathering system possessed, but as has been described, there still work to be done. Before the concept could be widely embraced, greater reliability and picture quality needed to be improved. These were pretty significant issues, but certainly not insurmountable. The design engineers went to work and by the mid 1970's these problems were solved with Sony's next step, three-quarter inch videotape recording. Out rolled the VO 3800 record deck as seen below in the archival picture. It was nothing glamorous, but it revolutionized the electronic image gathering process.

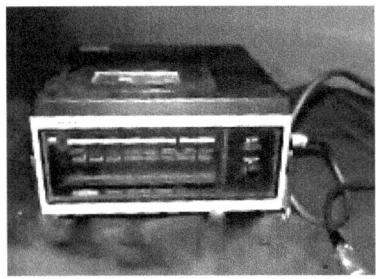

The three-quarter inch videotape recording system brought with it the innovative concept of the videotape cassette. Say good-bye to reel-to-reel video machines that needed to be threaded through a series of rollers. All you had to do now was drop in the plastic videotape cassette case, and the deck took it from there.

It was all pretty cool. When you dropped in the cassette and pushed down the top the deck took over. It opened up the front metal flap, gently pulled the three-quarter inch tape out of the cassette, and wound it around the audio and video record heads in the record deck and it was ready to go. All you had to do was to simultaneously push down the play and record buttons and they deck recorded each time you hit the roll button on the camera. When you ran out of tape, you ejected the cassette and dropped in another. It took no time at all and for TV News image gathering this was huge. It took less than one minute

The VO 3800 deck was battery powered and a bit heavy, but it could be easily slung over your shoulder with a strap when in use. As long as you didn't jostle it too much you could record as you walked if you had to, though running caused issues with the tape staying in contact with the record head.

Meanwhile, another Japanese company named Ikegami, developed a small, portable electronic color camera called the HL-33. When you put the deck and the camera together, the end result was broadcast quality, reliable videotape image gathering. For TV News it was a dream come true as the HL-33 with the Sony record deck became the way to go.

In ever increasing numbers, news stations began adding three-quarter inch videotape to their image gathering arsenal. Most stations gave it a catchy name like "Live Eye" or something like that to promote the instantaneous nature of electronic image gathering. That's me, top row, fourth from left in the archival picture below.

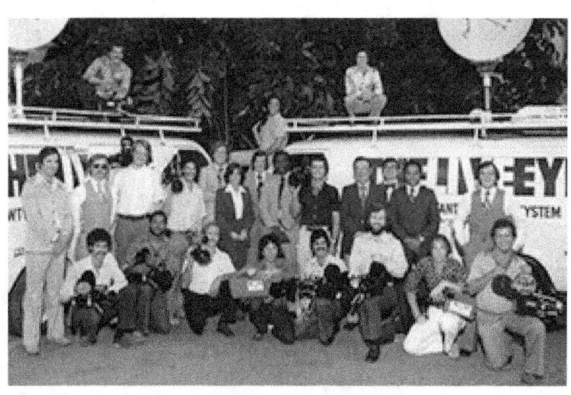

As you can see from the above picture, film cameras did not immediately disappear when videotape came along. Most news stations shot on both formats, saving videotape for late breaking stories, speeches, press conferences, and other events where it was more advantageous and cost effective to shoot tape.

However, it was obvious that videotape held the future in its hands and film would soon be gone. If nothing else, the financial benefit to newsroom budgets was a huge selling point. The videotapes could be used over and over again saving News Departments thousands of dollars in film stock and processing costs. This alone was irresistible to station general managers, but there was more.

Gone also was the forty-five-minute film processing time. Tapes could be edited and aired in a fraction of the time it took for film stories. Speaking of editing, taped news stories were completely built and finished in the edit bay. There were no more A-rolls and B-rolls or reporter audio carts. The final product was taken up to the control room completely cut and ready for air.

Finally, there was the live capability. The camera was electronic so its output could be relayed back to the station via a microwave signal and aired live from the scene. Nothing says breaking news like a live shot. Panel vans were converted into live trucks with microwave dishes on the roof, see above picture. The six o'clock news began to include a live report from the scene of breaking news even if there wasn't any. You could also transmit your shot tapes back to the station in this same manner if your story was late breaking and there was no time to drive back all the way back to the station and then still have to edit.

With all of these advantages three-quarter inch electronic image gathering was an immediate sensation throughout the world of TV News. However, while the news directors were jumping up and down for joy, the image gatherers faced some serious challenges. Whereas film was a manual medium, videotape was electronic. You turned on the camera and peered through a viewfinder at an electronic black and white image, kind of like a tiny TV set. The big, heavy batteries that powered the camera and deck did not last long and had terrible memory issues. The camera was attached to a control unit backpack with fragile cables that connected to the record deck. Whereas image gatherers had worked alone with their film cameras, videotape required a two-man crew to function properly.

You can see how it all looked in the archival picture provided by Frank Beacham.

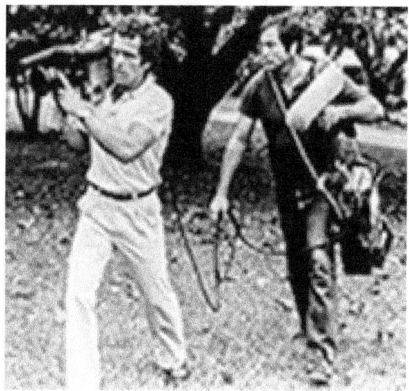

That's cameraman Warren Jones with the sound guy tagging behind lugging the deck and audio gear. Besides shooting what he had to shoot, the cameraman had better be paying attention to what was going on with that deck trailing behind him. Was it rolling? Was it recording? What about the audio? How much tape was left? The concerns were endless. Whereas with film, the image gatherer was in total control, with this rig you had to put your trust in the guy you were working with.

See the guy carrying the deck? If he stepped on that cable dangling between him and the cameraman, the camera snapped back and the viewfinder smacked the cameraman in his eye. Ouch!!! Meanwhile, the guy carrying the deck became the de facto soundman. This meant that he also had to carry the microphone and audio cable, while mixing the sound. He did all this while making sure the cameraman did not trip over something and break his neck. Try backpedaling with this rig. You needed a third hand to grab the cameraman's belt and guide him around corners and obstacles.

Video cameras also presented a whole new set of technical issues. There was this thing called white balancing that you needed to do to set the color on the camera. For exposure, well, throw away your letting meter. setting exposure was done in the viewfinder through something called zebra patterns. Even though the music was the same, the crew had to learn a whole bunch of new dance steps and it wasn't like the TV News departments spent a lot of time training everyone on this new equipment. Most of the learning curve occurred through on the job training.

Longtime Miami TV reporter Al Sunshine, remembers. Al started his career in the early 1970's as a TV News cameraman shooting film as you can see in the picture below. Al was there when video started happening. He put together a few of his memories of the early days of three-quarter inch videotape recording.

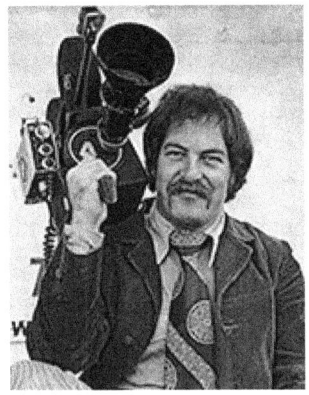

Recollections
Making the Change Part One

The downside to the emergence of video was that it came on just at the height of the 16mm film camera development. Cameras like the CP 16A had integrated, built in audio mixers. They were also smaller, lighter, and quiet as a mouse. Suddenly, I was handed the videotape camera.

Now I was shooting with a camera and a backpack attached to a record deck. It was like shooting while giving a piggyback ride to a small child. The camera was also constantly getting yanked by the guy carrying the deck who could not get used to the concept of the tether. Incidentally, the guy carrying the deck was another cameraman. We just doubled up for video shoots.

Nobody particularly enjoyed lugging that deck around, but we all had to take our turn. You only hoped that when it was your turn that the story being shot was not very important. There was nothing worse then having to be the deck guy on a major breaking news story.

In addition to all these manpower issues, there were also cables to hook up, and big batteries that had to be carried along all during breaking news stories. There was no place to put all the stuff you needed for back up, so we were constantly running back to the truck to get gear. Well actually it was not we, sometimes the guy carrying the deck ran back, or even the reporter. It all depended on who was most expendable at that moment in time.

The other thing I remember about electronic gear was the fact that you had to leave everything turned on if you wanted to roll. The deck also had to be left in record mode with the tape threaded up on the heads. Standing outside of a courthouse waiting for a defendant to emerge now posed serious issues. Do I leave the camera on and maybe the batteries die when I need to roll? Do I turn everything off and hope I can get it up and running before I miss the shot? It took about five seconds for the deck to thread up and the camera to warm up, would my shot be over by then? Film cameras did not have these issues, but tape cameras sure did. In the news arena this was a huge problem.

Bottom line, we had no idea what we were doing out there. The gear had just kind of shown up one day. We had no training on the nuances of videotape gear. We knew how to turn it all on and hook it up, but the rest of the time, we were just flying by the seats of our pants.

It's funny, the corporation that owned WTVJ, also owned a film lab called Reela Films. It was next door to the TV station and it was where we took our news film to be processed. It was a great business model during the film days. However, even with all the early problems, it was obvious which way the business was going. Videotape just had too many advantages.

Everyone could tell that film's days were limited. I always wondered if the folks up in corporate management realized that film was going the way of the dinosaurs, and that the parent company that owned it all, Wometco, in their effort to be number one in the news market, was pretty much going to put their own film processing entity out of business.

Recollections
Making the Change Part Two

Jim Duffy, seen below, is a Cameraman/Producer/Director and current Executive Director of Venture Media in South Carolina. When I knew him he was a news cameraman at WTVJ. Jim was around when the station made the move to electronic news gathering.

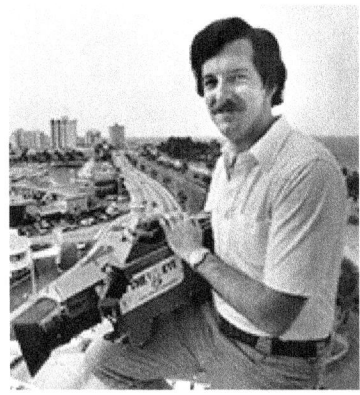

Jim remembers the transition from film to tape with all its bumps and bruises. At the time he was a cameraman assigned to the Broward County (Fort Lauderdale) bureau. These are his recollections.

From the tech side, I think the transition years from film to video are the funniest to look back on. I remember using that horrible Ikegami backpack that felt like it weighed eighty pounds. It required so much time to pull out of its cases and hook up. When you were trying to do this on the scene of a breaking story, it could be very stressful. The story could be over by the time you got it all together.

The other crazy thing I remember was that initially the station did not give us an edit system at our Broward County bureau where I was assigned. All the taped stories that we shot had to be fed back to Miami from our TV studio at the Yankee Clipper Hotel in Ft. Lauderdale. All the footage was recorded in Miami on those big two-inch quad videotape machines at WTVJ's studio. After feeding the tape, I edited the footage over the phone. Yup, I spoke to a video engineer over the telephone, while he manually edited the tape shot-by-shot as I edited the piece in my head.

Somehow we got it all done, but many were the days I looked wistfully at my good old CP-16 film camera. I was still in my twenties, but was already longing for the good old days.

PART III
Chapter Six
Recording Audio and More on Three-Quarter Inch Videotape

If you thought that shooting with three-quarter inch video sounded challenging, recording audio was even more ridiculous. Basically, a microphone was plugged into the deck, without any means of adjusting audio levels. The deck relied on this thing called automatic gain control, or AGC. Certainly great on paper, but in reality AGC had an annoying tendency to react to extraneous loud noise and clamp down on the signal, like right in the middle of an important sound bite. Take that into the real world of TV News image gathering and see what happens.

Oh and there were no XLR inputs on the deck. Instead, the audio input was through a mini plug. To make that work you needed to plug the male end of your audio cable into an XLR to male mini adaptor. Yup, one of those teeny tiny mini plugs that break off all the time, especially when weighted down with a heavy XLR cable. There also was no way to lock it in place, so having the cable get accidentally yanked out of the deck became another occupational hazard. Not sure who thought that a mini plug was a good idea, so whoever you are let me tell you, it was not.

Speaking of engineers, since this was electronic equipment it fell under the supervision of the TV station's engineering department. They were nice guys, but kind of clueless when it came to the finer points of news coverage. For example, at our shop, the entire unit, which consisted of three separate pieces, camera, control unit, and deck, was transported in our ENG van in specially designed drawers. That's right everything had to be disassembled and loaded into foam lined compartments in the van's cargo area. When you got to your location, it had to be unloaded and hooked up before you could use it. The process took several minutes at best, not exactly conducive to breaking news coverage. For guys used to opening the trunk and grabbing a loaded film camera ready to roll, well, it took some getting used to.

Then there were the batteries. The deck and backpack were powered by big, heavy battery packs that were impossible to carry around with you while you were shooting. It wasn't even realistic to try and haul them around in a bag or backpack. They were just too big and heavy, about the size of a small concrete block. To make matters worse there were not any battery meters on the camera or the deck to tell you that your battery power was running low. You would be in the middle of shooting when a light would start blinking in your viewfinder. About five seconds later, the camera just died. It was pretty much the same with the deck.

Those same batteries also had memory issues. You were not supposed to pull them out and charge them before they were full drained. If you charged them too soon, they started losing overall capacity. So we had to make sure to run them all the way down either in the field before changing them out. You did your best to keep track of how long the battery had been in use and leave the gear running between assignments to run them down. That way, when you got to a new location you could put in a fresh battery. Either that or when you got back to the station you'd put the half drained batteries back in the gear and let them run all the way down. That was the way it was.

For the image gatherers it was like being a rookie again. Veteran cameramen with years in the business, had to start all over to learn the intricacies of electronic image gathering. Not the shooting, the using. All the instinctual moves that were second nature to a film cameraman had to be thrown out the window and replaced by a whole new set of procedures. All of us were susceptible to those good old newbie mistakes.

Recollections
First Day Out

I was off on the Friday that the videotape gear arrived. When I showed up to work on Sunday, the weekend producer told me I would be shooting with this new video gear and that an intern who had been in the day before would show me how it all hooked up.

That's right, an intern. I found him in our equipment room and in fact he was able to show me the basic set up. The camera hooked up to the control unit by one cable and the deck connected to the control unit via a separate cable which was connected into the side panel of the deck like you can see in this archival picture. I hooked it all up a few times to practice, and then it was time to go. We loaded the gear into my news car and took off.

Unless there was a sudden breaking news event, Sundays were days we mostly shot feature stories so it was a low-pressure day to go out with new gear. We went to our first location, set up the gear, and shot the story. It seemed to work pretty well. The camera came on and the record deck rolled so I assumed all was functioning properly. The only issue we experienced was with the return button. See, the camera had this return function, which was supposed to show you what you were shooting when the camera was rolling. If you weren't rolling, when you pressed the button the tape rolled back five seconds and showed you the tail of your last shot. On this day, when I pushed it, I got snow. I asked the intern who assured me that this had happened yesterday, and everything was fine so not to worry. It was just a return button glitch, so we just kept shooting. Anyway the deck was rolling when I hit the camera trigger. If it's rolling it's recording right?

OK, well by now you have probably already figured out what happened next. We got back to the station and we had audio, but no picture. All we saw was some nasty old video snow. I can still picture it in my mind and recall that sick feeling in my stomach. Unbeknownst to us the video cable from the camera control unit to the deck was a multi strand cable. Each strand connected to a separate pin and transmitted different information to the deck. Apparently the strand that delivered video had broken at its solder point but the one that told the deck to roll was still connected. Since the early decks had no warning lights to tell me that the deck was not recording video, well I was up that proverbial creek with no paddle. Yes, we were big time screwed. I got one of those incredulous looks from the show producer and sheepishly grabbed my film camera and ran back out to the events we had covered, which luckily were still going on so I was able to reshoot the stories

The next day we found out all about the return button and the video cable. The engineering department also gave us a spare cable. Yes, correct, we'd have been screwed anyway because we had no spare. Better late than never I suppose, but that was how it worked with all this new technology. We learned from our disasters. Everyday was a new adventure, and by the way, those early cables were very poorly made and broke all the time. We just got used to it and checked playback constantly. We also always carried a loaded film camera just in case.

PART III
Chapter Seven
The New World of Video

In spite of the startup challenges, it was obvious from the very first moment that video arrived on the scene, that the end of the film days was a foregone conclusion. Even though video did not come close to film's ability to reproduce reality with as much richness, clarity, and color, management did not care. It was faster and cheaper than film and to them that was all that really mattered. After all they were the bean counters.

For the visual purists among us, the number one issue was contrast ratio, which is the ratio of the luminance between the brightest part of the frame, and the darkest. Film's ratio was around 1/256, while videotape fell in around 1/64. This meant that film had four times the range between the dark and light areas of a given frame. In essence, film was rich and textured while video was flat and boring to look at, but really, do viewers notice those fine points on their TV sets? Probably not, but image gatherers notice things like that.

To us, video images just looked like television. It was hard to consider yourself an artist, when you were faced with these limitations. However, there were other pluses to consider and they could not be ignored.

So even though TV image gathering took a step back in quality, it leapt forward in flexibility, capability, and cost with videotape. For the actual image gatherers though the struggle continued. It was kind of a love-hate relationship. Essentially, in the late 1970's a film camera in the hands of an experienced professional was like brush in the hands of an artist. A film cameraman was capable of creating fantastic images.

This was not the case with videotape back then. For image gatherers, shooting video in the early days was tantamount to giving Da Vinci a bucket of paint and a roller and asking him to paint the

Mona Lisa. There was only so much you could do with those early video cameras and the three-quarter inch format.

Recollections
What We Had to Learn

The biggest adjustment I had to make was leaving my light meter in the car. Auto iris on the video camera took care of all exposure calibrations, sort of. If the black and white viewfinder looked hot I could go to manual iris and adjust, but again this was just an eyeballing situation. There was nothing more to base it on other than it looked good in the viewfinder. We did not have access to a field monitor.

Then I had to learn how to white balance the camera to set color temperature. To do this I pointed the camera at something white that was reflecting the same light that was the predominate light in the room. That was key. It had to be the right light on the white that reflected the overall color temperature of the area I was shooting in. Once I hit the white balance button, the camera would adjust to white at least in theory. Again, like exposure I had nothing to base it on other than the fact that a light came on in the viewfinder telling me the camera was white balanced. Well at least the camera thought it was white balanced. Unfortunately, sometimes my overall color would be pretty close, sometimes not. It was not a perfect system and we received no degrees Kelvin value regarding overall color temperature of the white balance. That came later. We white balanced, shot, and hoped for the best.

Essentially, I was shooting blind. There was no such thing yet as a portable field monitor to check my work so I had no idea what the color really looked like until we got back to the station. Remember, the viewfinder was black and white. With film I had based everything on experience. With video well I hadn't worked with it long enough to have a reference point, so I prayed a lot.

Speaking of the viewfinder, well they were not very crisp, well actually, they were worse than that. They were just plain blurry.

Now, I was used to looking through the finely ground optics of a film camera lens. The early electronic viewfinders were not even close. Inside the early video camera viewfinders was a tiny television monitor and a mirror. The monitor reflected into the mirror and that is what you saw in your viewfinder through a magnifying eyepiece. There were little black nobs on the outside of the viewfinder that allowed us to adjust brightness and contrast, but these were crude and had little effect. It was like trying to adjust an old TV set. There was only so much you could do, so you made it as sharp as you could and got used to that being normal.

Focusing the lens was also a bit of a challenge. Normal focus procedure consisted of zooming in as far as you could, focusing the lens, then setting your frame. With our video cameras, I did the same thing, but the viewfinders were so fuzzy looking, it was very hard to be sure I really was in focus with my shot. The best I could do was to make the viewfinder look as sharp as it could look. Obviously, this was a value judgment, but, after working with the camera for a few weeks, I intuitively knew what level of fuzzy viewfinder meant an in focus videotape image and what level did not.

In spite of all these issues though, it was very exciting to be at the starting point of what I knew was going to be a major technological revolution. It was obvious that videotape was going to change the rules of the game. Though frustrating at times, we knew it would only get better. We especially appreciated the fact that we did not have to wait for film to come out of the lab, or for that matter worry about the lab screwing up our film. We also were thrilled with the fact that we could edit a complete package and not worry about broken film splices and missed cues in the control room. They were very exciting times.

And then there was "going live".

PART III
Chapter Eight
"Going Live"

For an image gatherer back then "going live" was new, exciting, and a major adrenaline rush. I mean, shooting live news images on a breaking news story? Knowing that an entire city was watching your camera work gave the image gatherers a sense of power and responsibility that had never been there before. Image gatherers were used to shooting stories, but going live with a breaking news story was a very different experience that required a totally different mindset. You had to slow down, keep your shots steady, and stay locked into what you were doing. All the while your heart is pumping like crazy as the adrenaline rushes through your body. There was no worse fear than messing up while live in front of an audience of millions.

Of course, going live gave the cameraman yet another job, TV engineer. The live truck was equipped with everything you needed for a live broadcast, except for a trained engineer. They stayed at the station. The two-man news crew drove the truck, set it up for the "liver", dropped the cables, set up communication, then shot the live shot. It pretty much looked like the archival picture below. Just a really big dish bolted to the roof of a cargo van and some cables running out of the back door. Nothing fancy about it.

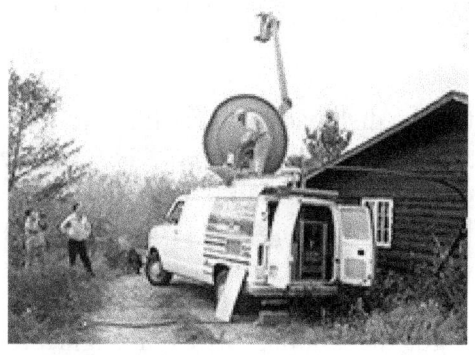

Here's how it all went down.

Recollections
The Image Gatherer Engineer

Our "going live" system was called The Live Eye. We had two big, full sized, panel vans that had been converted into microwave trucks and painted with all the station signage to let everyone know who we were. There was a big microwave dish bolted onto the roof of each truck that was held down with ratchet straps as we drove around town. Inside was the transmitting equipment and a video and audio board. It was very primitive by today's standards, but it worked most of the time.

Our procedure was always the same. When we got to our location, we fired up the truck's generator, and powered the engineering rack. Then we climbed up the truck ladder to a platform on the roof that held our microwave dish. We released the dish from its ratchet strap like restraints and raised it up, then bolted it to its upright moorings. The dish was mounted on a swiveling mount that allowed 360 degrees of rotation.

To find the station's microwave receiver we stood on the roof and rotated the dish more or less in the direction of downtown Miami where the station's receiver was located. South Florida is pretty flat so we had pretty good range from just about anywhere as long as there were no big trees or tall buildings in the way. Back in those days there weren't as many tall buildings around anyway so we were usually in pretty good shape as long as there weren't any tall leafy trees.

We rotated the dish back and forth as we fed bars and tone back to the TV station's receiving tower. The engineers would feed us back our tone on our walkie-talkie. We moved the dish around until we got the cleanest sounding tone. This told us that the signal back to the tower was solid.

Once we got the thumbs up from engineering, we locked the dish into place, climbed back down, and started setting up our camera and lights, well really light. The truck generator barely outputted enough power for a light and a camera, and by the way we didn't dare try to do a live shot on battery power. (see above battery discussion) We also had to string our audio and video cables from our camera position, back to the truck.

Here's where we often had our first major challenge. Where the camera needed to be and where the truck needed to be could be anywhere from ten feet away to inside a building. So we tossed cables out windows and ran them through the bushes, across lawns, sidewalks whatever.

We did not even consider the liability issues of people tripping over them. We pretty much put them wherever we wanted to or needed to. Our runs were anywhere from fifty feet to one hundred feet. Beyond that point, something about the resistance of the cable kicked in and you could have video problems.

The station eventually bought portable microwave relays called window ledge transmitters. This was a device that we could take inside high-rise buildings. We would set the transmitter by a window then point it down to our truck, and transmit the camera and audio output to the van. It was then, in turn, relayed to the station. So whether by cable or transmitter the camera was fed to the truck and we were ready to go live.

While all this was going on the reporter would have to gather the facts and figure out what they were going to say in a live broadcast. Communication with the TV Station was all done through walkie-talkies. This was way before cellphones. The reporter was fed program audio from the news broadcast via a small earpiece that allowed them to respond to the anchorman's questions.

Oh, and while we were shooting these live shots we also had to serve as the stage manager, cuing the reporter as we got cues via that walkie-talkie from the control room though they usually could hear program audio through a small earpiece. Of course there were times that stuff fell through the cracks and the anchor threw to the reporter when the reporter was not there. You know, stuff like that. Mostly though it worked pretty smoothly, well, more often than not actually.

Management loved going live. It gave an otherwise mundane report an air of importance it did not necessarily have. I remember the day we had set up outside of a hotel, waiting for Shimon Peres a high-ranking Israeli political figure. He was late and it didn't look like we were going to get anything before 6:30, but they decided to go with the reporter out front doing a quick "he'll be here shortly" type of report. Well, no sooner had they thrown to the reporter, then Peres' limo pulled up, he stepped out, the reporter ad-libbed and got Peres to answer a quick question as he walked by.

I remember another "liver" we did from the hospital room of a high profile Cuban exile who had been badly hurt during a political assassination attempt. Using those window ledge relay microwave transmitters, we were able to beam our signal ten stories down to the microwave truck. We were the only station in town that pulled this off. It was one of those exclusives that everybody loved.

"Livers" became so popular that the station started looking for other uses for this new capability. My Dad, Sam Hirsch, was WTVJ's critic-at-large. He was the first TV Critic in the country to go live with an opening night theater review. The crew would be set up in the theater lobby. When the show ended, he'd run out with pad in hand and ad lib a thirty second review of the show during the 11 o'clock evening news. These became very popular. In fact, I seem to remember the newspapers not being particularly happy with getting scooped. Sam Hirsch's review was always first on opening nights.

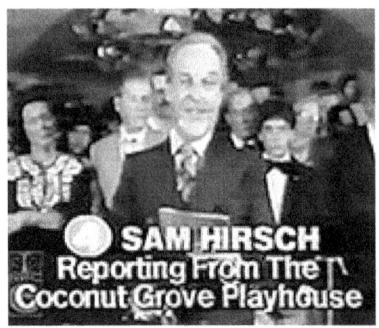

PART III
Chapter Nine
Early Video Limitations

Once everybody got over the excitement of going live and the last minute flexibility that videotape offered to TV News, they began to look at it more critically. It was clear that there was more work to be done. There was plenty of room for improvement, but there was expectation that with future research and development, these issues would be addressed.

Foremost in the assessment was the fact that those early video images really did not look all that great. While three-quarter inch videotape met the minimum requirements for broadcast, it looked well too much like video. Remember it had a limited contrast ratio, so the recorded images were basically flat. The cameras also did not do well in low light situations. They did have a gain switch, which added about a stop, but also added grain.

Then there were the camera tubes, anybody remember those? The early video cameras used red, green, and blue plumbicon and saticon tubes to create the color image. Oh boy were those fun. They were the weirdest things ever and often seemed to go out of their way to make your life miserable. The most important rule was to be very careful where you aimed the camera. If you pointed it too long at a very bright object, like a production lamp or the sun, the tubes were subject to burn-in damage. This was even true if the camera was not turned on. Burn-ins were loads of fun. You ended up with an ugly yellow smudge in your image. The only cure for this was to put the camera on a tripod, aim it at a very bright white surface, open the iris all the way, and leave it there for several hours. Somehow this cooked the burn-in away. Unfortunately, if you were out on the job, you had little choice but to keep working and shoot everything with a yellow smudge in all of your shots.

The tubes were also subject to something called "going out of registration." It's a bit complicated to explain, but suffice it to say that when that happened you'd end up with a red, green, or blue line surrounding the images you shot. You needed a monitor, a vector scope, and a registration chart to put humpty dumpty back together again. Of course, you did not carry those with you, so when it happened you had to go look for an engineer. Hot, cold, humidity, a hard bump any number of things could knock the camera out of registration.

There were also were some serious camera design issues. The first generation of video cameras were designed by engineers without any thought that they would be operated as a hand held news camera in fast breaking situations. Well, maybe that is a bit harsh. Let's give them the benefit of the doubt. In all probability, they knew all that. It's just that they didn't know how to reflect those types of requirements in the overall camera design. The biggest flaw was in the placement of the actual camera switches like power and color bars They were on the opposite side of the camera from the eyepiece so you had to physically set the camera down to access them. If you were in a big hurry, well you could feel around and start blindly flipping switches hoping you got the right one. If you guessed wrong, well you ended up putting the camera down anyway to figure it all out.

Even bigger than all that was the challenge that a whole new configuration of gear presented. We now had a camera, a backpack control unit, and a deck with two separate cables to hook up and two different batteries to plug in as opposed to what we were used to, a simple film camera. It was impossible for all that gear to be handled by one guy. It was just too much to haul around by yourself, so the station doubled up with two cameramen on the video crew. We took turns shooting and carrying the deck. Of course this meant that we had fewer crews going out, and they were not about to hire more guys. The video crews ended up working pretty much nonstop all day long.

Finally, there were new procedures. There were a whole bunch of new dance steps to learn and it did not always go according to plan. There were white balance surprises, cable problems, battery issues, and a million other bumps in the night. That is not to say that it was one disaster after the next. On the contrary, most of the time the videotape equipment worked great. However, human nature being what it is, what sticks with all of us veterans from those early days are the train wrecks. A complete and utter image gathering disaster sticks with you for the rest of your life. You just can't get them out of your head.

Recollections
Train Wreck Story #1

From the very early years we were instructed to roll color bars at the head of each tape. The bars gave the editor a means of setting up the monitors with something standardized so the color of your video footage could be properly evaluated. Not that there was a lot we could do about it if there were color issues, but that is what they told us to do so we dutifully obeyed. In addition to this necessity, the videotape on the early three-quarter inch cassettes was often a little funky at the head. Remember, we used the tapes over and over again, so the first minute or so would often be filled with dropouts and glitches. It was a good idea to roll about a minute in to get past all the junk.

Anyway, the problem with rolling bars on the first generation of video cameras was that color bars did not pop up in the viewfinder like it does today. The only way I knew I was rolling bars was by checking my return confirmation. If I saw bars when I hit that button, well I knew we were in bars. Now whose idea was that? Who knows, but it gets worse. In order to turn bars off I had to reach over and flip the toggle switch on the control unit to get back to camera. Try doing that while you are rolling. I don't know, maybe some design engineer thought I wanted to still see the camera when I had bars up or something. Maybe that was how they did it in the studio setting? Anyway, you probably already see where this one is going. Standby for the train wreck.

There we were covering a speech from then President Ronald Reagan. We were five minutes in when to my horror I checked the return function and saw that I had left it in bars mode and we were recording bars not news conference. OOPS!!! I could not reach the toggle switch from where I was standing so I signaled to the guy I was working with who was closer, and whispered bars rather frantically.

A look of horror crossed his face as he reached over and flipped the switch. Man, it really sucked having to tell the reporter we had missed the first five minutes, which of course according to our reporter, was the best stuff. Not a good day when stuff like that happened.

Recollections...
Train Wreck Story #2

Of all the horrific surprises with electronic news gathering that could jump up and bite you, you know where, the worst had to be the dreaded head clog. Here's how it went down. The recording mechanism in the deck was a big round drum that had the recording heads spaced evenly on it. The tape would be in contact with the drum and as it moved along it, it recorded the video. If any dirt or moisture got on the recording head it prevented contact between the record head and the tape and guess what? It did not record the video.

The only way to know was by checking playback. If I played back and saw snow and I knew for sure that all my cables were good, well it became a bad news/good news/bad news situation. The bad news was that nothing I had shot was recorded. The good news was that I found the problem and could fix it. The bad news was that even though I knew what to do, it was still going to take some time to rectify. Here's how we did it.

Head clogs were fixed by cleaning the head. Sounds simple, but of course it wasn't. First, I had to open the deck by unscrewing four screws that held the top in place. This revealed the inner workings of the deck. Second, using a head cleaning wipe and head cleaning solution, I carefully cleaned the head by slowly spinning it with one hand while the other hand held the cloth and cleaning solution on the record drum. I worked the drum around until all the heads had been lightly scrubbed, and then I prayed that the problem was solved. If not, I scrubbed it again. There wasn't much else I could do out in the field. We always carried little head cleaning kits to deal with these issues. A hair dryer was another option if you had one available.

Head clogs were especially problematic if I was shooting in the hot humid environment of a place like Miami. If the deck went from inside air conditioning to outside humidity I often got a head clog from the condensation that formed due to the sudden change in temperature and humidity. I remember traveling on a job in Southeast Asia where the humidity was awful. Each night I had to wrap up the deck in a towel and leave it in my hotel room bathroom with the door closed so it would not get too cold. If it did, the minute the deck went outside, condensation formed and bam I got a head clog from the humidity.

Head clogs were probably the most common train wreck back in the videotape days. Everyone who was there I am sure has a story to tell.

Recollections
Train Wreck Story #3

Had to throw this one in too. I've talked a lot about checking tape. Well, it was a great idea, as long as I remembered to cue it back up to the end before I continued shooting on that tape. Ok, so there was this one time when were out covering a late breaking story. I believe it had something to do with a big labor dispute at one of the hotels on Miami Beach.

We had just finished an interview with the leader of the protest. There was a lull in the action so the reporter I was working with wanted to save time and pick his sound bites so he could write the story as we drove back. He rewound the tape and found his sound bites. Then since we thought we were just about done he checked out some of the footage on the deck through the eyepiece of the camera. Note here, we did not have field monitors so the only way to view your footage was to play the tape back through the eyepiece. When he was done he hit stop on the deck and guess what I forgot to do? I mean, we thought we were finished.

Ok, so now you all know where this one is going too. All of a sudden a group of labor scabs started crossing the picket line. There was some pushing and shoving, so we grabbed the gear and ran over to where all hell was breaking loose. The police stepped in, and pulled the sides apart. I got it all on tape.

We left shortly afterwards and headed back to base. About forty-five minutes later I was in the edit bay cutting the piece and trying to find the sound bites from the interview we had shot. Ooops, it was gone. I had not recued the tape and we had recorded over the entire interview. Never could happen in the good old days of film, but tape had that nasty habit of allowing you to record over it. Oh well once it was gone, it was gone.

I'll guarantee you one thing. Every cameraman from the good old days of videotape had that same experience at least once. Another common train wreck experience.

PART III
Chapter Ten
The Videotape Editing Process

Let's move on to videotape editing. Much like the film days, the video image gatherers were expected to be video image editors. Ok, new challenge, everybody had to learn how to operate a videotape edit bay. This was actually a good thing. Just like editing film, video editing forced everyone to sit down and critically watch and evaluate your footage. Since there was a lot of new stuff to learn this was a good thing. You had a chance to see what worked and what didn't and make adjustments accordingly the next time out. It was invaluable for the learning curve.

Editing three-quarter inch videotape was much easier than the previously described process of editing the two-inch quad tape. Computer like electronic consoles linked to three-quarter inch decks electronically edited the tape. No more hand cutting. That was the good news. On the other hand, the early days of videotape editing had certain challenges much like the early days of videotape shooting.

Here is how it worked. In the late 1970's a video edit suite consisted of a three-quarter inch video playback deck, an edit console and a three-quarter inch record machine all housed in a room about eight feet long and four feet wide. Each deck sat on a shelf, while the console was in the middle. The decks, manufactured by Sony, were very large, heavy machines about three feet long, two feet wide, and a foot high. A company called Datatron developed one of the early editing consoles. It was housed in a big blue box that sat in between the decks and worked as a brain, coordinating the edit process.

Early video decks recorded all audio on one channel. There was a channel two, but it was devoted to a synchronization system called timecode. Timecode was an ingenious innovation. The field deck generated and recorded this code as you shot your tape so every frame of video had a corresponding timecode value. The code ran hours, minutes, seconds, and frames, with each second divided into thirty frames. You could actually here the sound of time code as it was laid down on the tape. It emitted a high pitched pulse. So, whereas before with film you timed your footage manually through a counter, with video it was all done electronically. You kept time for your edited piece through the record machine's time code window.

You started the process by finding your shot on your field tape and you hit the time code-in button and marked a timecode incue. Next, you went to the record side, marked an in-time and out-time where you wanted the shot to go. When all was set up you hit the edit button. At this point the edit console took control. The playback and record machines would roll back and synch themselves up. When they found the common synch point both decks would roll forward. At the appropriate timecode mark your shot was laid down onto the record machine. That was one edit. If you liked it, you moved on. If you wanted to change it you could add or subtract time to the in and out times by tapping the plus or minus key, then do the edit again. Anyway, you repeated this process over and over as you built your package shot by shot.

Once your piece was edited, if you wanted to go back and change a shot, bad news, you had to reedit everything that came after that shot. Much like film editing, editing videotape was like building a brick wall. You started at the beginning and edited to the end. If you made any changes you had to knock the wall down and start all over. You also were not able to do dissolves, wipes, or any other effects. All the edits were straight cuts.

One thing we all loved about videotape editing was the fact that it allowed us to lay down the reporter's entire audio track on the tape then accurately synch the narration track to the footage. This eliminated the need for the A reel and B reel that we used with film. Cutaways and footage covering the sound bites were all also all preassembled. Video only edits allowed you to lay picture over sound. When the piece was finished in the edit bay it was complete. For those of us who remembered the film days, this was great news. We sent off our finished pieces to the control with full confidence that they would air exactly as we intended them to air.

One other note, all the record tapes that your pieces were cut onto had prerecorded bars and a five second academy leader countdown. That's the strip you see that counts down from five. The tape engineer cued the tape to the two. The AD would count it down and the director in the control room pushed the button that rolled it and it dropped into the show as the anchorman read the intro. After the story aired, the record tapes were recycled. Management loved this aspect, even though three-quarter inch videotape lost a little bit each time it was recorded on. After about ten uses, the tapes started having dropout issues. It was only at this point that they were tossed.

All of this worked well in theory, however, those early machines, were, well, early machines. They got the job done, but they each had their little idiosyncrasies or personalities as we used to say which made editing a bit challenging.

Recollections
Editing Three-Quarter Inch Videotape
Story # 1

The Datatron editing console edited video very well, but then again we had nothing to compare it to. Well actually we did. We had edited film with the hot splices, A and B-roll, and oh those missed cues in the control room. We loved editing videotape packages that went upstairs complete with narration and B-roll. It's just the getting there was how do we say a bit of a challenge?

Videotape edits back then were not quite clean. They were cuts, but you could kind of see where they were especially if they were short shots. You'd get this one funky frame with each edit. It's hard to describe, and I am sure that the people watching never noticed, but it was there. Whatever, we didn't worry too much about it. Audio however was a different story. Each editing console had a default number of frames you needed to subtract to get your sound bites edited at the proper incue. I would find my sound bite, mark my in time, subtract the default frames, and then make my edit. When the edit was going through it would sound clipped, but when I played it back it'd be perfect. To make it even more difficult, all the edit bay consoles had a different default. No biggie, we knew which machine was which and acted accordingly.

Another minor wrinkle in those early days was the fact that when a TV News operation made the conversion to video, it was a pretty significant expense. Someone in management decided that we only needed two edit consoles to edit an entire newscast, even though we had five film editing stations and barely got the show done. Oh well, this gave us maybe an hour to get in and get out when editing about a minute and a half news piece. I learned to work quickly and efficiently while the next guy stared at me trying to get me to hurry up. Since we didn't have to wait for film to come out of the lab, we actually had more overall time to edit anyway. In the end, it was really nice to not watch our pieces go into the toilet because someone screwed up in the control room or a film splice snapped. We were in total control at last.

Recollections
Editing Three-Quarter Inch Videotape
Story #2

This was back in my WTVJ Miami days. We had been shooting videotape for about a year when the state elections rolled around. The decision was made that not only were we going to cover the Republican Convention to nominate the gubernatorial candidate, but we were going to do same day coverage from Orlando. This was not an impossible task. It is only an hour's flight, and there are flights back and forth all day. The biggest challenge was that the nomination would not happen until early afternoon, so how could we shoot the story, fly it to Miami, edit it and get it on the air? A plan was hatched to rig our Live-Eye ENG van with a complete three-quarter inch edit bay and drive it to Orlando along with our camera gear. This way we could shoot and edit the story, so all they would have to do back at base would be to pick up the edited piece at the airport and drop it into the news broadcast.

We arrived the day before in time to do an advance piece. The reporter grabbed a quick interview, we shot some local color, and a standup, recorded a voice over and started to drive to the airport as I edited the piece. Sitting on an equipment case I edited away while we raced across town to get the tape onto a flight that would get it back to Miami in time to make the six o'clock news. It became an interesting roller coaster ride as I slid back and forth across the floor with no seat belt to hold me down.

Anyway we made it to the airport, pulled up to the curb where I finished editing the piece. Airport logistics were much easier back then, and I finished editing while parked in the white zone. The reporter grabbed the cassette and ran to the airline counter where they shoved our tape in a bag and got it onto the plane to Miami. Day #1 success.

The next day was the actual nomination day. Of course it went late. When we finally got the acceptance speech we raced back to the van. The reporter had written his copy already, but he still needed to do the voice over. The only quiet place to do that was in the van. Florida summers are incredibly hot humid, especially when you are sitting in a van baking in the sun. Ummm well you can't record a voice over with the van motor running so we shut the engine and with sweat pouring out of our bodies, we recorded the voice over. The second we were done we took off for the airport as I edited while rocking and rolling back and forth on that unstable equipment case.

We made it to the airport with minutes to spare. I finished everything up, and handed it off to the reporter who was flying back with the tape. He grabbed his personnel stuff and raced to his gate, tape in hand, remember no security. He got back in time and we made local TV history. It was the first same day coverage of a big political event any station in Miami had ever done. This was another milestone even though the viewing public was totally unaware. They sat at their kitchen tables eating dinner and watching our story pretty much like they watched any other news story. We knew differently. We had made local TV history with same day coverage of a major out of town news story.

PART III
Chapter Eleven
Early Days of Three-Quarter Inch Videotape: Conclusion

And so it rolled literally and figuratively as film disappeared from the scene and videotape took over. By the late 1970's, TV stations all over the country had ditched their film gear and gone electronic. The good news for the image gatherers was that the technological development of the video cameras and decks made rapid progress rendering many of the rollout issues null and void.

By the late 1970's the engineers at Ikegami got rid of the backpack control unit and condensed everything into a single camera body. The quality of the picture also improved dramatically, though the tube issues still remained. The camera was still tethered to the record deck and this was not about to change. The crews had no choice but to learn to develop their own choreography. The guy lugging the deck had to watch the movement of the cameraman, staying close when he had to, letting out slack when needed. There were still tugs and trips over that video cable, but with time and practice, that happened less and less.

To be honest there remained some distant longing for the film days. We all got a craftsman like satisfaction shooting film that did not happen with video, because the electronics of the video camera did a bulk of the work. We turned it on, white balanced, and shot. Even exposure was determined by the camera, instead of a light meter reading. All of this removed you from direct participation in the creative process of shot making. All that was left was framing.

Gone also was the camaraderie of watching our finished pieces air on the evening news. Since we got to see them after we had edited them, there was no reason to hang around and watch them live. One other advantage for us though was the fact that we could now easily dub the pieces we liked onto our own tapes. It made it really easy to put together a show reel when you were looking for a job.

With all the pluses and minuses in the end our opinions were irrelevant. After all, the goal for TV News image gathering was to get the images on TV not create art, and it was obvious that video did this far more quickly and efficiently than film ever could. So, in the end, though there were some image gatherers who still waxed nostalgic for the good old film days, we all knew there was no turning back.

PART IV
ENG and Network News Coverage

INTRODUCTION

By the year 1980 video had become second nature for the image gatherers much as film had once been. TV News operations all over the United States had sold off their old film cameras and an era that had lasted thirty years had come to an end. Each day the local news crews went out and gathered the electronic images as if it had always been done that way.

ENG's biggest impact however, was really made at the network news level. Back in the "film" days, covering news stories for the networks way out in the middle of nowhere, came with limited options for getting those images on TV in a timely manner. If there was a local network affiliate TV station nearby, then no problem. The film was brought back to the local affiliate, processed at their film processing facility, then edited and fed to the network in New York via satellite. However, if there was no affiliate close by, the unprocessed film had to be taped up in film cans, thrown into an orange net bag like they use for citrus, then rushed to the nearest airport and put on a passenger flight to New York. Of course this could take all day, and oftentimes the footage did not air until the next day.

Videotape on the other hand offered an immediate electronic solution. Since videotape was electronic medium and did not require processing, once edited it could be fed back to the Networks back in New York from local affiliates or via telephone company lines. The networks charged forward.

Part IV looks at the impact of electronic image gathering on network news coverage. There are some amazing stories of how the early pioneers, came up with some incredible solutions to logistical problems. It will also describe how the networks encouraged the growth of the world of freelance image gatherers, and made entrepreneurs out of those willing to take the plunge.

PART IV
Chapter One
Network News ENG Style

Electronic news gathering revolutionized the image gathering game for network news. It gave them a shot at immediacy that film had never allowed. With ENG, all the networks had to do was to fly the camera crews and gear, the video editor, and the edit gear to the location of the breaking news story. The crew picked it all up in baggage claim, then went to work. The crews started shooting and the editor set up a suite.

The edit suites were the ultimate collecting points of the videotape output of the multiple crews the networks often employed on major news events. They were noisy, high stress rooms filled with reporters and producers freaking out as the feed deadline approached and the editor madly cut the story together. Depending on what time zone you were working in it could be the middle of the night, late afternoon, or whatever. The only thing that mattered was the air time of the network's evening news show on the East Coast.

Edit suites could easily be set up in hotel rooms, apartments, motor homes, basically anywhere they could find power to plug everything in. Oftentimes, much to the joy of the editors, luxury suites at hotels were the only rooms big enough to handle all the gear. Then again, there was always the bowels of an industrial complex as you see in this picture with former CBS editor Les Freed. That case he's sitting on sure looks comfy and so good for the back.

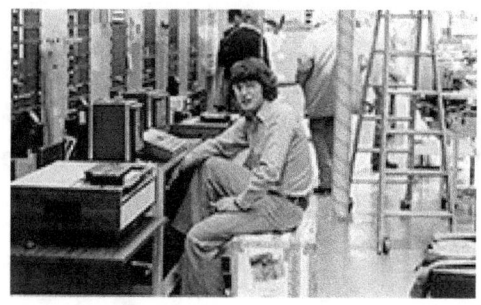

Once edited, all the networks needed was their local affiliate or a TELCO or Telephone Company office. These offices were everywhere and they provided specialized lines that were capable of carrying a video and audio signal from your location back to the network in New York. They were literally all over the world so subsequently, ENG gave the evening network news the capability of same day coverage of news from just about anywhere news was happening.

The networks expanded their daily coverage accordingly. Now, a major breaking story resulted in the deployment of multiple crews to the scene. Then the race began. Who would be the first to get this footage on the air. Edit suites were flown out to location along with editors and producers. News stories aired with up to the moment coverage on the evening news.

Along with this upgrade in news coverage capability came an increased need for gear and manpower which brought with it a new challenge. When the story was over, what would you do with all those people and all the gear? So an old concept was expanded, and the world of freelance network camera crews exploded. It was a great opportunity for the image gatherers who were willing to take a little financial risk.

The networks had always relied on a few freelance camera crews and their equipment packages back in the film days, so it was not a totally new concept. The difference was one of volume. Whereas before there were one or two guys who worked freelance in a given region, ENG expanded the list to ten or more freelance crews and their videotape camera packages working out of one city for the three networks.

These new freelancers were generally young image gatherer/entrepreneurs who recognized this opportunity, quit their local TV news jobs, secured a loan to buy a video camera package, and started freelancing for the networks. Since, a full package with lights, audio, and camera could run anywhere from $75-$100,000, freelance guys had to sign on to some sort of credit situation to pay for their gear. This left them with a monthly payment and a huge incentive to jump and run whenever called.

All freelance guys that wanted to eat and support their families were only too happy to put their life on hold and fly off to wherever at a moments notice to cover the news for the networks. Depending on what was going on, this could be a day, a week, or several weeks. Nobody was in a hurry to go home. The longer they stayed, the happier they were since it meant that they were making money.

It was a win-win situation where the crews got work and gear rental, and the network got extra manpower when they needed it. When the story was over, everybody took their gear, went home, and waited for the next call. It was a perfect situation for all parties concerned.

With this system in place, when a big story broke the networks could throw as many bodies at it as they wanted. All they had to do was pay a day rate. A major news event would often involve five or six crews freelance crews per network. By the way, for those keeping track, multiply that by three networks and you got a whole bunch of freelance guys getting work, and paying off their packages.

It was a natural next step for Frank Beacham whom we last met hauling around his Portapak. Recognizing this new opportunity, Frank was among the first in line to go out, get the necessary financing, buy gear, and start freelancing for the networks with a videotape equipment package.

Recollections
Freelance pioneer

In 1976, NBC's then parent company was RCA, a huge corporation that was heavily involved in the manufacture of TV sets and other electronic equipment. Recognizing a great opportunity, RCA began to manufacture a line of video gear featuring the TK-76 video camera. They not only rolled out the camera, but offered very favorable terms for financing the purchase as well.

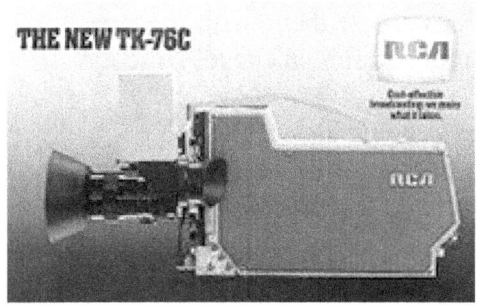

THE NEW TK-76C

RCA

This was a perfect situation for RCA as they were able to require that all NBC network and affiliate camera crews use their cameras. As a result, they held the paper on the gear at many NBC affiliated television stations in the U.S. as well as with many NBC freelance camera crews. In other words, if you wanted to freelance with NBC you had to buy a TK-76. Here's how I got involved.

In 1976 I attended the National Association of Broadcasters (NAB) annual convention, where RCA had a "financing tent" off the exhibit booth. Like a kid in a candy store, I went in and I told the RCA representative that I wanted to finance a TK-76 camera package. No problem, they said, and just like that it happened. Of course, all I had to do was to sign my life away. The sky blue RCA TK-76, which weighed 19.8 pounds without lens or battery, cost an astronomical $55,000 for the camera body alone. With the necessary zoom lens, batteries, recorder deck and other accessories, it soared to nearly $100,000 and these were back then prices.

I told RCA about my background as a Portapak cameraman and that I wanted to work freelance for the Big 3 television networks with the new gear as they made the transition from film to video. They asked how much money I could place as a down payment on the purchase. I told them all I had was $7,500. They said we had a deal. In less than a half hour, I gave RCA a check for $7,500 and bought close to $100,000 worth of broadcast gear. I had signed away my soul, but I couldn't have been happier. This was a great opportunity and as it turned out a pivotal moment in my life.

By the time I returned from NAB, my gear had arrived at my

home in Miami, Florida. It was quite a load of stuff. Fully outfitted, the camera was closer to 30 pounds. Then, tied to the camera through a thick, heavy cable, was the Sony VO-3800 recorder, which weighed about 30 pounds including battery. When you added to that audio mixers, microphones, headphones, portable lights, and extra batteries, you were carrying around serious weight.

My living room was filed with about 15 boxes. As I unpacked, I realized how insanely big and heavy this gear was going to be. The Ni-Cad camera batteries weighed a couple of pounds each. They lasted only about twenty minutes which meant that we had to lug more than the weight of the camera in batteries and chargers for a one-day shoot. The Sony U-Matic videotape record deck was no slouch either. It would take two very strong men just to carry the basic gear alone and a third to carry the extras in a serious news situation. By the time we got all the gear together, the TK-76 camera system took at least 20 huge Anvil-type cases to be transported on and off of airplanes, and in and out of vans.

Of course in 1976 there were many doubters unwilling to accept this new form of television news reporting. I clearly remember the chief engineer at a major network affiliate in Miami looking at my RCA/Sony gear and telling me that over his dead body would anything recorded on it be broadcast over his transmitter. A year later, very much alive, he proudly announced that his station would be the first in the market to adopt electronic newsgathering technology. I contained my smirk.

PART IV
Chapter Two
Network ENG Editing

As the networks expanded their coverage of major news stories, they discovered that they were also going to need more videotape editors and editing equipment. They could not buy and maintain that much gear by themselves. It took up a lot of room and it was very sensitive stuff that needed constant tweaking and maintenance. Also, the same labor issues applied as with the video crews, what would you do with all the extra editors when the big story was over.

Once again, Frank Beacham was one of the guys who stepped into the breach. Frank had smartly set up shop across the hall from the NBC News Bureau in Miami, Florida. He had two camera packages that he rented out on a day to day basis to the Networks as well as other clients. He also had an edit bay that was available to meet the overflowing editing needs off the Bureau. Here's a picture of Frank at the controls of his editing bay in the office of his company Television Matrix.

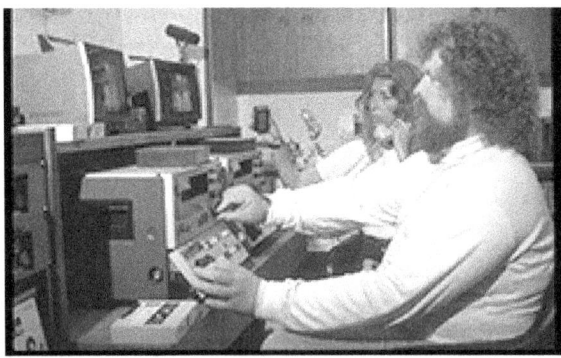

In fact, the edit bay concept was so successful that Frank had another brilliant idea. Why not figure out a way to load your edit bay into cases and fly with it to wherever you needed to go? Frank became when of the first to do just that. He put together a traveling edit bay. He packaged a three-quarter inch videotape edit bay into travel cases that could be checked in at the airport and transported to wherever it was needed, literally anywhere in the world with an airport, a road, and a truck. You also better have a pocket full of tip money to help get it where it needs to be.

While certainly possible, this was not always an easily accomplished task. As you can see in Frank's picture below, it took two airline carts piled high to just wrangle the gear out of the airport once you got to location. Then you had to get all that gear into a vehicle for transportation.

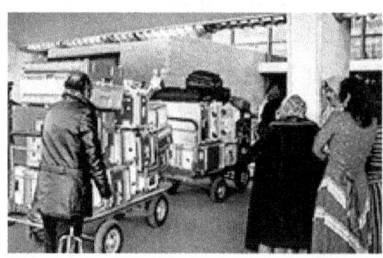

Even once you got to where you were going, finding a place to set it all up, well that was a bit more challenging. Since the news stories happened where they happened, and the edit bay needed to be relatively close by, well therein lay the challenge. There were certain basic requirements. Edit bays need power and they need to be inside in at least subdued lighting so you can see the monitors. You can't edit out on a sidewalk in the bright sun. They also work much better in a clean climate controlled environment. Since news stories break anywhere from a big city to out in the middle of nowhere, finding a place to put build your edit bay could be a bit challenging. Once again, let's hear if for that old necessity is the mother of invention thing.

Frank remembers this classic story from those early days. Ever heard the story about the chicken truck edit bay conversion?

Recollections
The Chicken Truck Conversion

It was in December of 1977. Egyptian President Anwar Sadat had invited then Israeli Premier Menachem Begin to Egypt as part of their continuing negotiations to achieve a peace treaty between the two countries. This was a huge news story and the news networks responded with an historic response as everyone converged on a city called Ismailia on the western bank of the Suez Canal. We're talking multiple camera crews, producers, and reporters. Everyone was there.

At my company, Television Matrix we had designed our bay so that it could be quickly taken apart, packed into cases, shipped off to wherever, then put together again out on location. Sure enough we got the call to go to Egypt. This was really good news as there was nothing better than getting gear out the door on an overseas trip. The gear could conceivable be gone for a month as the rental tab just kept growing day by day.

My only problem was that I had just taken delivery on a new edit controller. It was the world's first Sony RM-440 video controller. We tested it out as best we could in our shop, putting it through its paces. It seemed to work, so we rolled the dice.

We packed it all up, threw it on the plane, and off we went to Egypt. I won't say I wasn't worried. If it failed there weren't many options in the middle of Egypt. Whatever, life on edge can be exciting too, though I have to admit, I had some excuses ready to go though somewhat confident I wouldn't need them. At least that what I kept telling myself on that long plane ride.

We arrived and found the usual chaos going on. All the television networks were scrambling like crazy in this small Egyptian resort town to find local facilities to set up their edit bays and news offices. The space was very limited. We were a bit late to the game, so it was time to get creative.

We found our solution driving around on the streets of the city. The local chicken farmers transported their live chickens in big hollowed out trucks, which, as it turned out were the perfect size for an edit bay. Hmmm. Yup, we rented an old chicken truck from a local farmer and created the world's first and only chicken truck edit bay conversion. See picture below, yes, that is our chicken truck.

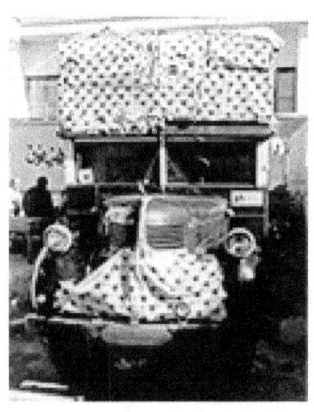

We cleaned it up, painted it blue, installed some shelves and tables, and covered the rest with network stickers. It was the world's first mobile videotape editing facility. We were the envy of the other networks. We could drive our edit bay to location, plug it in, and start editing, while the other crews were scrambling to get tapes back to their edit bays through the congested streets of Ismailia.

I saved this picture for the end of my story. You really need the whole back-story to appreciate this image. And yes it still smelled like a chicken truck. Something about trying to make a silk purse out of a sow's ear, or something like that. Really though, nobody complained and it made for a great story when we got home. Here it is, the chicken truck that saved the day for NBC News

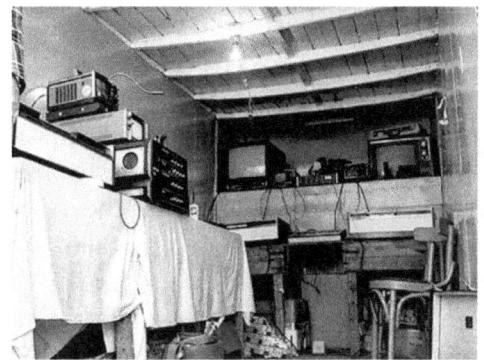

PART IV
Chapter Three
Telco Transmission

The last part of the editing adventure came when you were finished editing and it was time to transmit your piece back to the network. We mentioned earlier how the Telephone Company was an integral part of this process. Frank Beacham had many adventures with Telco. He continues his recollections and explains how that part of the process played out and how actually just getting there could be half the battle.

Recollections
Telco

Once videotape came into play, it gave us access to Telco lines and satellites anywhere in the world. Satellite feeds mostly happened at local TV stations in the US, where we simply hooked up to their satellite dish and uplinked to the network in New York City. It was all very straightforward. The bird went up at a certain time, we fed our edited pieces, and were done for the day. When we were in a remote location it was a bit more challenging as we relied on the Telephone Company's Telco lines.

Here's a quick look how Telco worked. Telco lines had been around for many years. They had connected the first television networks in the 1940's. These were not ordinary telephone lines, but leased lines specifically used for video transmission from point "A" to point "B". As long as you had access to a telephone company office, you could transmit your video via the Telco lines. The key of course was locating the office and getting there in time to feed.

So we'd arrive at location, and establish a base. Usually it was in a hotel somewhere in town, but not always (see above chicken truck story). The tapes would be brought back from the field to our edit bay set up. The news correspondent and producers would write the story, get the script approved by New York, and then record a voice over. This would all get edited together and off we'd go to the local Telco office with our field deck in hand and a deadline to beat.

Once there, we'd hook up the field recorder's output for audio and video to a panel and hit play. The network had a receiving set up in New York and they'd record what we sent and it aired on the evening news. Sounds simple right? Well the transmission part was anyway, finding Telco and getting there was another story. Remember this was before the days of GPS on your cellphone.

We had a lot of adventures going to Telco. There were many wild rides through all sorts of conditions in all kinds of towns to get to the Telco office before our deadline. I remember during a hurricane in Brownsville, Texas almost getting killed looking for the Telco office in the middle of howling wind and pouring rain. Electrical lines were popping in the street all around us as we drove around searching for their office.

Once there, it was great. Telco central offices were the most secure bunkers in the world. When you got it all hooked up, it was very reliable. It was only later in the hotel bar that we'd realize how crazy we were. Never could figure out what drove us, but we let nothing get in our way. Like they used to say about the post office, neither snow nor rain nor heat nor gloom of night prevented us from the swift delivery of our news piece.

Let's just call it professional pride. It sure felt good when it worked.

PART IV
Chapter Four
Working ENG Freelance

The lure of making big money and working at the network level was very tempting. When you added to that the excitement of shooting major national news events, many image gatherers could not resist. What started as a trickle soon turned into a major flood. Many camera people quit their local news jobs and jumped on the freelance bandwagon. It was a little scary for those with families and overhead, but then again, fear is a great motivator.

The first step in the process was getting a hold of a camera package to shoot with. Obviously the big money came with owning the gear. That way you got paid for labor and gear rental with every job. The rates for gear back then were around four to five hundred dollars a day, a figure higher than your eight-hour labor-day rate. There was risk though. Signing on the dotted line came with a monthly commitment that lasted four years. This is where it got a bit hairy. You literally signed your financial life away. It was one thing to quit your job, quite another to sign your name to that much debt. Nevertheless, there were many willing to take the plunge.

Recollections
The Freelancer's Camera Package

I quit my news cameraman job at the TV station in 1982 and decided to freelance. I was at the top of the pay scale and kind of stuck there, so I figured why not. I was also getting a little bored covering city commission meetings. The lure of the networks was strong. I knew a lot of guys that had done it and doubled their income their first year out, so it kind of made sense. I mean, I could always go back and get another full time job if I had to. At least that's what I told my wife and horrified parents.

The first step was to get my hands on a camera, or as we called it a "package." If I wanted to freelance for network news, and back then that was pretty much all there was, I had to be ready to blast out the door at a moments notice. Therefore, I either had to buy the gear, or someone else had to buy it and let me keep it at my home. I decided I wanted my own.

The "package" consisted of first and foremost the camera which at this point in time was either the Ikegami 79E or RCA's TK-76. Add to that the lens, camera batteries, the three-quarter inch record deck, a tripod, an audio mixer, a stick mike, a shotgun mike, a couple of lapel mikes, and a lighting kit which generally had three open faced 650 watt lamps and a bundle of diffusion and color correction gel. To round things out I also needed some extension cords and mike cables. It was about $90,000 worth of gear. Gulp!!! I signed my name to a four-year lease with option to buy and I was done. "Don't worry", the salesman said, "you only need to work three days a month and you've covered your nut. Anybody can work three days." It certainly sounded simple. I mean I only owed $90,000…yikes!!!

I didn't have an office so I took the gear home and stashed it in a spare room of my house. This of course thrilled my wife who just loved the idea of me carting production gear in and out every time I got a job. Something about smashing up walls and tearing up carpet bothered her a bit. I just told her not to worry, then cringed every time I nicked the wall with the gear.

Then there was the transportation issue. How was I going to drive the stuff to jobs? Car trunks were not big enough and this was in the pre-minivan days, so I bought a used panel van. Of course it was an empty shell so I had to take to a van conversion place and have them build it out with shelves and a security cage. I had a lot invested in that gear, so I had to keep it safe.

While freelancing was good for me, my poor Mother could never understand why I quit my perfectly good job at the TV station to go out on my own. Moms did not like the freelance concept. Wives also were a bit nervous about it. Especially the part about buying your own health insurance, no retirement, and having to drop everything you were doing whenever the phone rang or your pager went off. Wives became believers though when the money started flowing in. Mothers on the other hand just kept worrying.

Whatever, I loved being an owner/operator. I wouldn't have traded it for any other way of life. It was a pretty simple formula. The more I was willing to work, the more money I made. I liked that concept. I only had to come up with about $1500 a month to pay the loan and general maintenance expenses. They were right that was three days' gear rental. There was no way I was not going to work three days a month, right? Ok so I was wrong, but in the end I figured out that some months I worked ten days, some fifteen, and some one. As long as the average was good, it worked. I just had to be smart with my money and always keep something in reserve to get past those slow times.

Looking back, freelancing was the best career move I ever made. Over the years I made way more money than I ever could have working at a TV station, but that is only part of the story. More importantly, I was constantly challenged to up my game. I had to be on everyday and be able and prepared to meet whatever challenges came my way. Freelancing also gave me the opportunity to meet and work with some amazing people over the years.

Freelancing took my career further than I ever thought possible and enriched my life in ways that I never dreamt that it could. I will say that it is not for everybody. If you need a regular schedule with set hours and a set salary, don't do it. If you don't mind rolling the dice to see what comes up, then try freelancing. It is just that simple.

PART IV
Chapter Five
The Foreign Legion

As has been described when a big story broke, the networks would man the trenches with crews until the story ended. Competition was fierce between them and they wanted crews everywhere so they didn't miss anything. The producers were also always afraid to leave first for fear that a competitor would get something great after they had left. As a result, nobody ever wanted to leave until everyone else left so you could end up on a big story for a day, a week, or a month, at least until the next big story broke.

Shooting network news as a freelancer was a huge departure from the life of a local news cameraman. Working at a local TV News operation, you worked an eight-hour shift with an hour meal break. Shooting for the networks on the other hand was like joining the foreign legion. You kissed your wife good-bye and headed out the door. There was never an answer to the question, "When you coming home?" You just didn't know and you didn't care because you got paid for your time and for each day the camera package was out, so the more days the better.

Besides working for the network was a huge ego trip. You traveled first class, often in private jets. The networks covered all hotel and transportation costs and gave you a per diem for meals, so traveling was especially lucrative.

A smart freelancer kept a suitcase packed and his gear ready to roll at a moment's notice. You also learned the number one rule, never say no. When you got the call you went. If you dared say no, then your name went to the bottom of the list and you might not work again for a while. Not much has changed with this formula over the years.

The real beauty of those early freelance days back in the 1980's was the fact that the networks were free spenders. Cost of coverage was not a concern and they were willing to throw massive numbers of bodies at a news story. They covered every angle imaginable. As a result, many freelance crews made a great living just doing network news stories.

Actually, back then news was the number one game in town, whatever town you lived in. Other than shooting an industrial video for some corporation from time to time, news stories were pretty much it. You almost didn't want to commit to anything else anyway. The worst scenario was to be working a day job somewhere and have to turn down a network gig.

For the freelancers, the biggest challenge was schlepping the gear. You held the paper on the package so you had to be extra careful to not lose or break anything. If it happened, well the fix or replacement came out of your pocket.

Transportation in town was no big deal. Owner operators bought panel vans, rigged them with shelves and cages, and drove. Trips out of town for the network were an entirely different story. All the gear had to be packed into cases and loaded onto commercial airlines. Generally, the average package consisted of seven to ten cases. If you were traveling out of the country, you took even more backup stuff and backup-to-backup stuff.

Once you got to where you were going, you'd unpack the gear and dump the cases in your hotel room. Everything then had to be configured in such a way that you could work with it. You had to have quick access in breaking news situations. Lincoln Continental Town Cars, with their gigantic trunks were a popular choice. Believe it or not an entire package could fit into the trunk of the 1980's versions anyway.

Once you were part of the network roster you sat waiting in the starting gate like a racehorse. Actually, even if you weren't working on a given day, you prepped everything as if you were so you'd be ready to jump and run if you got the call. Working as a network news freelancer was like being an on duty fireman. When the bell rang, you were out the door. So what was it like when the alarm bell sounded?

Recollections
Breaking News

I had just dropped our daughter off at nursery school when my pager started beeping. In those days we had voice pagers. When the pager went off, it beeped and a voice message followed. So, sure enough there was a message from the Miami NBC News Bureau telling me to call in. I immediately went into response mode and searched frantically for a pay phone, no cellphones yet. I found one at a local strip mall, dropped in my quarter and called. Apparently a plane had been hijacked in Curacao, a resort island off the coast of Venezuela. The bureau needed me to jump. Of course I said yes then I raced home to get the gear and a change of clothes. I called my wife at her work to let her know, arranged for my parents to pick up the kids at school, then threw stuff in a suitcase, packed my gear, and ran out the door. I had this down. It took me fifteen minutes max.

I made it as far as the truck. Another page and phone call revealed that the Curacao airport was closed to all air traffic. Not to worry, network producers had a new plan of action. We were going to fly to a tiny Caribbean island called Bonaire on a private jet. That island was fairly close to Curacao. We just had to figure out a way to get the rest of the way by boat. No worries right? Off we went.

After about a two-hour flight, we landed, grabbed our gear, and took a taxi to the local marina as in fishing boats and pleasure craft. Our producer negotiated with a local guy who owned a charter fishing boat. He agreed to transport us across the Caribbean to Curacao. Meanwhile, the hijacking was now in a standoff phase so we moved forward.

We loaded our gear onto a sport fishing boat and shoved off. We had no idea what we would find once we got there. Since there was no communication on the high seas, we hung out on the boat and enjoyed the cruise while our producer nervously paced.

It took us several hours to get to Curacao, but our timing was impeccable. We hopped off the boat, hired a cab, loaded everything into it and drove to the airport. When we arrived at the airport we grabbed what gear we needed, paid the cabbie a pile of cash to wait for us, and ran out onto the airport tarmac. There was no such thing as airport security so we had free run of the place.

We immediately learned that local soldiers had just stormed the jet and killed the hijacker. We ran across the tarmac as I went into auto mode and started covering the action. There was no time to think in those situations, I just shot by instinct. I'd swing the camera around, my brain would register the image and I rolled. I was not conscious of the passage of time as I recorded amazing image after amazing image.

There were survivors weeping and hugging each other. There were soldiers with assault rifles at the ready just in case anything else came down. There had been a couple of civilians wounded, so there were medical personnel administering first aid. I rolled on it all. Then something caught my eye and I looked up. There was a gripping image of the dead hijacker's legs hanging out of the plane's open door backlit by the airport lights. I whipped my camera up and rolled. I can still picture that image in my mind, now almost thirty years later.

There are a few frames like that I have gathered over the years that are etched into my brain. They are striking images that tell an entire story in five seconds. My career was all about the images and that hijacker shot was one of the great ones. It was one frame of video that carried all the raw emotion of a human tragedy that had just occurred. Our producer was ecstatic. Reputations were made on coverage like this. We were also the only network crew there, yup, a real exclusive.

By the time we finished up it was late at night. The producer grabbed the raw tape and was off to the Telco office to feed it back to the News Bureau for editing. The poor sound guy had to take the deck and go with him, while I grabbed a couple hours of sleep in a local motel. We were up early the next morning and flew back to Miami for a heroes welcome at the Bureau.

The good news was that the bureau chief was thrilled with what we had done. The bad news was that we were only gone for a little over twenty-four hours in spite of the long and arduous journey. We were paid for only two days of work. Oh, and back then, when you went out of the country you got paid a flat rate, so there wasn't even any overtime. That's ok though. Our success meant there'd be more calls in the future and soon. All good.

I also came back with a swagger. Shooting footage like that made you feel like a true network news veteran. Now I had an amazing story to tell. You could be a real big shot with your friends when you told stories like that. Their day at the office was never as exciting as mine.

PART IV
Chapter Six
Freelance Motivation

Freelance image gathering is something you do because you love it. You love the adventure of travel, you love the adrenaline driven excitement of breaking news in foreign locales, and you love the exhilaration you get when you came through the smoke and fire with a shot that nobody else was able to get. The praise you got from everyone was great, but what you really loved was the knowledge that millions of people across America saw your work.

The downside to it was that you are working at the whim of the guy who hires you. If you piss him off, or let him down, you are screwed, mainly because there is nowhere else to go for work. There are no excuses for failure, especially if a different crew at another network is successful.

As a result, the freelance world is full of highly motivated individuals willing to walk thru the fires of hell to get the shot. Each and every day you have to bring your "A" game. The smart bureau chief understands this and uses it to their advantage. It takes a special person to recognize this fact, and I had the pleasure of working with one, a man named Don Browne.

Recollections
More Network News Adventures

In the early 1980's, Don Browne was the NBC bureau chief of the Network's Miami Bureau. Don went on to have an illustrious career at NBC News. Back then, as a bureau chief, Don was a passionate and aggressive leader. He loved freelancers because he understood what motivated freelance crews.

Freelancers will work anytime, anyplace. Call them up in the middle of the night, ask them to leave their kid's birthday party, or really just about anything else, the freelancer will always jump and run. Don knew that a freelance camera crew would crawl across a field of broken glass to get him the news coverage he needed, and he was right. After all, the freelancer's code begins with the fact that nobody makes any money sitting home on your butt. So when the phone rang or my pager went off, I answered the call.

When I quit my local news job and started freelancing, I knew a bunch of guys that were freelancing with NBC so with their help I tried to get in with Don. My first big chance came in 1983 with the war in Grenada. President Reagan had authorized the invasion of the island to thwart a Communist takeover. We worked out of the Miami bureau which was the closest one to Grenada.

When a big story like this broke out it was all hands on deck and a great opportunity for me to get into the mix. The idea of going off to war was a little scary, actually no, it was a lot scary, but I had a package now and a monthly nut to crack so whatever. I sucked it up, loaded up the gear, kissed the wife and kids goodbye, and off I went. Fortunately, they paired me up with a network veteran named Larry Ashley, so I had him to show me the ropes.

We arrived in the Southern Caribbean, and got our assignment. The US military had closed down all airspace around the Grenada. We were told to hop on a boat and try and get onto the island that way. The military had blockaded the island, but we were instructed to try anyway.

We chartered a local sport fishing boat and made a run for Grenada. Before we ever got close, we were greeted by a Navy PT boat, which told us in no uncertain terms to leave. We went back to where we started and tried again the next day. Again we were turned back. We did this for a few more days.

Then someone got a new idea. Let's put the boys on a helicopter and let them try and fly around and see what the invasion force was doing. Looking back, it was an almost suicidal concept, but what did we know. I mean flying around in the middle of a war zone? Seriously? We did not question though. As a freelancer, they said jump we said how high?

Anyway, it was not just any helicopter. Check out the picture below. It was stars and stripe helicopter service. Our pilot Steve was a Vietnam vet who had moved to the Caribbean and opened up a helicopter tourist business. He was a combat veteran and totally fearless.

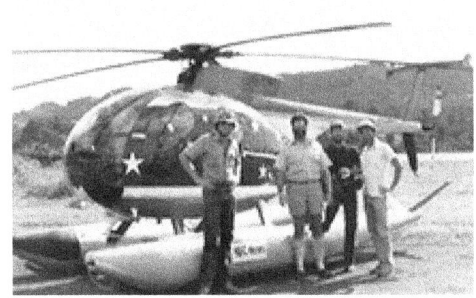

Can you imagine what it was like flying around a war zone in that thing? Fortunately, before we got airborne, Grenada had been secured, and the press was allowed in, so our assignment was revised to buzzing around looking for the US troops doing mop up on the many outer islands in the area.

The troops were finding caves on the outer islands where the Cuban Communists had stashed weapons, ammunition, and propaganda in preparation for their planned assault. The soldiers were thrilled to have us there as the images we were recording graphically illustrated the threat to the region that President Reagan had been talking about. This really gave us a sense that we were a part of history. Being able to gather the images that backed up our government's justification for this invasion made us all feel a certain pride in what we were doing there, and a definite pride in being image gatherers.

On a less serious note the producer had to get our tapes back to the nearest Telco feed point that was on an island called St Vincent. This was about a two-hour helicopter flight from where we were. The problem was that the chopper did not have enough fuel to make it back with all of us on board. Steve, the pilot, came up with a great solution. He dropped us off at a beautiful resort island, the only accommodations out there in the middle of the Caribbean. The owner of the resort a buddy of our pilot, was thrilled to have some business. The war had pretty much shut him down. Our producer flew back with the tapes to St. Vincent while we ate fresh island lobster and drank piña coladas courtesy of network news.

They came back to pick us up the next day and we had another amazing adventure. We found some American troops gathering on yet another island. We landed nearby and found out they were being deployed to check out a tiny little island in the middle of nowhere. They invited us to come along so we jumped into their Blackhawk helicopter and took off in full combat readiness. Let me tell you, those army helicopter guys do not fool around. They take off and land really fast, and you better be holding on to something when they do.

We landed on this tiny nameless island in the middle of the ocean. We were totally focused on shooting the soldiers as they deployed with guns in hand. It was only after they were all in place that we looked up and saw the alleged enemy, some curious goats and a few little shepherd boys staring wide-eyed at the soldiers. Clearly, there was nothing of any significance going on here.

None of this mattered to the network. NBC news loved our footage. They led their evening newscast that night with the story of how troops had secured another island and NBC had the exclusive footage. We got huge kudos from the honchos in New York for our dedication and bravery. All we could think of was the wide-eyed kids and curious goats. Whatever, we said thanks and acted like heroes.

That is the way it is with gathered news images. They get gathered and put on TV, and the viewer reacts to them. It is up to them to come to their own conclusion as to what these images mean. For this reason, we as image gatherers have an obligation to make sure that the images we gather are honest and neutral. We are not making a political statement and we cannot allow ourselves to have a point of view. We gather the image and let the viewers come to their own conclusions. In this case the viewer saw war is hell, while we contemplated whether tonight we'd stick with lobster or try some of the other local seafood delicacies while the producer flew the tapes back to St Vincent.

PART V
Image Gathering Goes Prime Time

INTRODUCTION

For several years, three-quarter inch videotape was pretty much relegated to news shows. The world of prime time TV, looked down at the whole thing, labeling three-quarter inch video as the "news format". Image gatherers with their video cameras were not yet ready for prime time. Well all this was about to change.

Back in 1970, the Federal Communications Commission (FCC) had enacted the "Prime Time Access Rule". It stated that local stations were prohibited from accepting any network shows during the 7:30pm-8pm evening time slot. This time was to be reserved for local stations to run their own programming or buy what became known as syndicated shows.

Initially, game shows filled the slot, but with the advent of three-quarter inch video tape, and its lower production costs, a new type of TV programming was developed. It was called the Magazine Show. These shows provided more depth, with stories that were four, five, or even six minutes long.

Magazine shows gave the viewers what was generally called infotainment or a combination of news and entertainment. Think of a magazine versus a newspaper. Instead of probing news, these shows told true stories of inspiration and humor. They were all shot on three-quarter inch videotape at a fraction of the cost of prime time programming. Local stations were quick to sign up.

Part V examines how these magazine shows ultimately led the image gatherers and their video cameras to prime time television. It will discuss some of the shows that led the way and once again how the image gatherers adapted their skills to new image gathering challenges. The Recollections are provided by image gatherers that were working during this time period.

PART V
Chapter One
PM Magazine

In the late 1970's Westinghouse Broadcasting Group, better known as Group W, was one of the first to roll out a prime time access magazine show that they called PM Magazine. This was a syndicated, nightly magazine show. The main goal of *PM Magazine* was to fill that prime time local access slot with a light, feature oriented news magazine show.

The overall concept was for *Group W* to provide the *PM Magazine* name and one national story, while each local market had its own hosts and produced local stories to go with the national feed. *PM Magazine* soon became a national institution. *Group W* was thrilled as they were able to sell the rights to the highest local bidder in cities across the United States.

PM Magazine was a high-energy, happy news type of show. It preferred positive stories with happy endings. The hosts were young, upbeat men and women that could easily have been mistaken for Ken and Barbie. Of course, the entire show was shot in the field on three-quarter inch videotape. This included the host wraps that were shot on location all over the different local cities where the show aired. These host wraps as they were called helped tie the show together kind of like video bridges.

PM Magazine offices were set up at local TV stations usually within view from the station's newsroom. The hard-boiled news guys looked with disdain at this upbeat upstart with their ever present cheerfulness.

Recollections
Shooting PM Magazine

I was a grizzled veteran news cameraman when *PM Magazine* rolled into town. They reminded me of Barnum & Bailey Circus. *PM*

Magazine was all about bright colors, painted vans, and terminally happy hosts. Over in the news department we looked at them like they were a bunch of clowns. The pieces they did were "good news" stories all about people with a "zest for life." To us it was all a bunch of trivial nonsense, only we didn't use the word nonsense. Remember, we were grizzled news veterans.

Well sure enough one day one of their camera guys was out sick, I knew some of the people at *PM* and they asked me if I would come in on my day off to shoot a story for them. I was up for a little overtime, so I said yes. Though I wouldn't have admitted it, deep down I was also curious what it would be like to shoot those types of stories. I had always enjoyed working on news features, lighter stuff, instead of the usual death and destruction. *PM Magazine* emphasized the positive side of life, and from the stories I had seen on their show, they loved creative shot making. It seemed to me that I might actually enjoy shooting for them, though I would never had admitted it to my news buddies.

I went out on their shoot and I really got into it. I bounced around getting all sorts of angles and coverage for their story. At a certain level I really surprised myself with the shots I was getting. It amazed me at what I could do when I really let myself go. I had shot feature stories before, but news format stories rarely went over a minute and a half, so I was always limited with what I could do. I also always had to deal with reporters who were not interested rack focuses, pretty sunsets, and all that artsy type stuff. They just wanted to get in and get out with the bare essentials. These stories were longer and more involved and more challenging to shoot. *PM Magazine* also devoted several hours to shooting the stories, not the quick in and out of a news story. They definitely appreciated good shot making.

I enjoyed shooting *PM Magazine* so much that I told them anytime. I ended up working for them a few more times before I left the TV station and began my career as a freelance cameraman. As things turned out, my *PM Magazine* experience served me well once I started freelancing. My freelance career took me down so many different paths and shooting styles. I worked on many different shows and projects. The ability to flip into a different shooting mode was very important, as was understanding how to shoot longer more involved feature stories and apply creative shot making while still keeping it all honest.

PART V
Chapter Two
The Birth of Primetime Reality TV

The success of these syndicated magazine shows got the TV networks thinking, "Can we make this format work during prime time?" These shows were way cheaper to produce, while the prime time ad rates still applied. This equaled greater profits and so the networks started to take a really hard look. It was certainly doable. The talent pool of image gatherers certainly existed, as did the technology. The public seemed to like watching, so maybe with a little tweak here and a little tweak there, hmmmm.

Then along came a TV producer named George Schlatter. A creative and fearless executive producer, Schlatter had made his name several years before as producer of *Rowan and Martin's Laugh-in,* a zany show that broke new ground for primetime comedy. In 1979 he turned his gaze to this new magazine format and rolled out a show called *Real People* that successfully took the reality magazine format to network prime time.

Real People was a hybrid show, sort of a stepping-stone into the world of reality TV. The show still followed the old format of hosts in the studio with a live audience, but they introduced segments that had been shot by our image gatherers in the field on three-quarter inch videotape, just like the prime time access magazine shows. Each show contained numerous taped segments that had been shot all over the country. Nothing of this magnitude had ever been attempted before.

To shoot it all *Real People* sent out a combo producer/director called a field producer to go out into the field set up the story, do interviews, and direct the freelance three-quarter inch videotape crew. When they were done shooting they boxed up their tapes, and traveled back to Los Angeles, then flew out somewhere else and did it all over again. Each story was shot on five to ten, thirty-minute videotape cassettes, and when you multiply that by seven or eight segments per show, well you get the picture. There were a lot of videotape cassettes to view, log, and edit. With these kinds of numbers, the biggest challenge faced by Schlatter and his production team was figuring out where were they were going to edit all this tape. It was a huge amount of work that required a full on three-quarter inch editing facility which at the time did not exist anywhere in the world. Where were you going to find a place with enough three-quarter inch edit bays to get the post work done and meet a weekly production deadline?

One of the great things about three-quarter inch editing was the cost of the equipment. Compared to online machines, three-quarter was a lot of zeroes cheaper. This made the answer to the question where are you going to find enough edit bays very simple, you build it yourself.

Image editor Larry Shulman once again helps us out with some great memories from back in the day. He was on staff with George Schlatter Productions and was part of the team that built the first three-quarter inch edit facility in Los Angeles. As Larry tells it, it didn't seem like a big deal at the time, but looking back it totally changed the history of prime time TV.

Recollections
Building an Edit Facility

In 1978 I started working on a show called *Real People* for George Schlatter Productions in West Hollywood. This was the first reality show on primetime network television. We had at least eight video crews crisscrossing the country weekly led by eight Field Producers. The freelance crew market had been pretty well established by network news, so we had few problems finding the camera crews. They also mostly owned their own gear, so equipment was not a problem either.

Our biggest challenge was post-production. There were no facilities in existence that were prepared to handle that much three-quarter inch videotape. The solution for George Schlatter was simply, "build it yourself." I was a twenty-four-year-old production assistant back then, but nevertheless George assigned me to work with an edit bay engineering genius named Dave Morgenstern and a wonderful wire man named Karl Levin to build an edit facility they called "The Editing Company". And build it we did. There was available office space upstairs from our production office at Beverly and Sweetzer in Hollywood. We tore it up and put it back together and suddenly we had a three-quarter inch edit facility. We'd start the process by dubbing the shot tapes to a three-quarter inch work print with the time code burned onto the lower third of the video. A copy was also made directly to two-inch videotape as the master. Now the editors went to work.

The "off-line" editors were the creative ones. It was their job to take all the tapes from the field per story and edit it down to a *Real People* segment, of varying lengths. To do this they used were eight smaller rooms with Convergence off-line editing. This consisted of basic editing equipment controlling a three-quarter inch playback machine and a record machine. This system did simple cuts only, but that was all we needed for the off line work.

After they finished a first cut, they would show the rough cut to the producers of the show who would make their changes. The editors would do the revisions then manually write down the visible time code that they were looking at for each cut in the rough cut. Remember that this was linear editing. If something had to be altered everything that followed that change would have to be reedited. It was a time consuming process.

When it was done, all this information was turned into our edit list. This was used for the next step in the process, the CMX bay. In the CMX 340X bay, the edit was refined. With 3 U-Matic machines, we could do dissolves and wipes, and create a new electronic list on punch tape. After final approval from the exec producer, we would take our list over to an online edit facility called Vidtronics, where the list could be "automatically" controlled based on the time code and reel numbers, and our final two-inch videotape version would be completed. A visit to audio sweetening allowed the application of sound effects and a general cleaning of the audio. The segment was then ready for broadcast.

Inspired by George, we made it all up as we went along. None of this had ever been done before at a level high enough for prime time broadcast. Three-quarter inch videotape had made it to primetime as a procession of similar shows followed *Real People* to the national airwaves.

PART V
Chapter Three
Tape is Cheap

"Roll on everything, tape is cheap!!!" soon became the battle cry of reality show production and it was true. A thirty-minute cassette cost only a fraction of what an equivalent amount of film would have cost.

As a result, the image gathering style of reality based TV became one of shooting piles of tape in the field, then editing it down in post. It was better to shoot it and not use it, then need the shot and not have it, so it was just easier to shoot it all.

The producers scheduled insanely packed days, so the image gatherers had to learn to work quickly and efficiently while maintaining a creative style of shot making. They had to shoot lengthy interviews then an interminable list of what was now called B-roll a term that was adapted from the film days when editors would use B-roll shots to cover film splices and to visualize sound bites. "Shoot everything that moves!!!" was the basic instruction given by the field producer to the cameraman back then.

So, it fell upon the shoulders of the image gatherers to make these shows work. It was their ability to work quickly but still create quality content that drove reality format shows. We used to call it "making chicken salad out of chicken poop", only we didn't say poop.

Cameramen had to have the physical endurance to work a ten-hour day with only a short half-hour lunch break that usually consisted of take out picked up by a PA. They also had to be able to maintain their creativity to keep cranking it out though exhausted. Shoot days became an endless procession of set up, shoot, wrap, set up, shoot, wrap as the two-man crew moved from one location to the next. The image gatherer was the Director of Photography, camera operator, gaffer, and electrician, while the soundman did audio and served as a camera assistant and grip.

Recollections
Reality: My First Time

I had been freelancing in Miami for about a year, shooting mostly network news. I got a call one day from a show called *That's Incredible* a network reality show that ABC had rolled out to compete with NBC's Real People. They were coming to town to shoot some stories and someone I knew had recommended me. I said sure. It was clear that network news was no longer the only game in town. It seemed a good idea to jump on this new bandwagon.

Now I was used to a news type work schedule where you ran out, shot for about an hour, handing off your tape and had lunch. Or you showed up, sat around for several hours, jumped into action for half an hour, and then, yup, had lunch. I was about to find out that this reality world was very different. It was crazy from the start, sort of on your mark, get set, shoot! Very few breaks were scheduled, and everyone seemed to be in a big hurry. We were always behind schedule.

Anyway, here's what my days were like on my first magazine type show. On the first day we met at five in the morning at a local marina and hopped on a chartered fishing boat to shoot a story about a ten-year old kid who had broken some kind of fishing record. Off we went to Florida's gulf stream fishing area to shoot the kid fishing and do an interview.

I had the camera on my shoulder pretty much the entire morning shooting the kid baiting his hook, casting his line, and yes eventually catching a fish. Of course I had to roll constantly because the producer wanted that moment when the kid hooked one. By the way shooting on a small boat was not easy. The boat was bobbing like a cork, and if I saw the horizon going up and down in my viewfinder, well, let's just say that is a good way to get sea sick. Anyway, we finished the shoot then ate lunch on the boat on the way back. We hit the dock, loaded the van and were off and running for our afternoon shoot. Afternoon shoot? Yup.

Next stop was Jackson Memorial Hospital to do a story about some doctor and his cutting edge medical research. By the time we started shooting that story it was already two o'clock in the afternoon and we'd been working for nine hours. It was at this point that I realized that they didn't care about overtime, so at least we'd be making a pile of money while getting our asses kicked.

We ended up working for five more hours, shooting two more interviews and B-roll. I was starting to really love shooting interviews. It was the only time I got to sit down. We wrapped our location and as we were loading the car, the producer gave us the info for the next day. We had a seven o'clock in the morning call time in Fort Lauderdale, which was about an hour and a half hour drive for me. Oh, and it was now eight o'clock at night.

I got home, grabbed some dinner, showered, and threw my self in bed. The alarm went off at four-thirty the next morning and on and on it went. We did this drill for four days, shooting two stories a day all over South Florida. In the midst of all this, I became an image gathering machine. The more we worked, the better and stronger I seemed to get. Shots popped into my head and lighting setups fell together with ease. I was on a roll.

After four days of shooting at that pace, though, I was physically exhausted and my brain was fried, but the producer seemed happy with our work. When he left, we shook hands. He smiled and said Welcome to reality TV. I smiled, went home, and crawled into bed, and slept for two days. Had another show coming in to town so figured I better get some rest.

PART VI
Betacam

INTRODUCTION

Three-quarter inch videotape had a great run, but in the end, there was no getting away from the fact that a cameraman and a guy lugging a big heavy deck was just not a good enough option to meet the growing demands of TV image gathering. At this point in time there were still enough film veterans around who remembered how easy it was to shoot with a film camera. You picked it up, threw it on your shoulder and off you went. If only they could make a one-piece video camera that could do the same thing was the general plea. Sony Corporation was listening and after several years of research and development, they introduced a revolutionary product that solved this dilemma.

In 1982, Sony engineers developed a videotape format called Betacam. The size of the videotape went from three-quarter inches wide to a half-inch. This reduction in width allowed for a smaller record deck design that was small enough to be mounted to the back of the camera.

Sony rolled out a video camera with a dock-able deck that was a "one-piece" unit known as a camcorder. No more cumbersome deck, no more tethered second guy trailing behind lugging that big heavy box. Betacam gave the cameraman the same ease of movement that the film camera had provided, but this was only a part of the new technological landscape. The Betacam record system also t provided a significant upgrade in the quality of the taped image that was several steps above three-quarter inch videotape. Betacam was a major game changer.

Part VI discusses the impact of Betacam on image gathering and how it broke down the final barriers to all electronic prime time shows shot on location. With the arrival of Betacam, the golden age of video truly arrived. While three-quarter videotape had only been considered "news quality", Betacam was definitely ready for primetime. It took videotape from the limited world of taped segments, to a production tool that met network standards for an entire show.

All this was great, but once again the image gatherers had to adapt to an entirely new technological landscape which came with a whole new set of challenges. As always, my generation provides the thoughts and memories.

PART V
Chapter One
Betacam: The Next Big Thing

As mentioned the reduction in size of the Betacam format allowed for a record deck that was small enough to be mounted to the back of the camera. This created a one-piece videotape camera that could go anywhere just as this ad declares. Yes, that is me shooting comedian Milton Berle for the TV show, *Lifestyles of the Rich and Famous*. There will be more on that show later in this history.

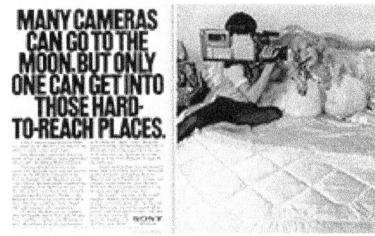

As you can see in the above picture, the Betacam camera sat on your shoulder with a padded and rounded bottom that was molded to the shape of your shoulder. Of course, adding the deck made the camera significantly heavier, but the design engineers balanced it so well designed that you could let go and the camera would pretty much sit there. Of course you didn't do that, but the balance of the camera took the strain off of your arm and increased your overall mobility. The shoulder and back was another story, but that was pretty much the cost of doing business.

Betacam was truly designed as a hand held camera. Its primary market was TV News and magazine shows where most of the image gathering was done by a cameraman with a camera on the shoulder. Ok, but what about the times that you needed to use a tripod for a speech or interview? There needed to be a way to mount a Betacam camera to a tripod. With a rounded bottom, how were you going to make this happen? All other cameras in history had flat bottoms with a threaded hole in the middle that matched the mounting screw of the tripod head.

Well, this is where some genius stepped in and designed what became known as the quick release plate as seen in the picture below. It was an ingenious innovation that solved several problems and was actually a big improvement over that old tripod screw.

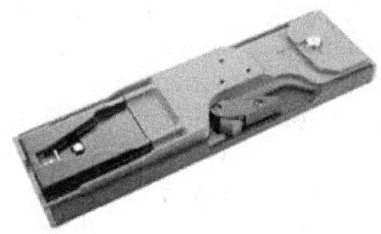

As you can see in the picture, the flat plate had special grooves in the front and back that corresponded to a toe and heel on the bottom of the camera that slipped into those grooves. When the camera was properly seated, you slid the camera forward and a spring clicked a lock in place mounting the camera to the quick release plate. If you wanted to remove the camera, you put your thumb on that red button and pulled back on the lever. The spring released and the camera could be easily lifted off of the plate. Hence the name quick release plate. When you bought the camera, the plate came with it.

Of course this necessitated a new design for the tripod heads. They needed to be redesigned with a fitted piece called a wedge plate. The wedge plate, like the one you see here, was designed to be screwed onto the under side of the quick release plate. The tripod head had a corresponding space on top to which the wedge plate would be slipped in and locked. Two screws were used to attach the wedge plate to the quick release plate so that the camera didn't swivel.

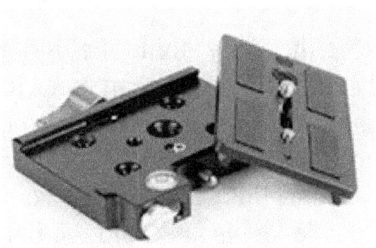

Ok, now let's move on to the Betacam format which was the real quantum leap forward. It's a little complicated so we'll keep it as simple as possible.

The Betacam format was a high-speed record format that used component video signal separation. This meant that the YUV video signal, which in three-quarter inch composite video had transmitted the brightness and color/chroma in one signal, was now separated into three separate channels. The result was a much sharper image. If none of this makes any sense to you, suffice it to say that Betacam was easier to use and looked way better than three-quarter inch video. The minute you picked one up and shot with it, you knew you were holding the future in your hands.

Recollections
That Betacam Feeling

I had started my career shooting film. Back in those days, with my film camera perched on my shoulder, I had had fantastic mobility. Then along came videotape and everything changed. Suddenly I was tethered to a guy who was carrying a fifty-pound deck. We were not used to this. As a result, we were constantly getting tangled and when that happened my camera got yanked, and I got viewfinder punched in the eye.

I always felt like I was hauling around a load of bricks behind me, the deck not the sound guy. Betacam solved this problem in a big, big way. Even though the camera was a bit box-like in its design, the fact that it was one piece meant that it was so much easier to use.

With Betacam, the only thing behind me was a soundman wearing a small mixer as you can see in this early Betacam production picture. That's soundman Roy Chase behind me. Speaking of sound guys, this configuration was great for them too. The small mixer around the neck left the sound guys with two free hands. They could ride levels and hold the boom at the same time. It was also so much better for the health of their necks and shoulders.

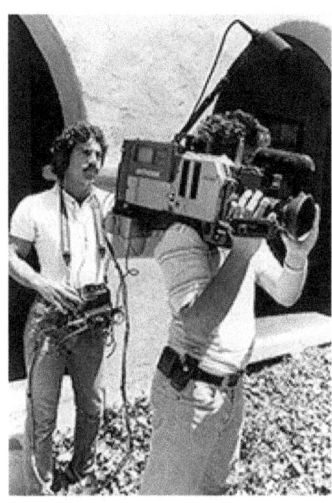

I especially loved it when we shot our B-roll. Betacam came with its own camera mike as you can see in the picture below. This meant that I could unhook from the sound guy, switch on the camera mic and go get my shots. It was perfect for shooting the "B-roll" which was the label now given to everything that was not an interview. The camera mike gave the b-roll ambient sound. I was free to dart around and find my shots, just like I used to do in the good old film days. I had a camera on my shoulder, and the comforting sound of tape rolling next to my ear. The swiveling viewfinder gave me low angle, high angle, and everything in between. I was an untethered shot maker again and I loved it.

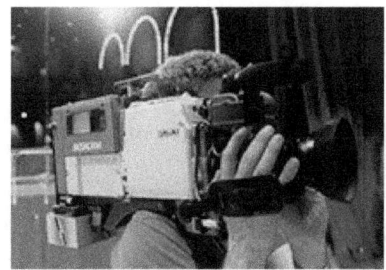

Then there was the quality of the image. Everyone was blown away by how good Betacam looked. Three-quarter inch had always been considered the "news" format. It was ok for TV News but certainly not good enough for more demanding levels of production.

Granted three-quarter had made its way into network prime time, but it was relegated to field pieces dropped into a show. It was looked down upon and with good reason. Three-quarter inch tended to be soft and grainy. Betacam was different. It had that sharp, crisp image of big time video production at about a tenth of the cost. We all immediately fell madly in love.

PART VI
Chapter Two
Syndicated Network Reality

It took a while for people to realize the fact that Betacam's quality exceeded network standards for the airing of videotape, but when they did it opened the door for a whole new genre of TV shows that could be completely shot in the field and broadcast on network television in prime time at the fraction of the cost of any other type of production. We're not just talking about taped segments. We are talking, the entire show. The Betacam camcorder could deliver the image quality that the networks' specs demanded. It was just a matter of time until someone decided to give it a try.

In 1984, a TV show called *Lifestyles of the Rich and Famous* led the way. It was a pivotal step in the history of reality television. It was the first network syndicated prime time reality type TV show that did not have a studio presence, saving thousands of dollars per show. The show was shot entirely in the field on Betacam.

Lifestyles of the Rich and famous was the brainchild of a man named Robin Leach who also served as the show's host. The show, which focused on the private lives of big name celebrities and filthy rich business moguls, was shot at their sumptuous homes, exotic vacation spots, and exclusive watering holes.

The production costs of *Lifestyles* were a fraction of the costs for a standard network prime time show. It was the low cost and high quality of Betacam production along with the skill of the crews to quickly and efficiently gather images that made this show and others that followed possible. The networks were thrilled as they realized the new possibilities. They could now fill prime time programming slots with these new types of shows. They could get great ratings with a one-hour show, and make huge profits because of the low production costs.

Frank Beacham, once again, provides the memories as once again he was right in the middle of what was happening. Remember,

Frank had started with the Portapak, jumped at the opportunities offered by the TK-76, so it was only natural for him to be one of the first kids on the block to own a Betacam camcorder. This purchase led Frank on a path that eventually intersected with a man named Robin Leach. Together, these two individuals moved forward with a totally new concept that would have major future ramifications. Frank recalls the details of this encounter, and I follow those memories with some of my own.

Recollections
Lifestyle of the Rich and Famous

Prior to Betacam, one hour of prime time TV cost one million dollars to produce. When shows like *Real People* arrived the cost dropped to $300,000. Each taped segment, which made up a bulk of the show, cost the price of an airline ticket and a day or two of labor for a two–man video crew, though there were some bump up costs to get three-quarter up to prime time specs. One or two studio hosts replaced the cast of actors, and the same studio set was used for each show. The shows were shot like news shows with the taped segments dropped in. An entire season could be shot over a few weeks. Ad revenues were the same no matter, so down came the costs and up went the profits.

Meanwhile, in 1984 I was running a small production company called Television Matrix. We provided crews, equipment, and editing for network news and the occasional national show like *Entertainment Tonight* that came to Miami to shoot segments. That year, a production company came to South Florida to shoot some tape pieces for a new pilot. It was called *Lifestyles of the Rich and Famous* It was the brainchild and starred a man named Robin Leach.

Robin Leach sold the show as a look into the lifestyles of the very rich. However, he had only been offered a $100,000 budget per one-hour episode. Everyone, and I mean everyone, had told him it was impossible. Now, he was looking at my Betacam package and asking if maybe this was the answer. Betacam quality was head and shoulders above the older tape formats. It was totally up to network video standards. What if he shot the entire show out in the field on Betacam? I stalled and told him I needed a little time to do some research. He then countered with a promise. If I could help him do a show for a per episode cost of $100,000, he would give me a contract for the show and move my entire company to Los Angeles.

Of course I was intrigued by the idea. It would be very hard, I imagined, but not impossible. The biggest challenge I faced was that the network would not yet accept a finished prime time show on Betacam tape. Even though the quality was there, it was still too new for them to accept. I would have to create an inter-format edit bay that took the beta tapes and edited them to one-inch Type C format videotape system which at the time was the standard for television broadcasting.

The next day I called Charlie Felder, then president of Sony Broadcast in New York City, and told him of Leach's inquiry. Sony was a very small company back then and you could get its executives on the phone easily. I also knew Charlie as a deal maker, and a man open to new ideas. He knew me as a very early Betacam customer.

I explained in detail what Leach wanted to do. We'd have to build an inter-format room, one where the Betacam could be edited directly to Type-C one-inch videotape. Sony had all the pieces, but had not put it together yet. Charlie was intrigued and told me that Sony had been thinking along the very same lines. A little more negotiating and the deal got made. Robin Leach got his show. Television Matrix moved to Los Angeles, and set up a groundbreaking edit bay at Sunset Gower Studios in Hollywood.

I was lucky enough to hire a man named Jim Fancher to build the facility. He was far more than a brilliant engineer. As a hands-on "can do" guy, he was also a natural born negotiator who could coordinate the different technical approaches of companies whose gear would not work together.

I can still picture Jim lying on his back under a rack of gear talking on the phone with tech support at some company about why their product wouldn't work. Thanks to Jim, it all came together on time and on budget. By fall, we were ready. We had built the first inter-format edit bay in the nation, Betacam to one-inch, and *Lifestyles* was the first major magazine show to be shot using the new Betacam format. Even though nobody else knew or cared, we had made television history.

Recollections
My Time with Lifestyles

I had spent almost ten years as a news and public affairs cameraman at WTVJ in Miami. I left my job and started freelancing at NBC News, but still hoped that as a freelancer, I would get the opportunity to shoot stories outside of the strict news format. My passion was shooting feature stories where creativity was more valued. A few shows like that came along, but they were rare. Then along came *Lifestyles of the Rich and Famous.*

I had shot a couple of segments for their pilot in South Florida, and though I loved the work, I pretty much forgot about it. I mean as a freelancer you are always moving forward to your next day's work. A few months later, early in the summer of 1983, Frank Beacham, came to me with a proposition. He had put his deal together with Robin Leach and part of that deal included a camera crew and Betacam package in Los Angeles. Was I interested in moving to Los Angeles to be part of that camera crew? I thought it over, discussed it with my family, and then took the plunge. Off we went to Los Angeles. I know it was pretty crazy, but it just felt right. I mean who could turn down a chance to shoot in LA with the Big Boys? Who knew where this could lead?

We shot *Lifestyles* on the first generation of Betacam equipment. The audio guy fed the camera with an FP-32 Shure mixer so all he had to carry around was a little two-pound mixer and his boom pole. A small box with a toggle switch was used to flip back and forth from the mixer to the confidence track of camera audio. Betacam also had two tracks for audio as time code had been shifted to its own separate third track.

I loved working on *Lifestyles of the Rich and Famous*. Because we shot interviews and b-roll with major motion picture and TV stars, it really forced me to up my game, especially in the lighting department. We also shot their homes and they were even more picky about how that footage looked than they were with their own appearance.

We did long sweeping pans, and achingly slow zooms of the interiors and exteriors of their homes. Then we shot the stars in short, movie like, scenes around the house. We shot them in their home office, picking roses in the garden, or reading a script by the swimming pool. Everything about these shots had to be perfect. I learned early on that actors know the difference. They can sense when the lighting is good and they are very protective of their image.

A show like *Lifestyles* had never been done before so there was no model to follow. I look back with amazement on what we were able to accomplish with a minimal crew and limited lighting package. It was me and a sound guy with a four fixture light kit consisting of two open face 650's and two open face 1k's. We had a few pieces of diffusion, color correction blue, scraps of party gels, a bounce card and a roll of black wrap. That was it, no C-stands, sand bags, or flags. All that grip equipment was just extra stuff we'd have to drag around. We had no place for it and no time for it.

Fortunately, the Betacam camera of the day was somewhat light sensitive. Our camera lens was a standard 12x120mm zoom lens. Wide-angle lenses did not exist for video cameras yet. Instead we used a wide-angle adaptor. This was a big hunk of glass that fit on to the end of the lens and gave us a bit more on the wide end of the lens while still allowing us to focus and zoom through. It was perfect for those long slow pans and zooms of the design elements of the stars' homes.

With my limited manpower and equipment package, when all was said and done, I had to get smart really quick. I had come from a news background anyway, so I was used to figuring out how to make good with what I had to work. I had also learned to work quickly. I knew how to blend color temperatures from my film days. I employed all those same instincts to shooting with Betacam.

Blending the light sources and white balancing was the key. After that it was just a matter of putting the camera in the perfect place to take full advantage of the lighting. I put my back to the windows, gelled the lights as necessary and went to work. I discovered that it was really amazing what you can do with limited resources when you have no choice and you have to make it work.

I never scouted. I arrived at our location in the morning, figured out where we'd be shooting, and went to work. I had to come up with a plan of how I was going to get it all done. I learned to trust my instincts and my eye. Good framing and composition became instinctual after a while. My eye connected with my brain and when everything was right something in my head said yes. I could never explain what made a good shot, I but I knew it when I saw it.

The really crazy part for me though, was finding myself on a job with some of the biggest names in Hollywood in 1984. We shot with Lucille Ball, Zsa Zsa Gabor, Milton Berle, John Forsythe, Greer Garson, Joan Collins, and the list goes on and on. I even did an interview with Clara Bow the "it girl" from the early days of Hollywood. I loved shooting celebrities. There I was, the old news guy, rubbing elbows with all the big stars of that day. There really is something magical about gathering images of famous people. It is very hard to describe, but anyone who has done it knows what I am talking about. It is so surreal to shoot someone you have seen in movies or on TV.

It was also astounding how friendly these celebrities were back in those days. We would spend an entire day with them shooting their homes and recording their lifestyles. I found that if they sensed I was on their side, that I was doing everything I could to make them look good, they would happily jump in and work side by side with me. The fact that they were all physically beautiful certainly made my job easier, but I was still faced with the challenge of making them look good. They trusted me so I could not let them down.

We were basically hanging out and with some of the biggest stars of the day. Oftentimes their publicists would stop by, say hello, and leave. They knew us and they knew we would take care of their clients. The stars were always cordial and cooperative and treated us like guests in their homes. They would often stop and say hello if we saw them at some future red carpet event. Those were really the good old days.

PART VI
Chapter Three
More Celebrity Shows

When Lifestyles premiered a new wrinkle was added to the image gatherer's list of responsibilities. Up to this point in time most image gatherers had come up through the ranks of TV news. They had learned to work fast and efficiently while still capturing quality images. Shows like *Real People* and *That's Incredible* had forced the image gatherers to extend their repertoire. Adding celebrities to the mix took everything to a whole new level.

The image gatherers found themselves working with TV and movie stars who were used to plying their craft in big Hollywood productions. Just because they were involved in a reality type show didn't mean that their needs and demands were any different. They had to look good in every shot. Their face was their livelihood after all, and they were fiercely protective of that asset. This was a fact that had to be respected by the camera crews working with them or things could get ugly really fast.

Recollections
Cranking It Up to Hollywood Style

There was nothing more insane than shooting with Hollywood celebrities armed with my Betacam and a limited lighting and grip package. These were people used to shooting on movie sets, with big crews, and multi million dollar budgets. Most of them had worked with the top directors of photography in the business. As a result, they were very aware of the effect of light on how they looked and knew what the best lighting angles were. They assumed I was going to do the same for them in spite of the fact that it was just me and the sound guy with four lights.

Celebrities also always had their publicists on the shoot. They were charged with the task of image protection. The publicists took their job very seriously as it justified their existence. Though most were nice, some were very picky. They would sit there with their faces buried in our field monitors critiquing every aspect of my work as a means of justifying their existence. So how did I survive?

Every image gatherer has their bag of tricks. In my bag I carried heavy diffusion for the lights, bounce cards for fill, home made dimmers, 25w bulbs for the practicals, and lots of black wrap. C-stands, flags, cutters, sand bags and all the grippage of Hollywood, were not realistic in our fast moving world of production. It was just more stuff for me to carry and move around. I just didn't have the time. Of course in addition to all that was the fact that I was a converted news guy from Miami and didn't even know what most of that stuff was. Hey, I got the job done, and it looked good. How I got there was up to me.

Instead of relying on gear, I developed a set of rules for quickly and easily creating quality images. I always put the windows at my back and supplemented the existing available light and let the white balance of the camera take care of the blending. I learned that it was not how many lights you used, but more importantly how you used them and where you put them. I learned to find the best angle of the key in relation to my camera angle, and then fill as needed. I learned that aging actresses needed to believe that I was taking extra special care of them. They loved white bounce cards, so I always applied them liberally to my lighting set ups. Finally, I learned that no matter what, keep smiling, never let them see your pain. Working with celebs could spiral out of control really fast and I would always lose that argument. I was there for them, not vice versa.

Beyond lighting there were also some camera tricks I picked up along the way too. My favorite technique was manipulating the white balance to the proper color temperature for my set up. The video cameras of the day did not have dial up color temperatures like they do today. I figured out how to play with the white balance and warm up or cool off a shot to better blend ambient light in the room with my tungsten light fixtures. To do this I would white balance through a piece of color correction blue, to warm up, or orange to cool off. The camera would be fooled and it would remove just enough blue to blend the light sources. It really worked well as it fooled the camera while giving me a slightly warmer image.

This technique was good for me on two levels. Warm always looks better than cool for me and for those peering into the monitor. For them I even cranked up the chroma on the field monitors. The publicists had this thing for overly warm images. What they didn't know couldn't hurt them. I needed to get the day moving, without compromising what I knew was right. A warmed up monitor image made them happy while I still got my shots with proper color balance.

The last rule for shooting celebs was, do not under any circumstances attempt to shoot aging women movie stars outside in direct sun. Big no, no. You either back lit them and filled them in with a bounce card, or shot them in the shade, but no direct sun. That went for bald headed men too. Hey I was all about the image. I really wanted them to look good. It only made me look good too and my ego enjoyed getting a thank you from a movie star.

Our days were jammed packed. I found that my news training that had taught me to work quickly, served me well. I developed the knack of walking into a room, quickly figuring out the best camera angles, and then making it happen. I learned I had to commit to my concept. My goal was always to bring the highest quality lighting and camera work that time would allow.

I won't deny that looking through the viewfinder and seeing some of the biggest stars of the day was a huge thrill. Of course I had about two seconds to revel in all this and then we were off to the next shot. However, shooting with actors who knew how to interact with the camera was a fantastic experience for this old newshound. Many was the time when I'd capture a look to camera that just blew me away. They all had a knack to make even the slightest gesture seem so natural. I mean they were actors and they knew how to do this stuff.

I'll never forget shooting movie star Greer Garson at her home in New Mexico. We were shooting her crossing a wooden bridge over a small river on her property. I was following her on a long lens when she paused on the bridge, picked a flower, sniffed it as she looked wistfully off into the distance and continued her way across the bridge. I'm telling you it was magical. She was back lit by the sun and the effect was incredible.

Of course there was the day I asked Steve Allen if he would shoot without his glasses. They were coke bottle thick and no matter where I put my light, I got a major kick in his lenses and horrible shadows across his eyes from the frames. Bad idea that one. I got a stern lecture about his trademark image and how he had worn them on camera for forty years. I got it, and never made that mistake again. I mean it was their world and I was being allowed in it for this very brief period of time. They made the rules not me. It was and is a world of show up, shut up, and shoot.

Anyway, the Steve Allen thing worked out fine as you can see from the picture below. That's me shooting host wraps for his show *Start of Something Big*, a syndicated show from the 1980's.

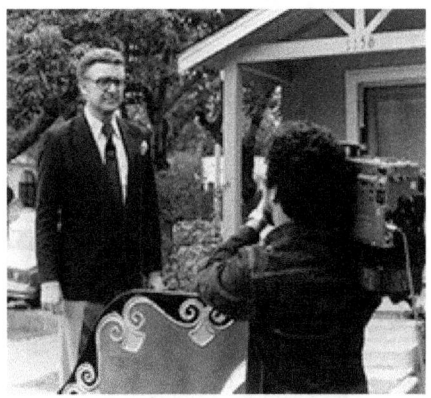

And then there was the time I was covering a big event for Entertainment Tonight. Whitney Houston was in her prime and was going to sing a song as part of the event's entertainment. She was a huge presence and there was a mob of camera crews waiting backstage hoping to get a brief moment with her. Suddenly, she emerged from her dressing room and started walking who knows where. We all reacted like a herd of cattle and just blindly followed.

I was frantically backpedaling and working hard to hold my position amongst the crews.

Finally, she ducked into a door and we all stopped. The door closed to reveal that Whitney Houston had just entered the ladies room. Of course, we all waited for her to finish, then followed her back down the hallway to her dressing room. True story!!!

Oh, and one more story. I was out covering a celebrity ski event. A very well known actor, whose name I have sworn not to reveal, was standing in a group that I was shooting. He slipped on some ice and went down. No biggie, except his toupee went flying which was a biggie. He came over to us and in so many words begged us not to use the footage, pleading that his career could be on the line. We respected his wishes which is what you did back then.

All in all, shooting these "celebrity" based show was a great experience for me. In the end I got really good at combining news speed with production savvy. These skills served me very well for the next twenty-five years as I grew from the role of a cameraman to that of director of photography.

PART VI
Chapter Four
The Next Big Step: Cable TV

In the early 1970's a communication satellite orbiting the earth was made available for domestic use. A national domestic satellite distribution system was created and Cable TV was off and running. The biggest selling point was that with the access to a satellite, Cable TV could now be accessed anywhere with perfect reception in an age when TV's were hooked up to an antenna on your roof or rabbit ears on top of your TV. In those good old days, you got some networks well, others, not so much as everything depended on your location in relationship to the broadcast tower of the TV station.

Cable provided perfect reception for its subscribers hard wired into their homes. The monthly rates were also reasonable, so many people were only too happy to pay the fees especially when Cable added original programming on its own Cable TV stations. All this new programming ushered in the golden age of freelance image gathering.

With the addition of Cable TV shows, the workload and the variety of image gathering opportunities for freelancers exploded. There were just so many shows that needed to be shot. Here's the story. Network TV had been king of the hill since its inception in the 1940's. Then along came two men, Charles Dolan and Gerald Levin. They founded Sterling Manhattan Cable and on November 8, 1972 they launched the nation's first commercial free pay TV network called Home Box Office or HBO. Ted Turner soon followed with Turner Broadcasting and rolled out a twenty-four-hour news service called CNN.

In 1978 Cable TV gained increased channel capacity and everybody plunged in with what was called "boutique broadcasting". *ESPN* covered nothing but sports, *MTV* tapped into the music scene, *The Playboy Channel* offered viewers adult entertainment, *The Food Network* created celebrity chefs, and a whole potpourri of other TV programmers jumped in with their own cable channels.

By the 1990's there was virtually a channel for every interest and the viewing public loved it. Everybody had a cable box, with a button for each cable channel, attached to the TV set. You manually pushed one of those buttons to select the station you wanted. Each one of those channels was filled with original programming that was only available on that cable channel.

The effect on the community of freelance image gatherers was profound. All these new channels needed to fill their airtime with programming and someone had to shoot these shows, which were all reality based programming. The industry once again turned to the freelance guys and their camera packages. Even more guys quit their TV News jobs as image gatherers, bought Betacam packages and joined the freelancing world. Amazingly, everyone stayed busy

Recollections
Cable TV: 1990's

The 1990's took freelancing image gathering into a whole new stratosphere. I know that my freelance career really took off. New production companies were popping up all over town to meet the voracious appetite of Cable TV. Since buying camera packages was way too costly, these companies looked for cameramen with packages to shoot their shows. That was the good news. The bad news was that most of the shows had very small budgets, which meant that when I worked on a Cable TV show, I really worked. The days were packed like never before in order to maximize the value for each shoot day.

The first Cable TV show I shot was a house tour design show called *Awesome Interiors.* The show had a lovely female host, Jennifer Convy, who would walk around the rooms of a uniquely designed home with the homeowner talking about the specific design features.

My job was to shoot the entire interview segment hand held while following the host and her guest. I had to light the entire room so they could walk anywhere and talk about anything without seeing any sign of production. It was quite a challenge as I am talking about lights on stands, cables on the floor, and nobody to help me as I figured out where to hide the stands and cables to give the host the most room to freely roam.

The days were relentless. I would have to move the gear into the room, set everything up, shoot it all hand held, then break it all down and drag it all off to the next room and do the same. This was repeated many times during the day with only a half hour to sit down and eat lunch. It was kind of like painting a room with a spray gun instead of a brush.

Listening was also an important part of the process. I always had to listen to what the people were saying and as they talked, I'd pan over to what they were talking about, then drift back to the host and her guest. These were all on air type moves, not easy stuff. There was also a lot to keep track of. If I let them walk out of frame, I had to remember which direction they walked. If they exited frame left, they had to enter the next shot frame right. All that stuff.

When we finished shooting the interview portion we had to go back through the rooms and get B-roll shots of everything they had talked about. If the guest had described Grandma's antique chair, I had to get a pretty shot of Grandma's antique chair. I also had to keep the light consistent with the interview set up so that it would cut, even though we might be shooting it a couple of hours later. It was up to me to remember the essence of my lighting setup and match it for the B-roll.

This show was only the beginning. For the next ten years I shot every imaginable type of cable show. All of them were very narrowly focused on a very specific subject matter. I even shot one called *Simply Quilts*, which consisted of interviewing a quilt maker then shooting her finished quilts. I've got to tell you, shooting a quilt hanging on the wall after lunch is a real challenge. Not the shooting, the staying awake.

My favorite shows were the cooking shows where we got to sample the food after we were done shooting. That was the good part. The challenge was shooting hand held in a hot kitchen while following a chef step by step. I did not have the luxury of multiple cameras. I was the wide shot, the tight shot, and the over the pot shot. FYI, little mountable cameras also did not yet exist. I worked out a technique where I'd call out freeze. Then I'd jump around over the chef's shoulder to get the shot of the ingredients going in. Freeze!! Back to the wide shot, and on and on it went. I was always tempted to slap on a pair of roller skates or maybe a use my son's skateboard.

No matter what the subject of these cable shows, I was constantly challenged both physically and mentally. It was an endurance contest to spend ten straight hours running around someone's house with a twenty-five pound Betacam camera on my shoulder. It was mental gymnastics to figure out ways to shoot the endless shot list and make it all look amazing. I relied on my experience, remembering what worked well in the past, then applying it to the new project. I instinctively knew what to do in just about every situation.

These shows also always had hosts. They were male and female, tall and short, and representing every ethnicity which created many unique lighting challenges. I've got to say, the tall ones were the worst. Trying to shoot a tall host standing next to a short home decorator was impossible, especially in a home with low ceilings. I mean where you supposed to put your lights?

Then there were the kitchens for the cooking shows. These were not built on sound stages. These kitchens were in people's homes. Ridiculous. I mean, chrome kitchens are beautiful, but they reflect every light you turn on. I still have nightmares about some of those locations. Whatever I figured out ways to make it work, and somehow it always did.

I also tried hard not to judge content. I realized that my job was about quality images. I was about pretty pictures artfully crafted. The producers were about content. Over the years I worked on hundreds of shows. Some were funny, some were inspirational, some were insightful, some were instructional, and yes some were really lame.

Whatever, as long as I stayed all about the images, I was good. I mean some shows were really great to work on. I met interesting people doing great things. Other shows, well, not so much, but again, as long as I kept my eye to the viewfinder I was fine.

PART VI
Chapter Five
More Media Expansion

Next up were the tabloid TV shows. These were newsy types of shows, that basically decided to completely ignore the stern rules of engagement that news coverage demanded. Many of those rules that TV News had implemented over the years were loosened or ignored. Everything and everybody was fair game.

The image gatherers still gathered images as producers encouraged certain activities from the subjects to help tell the story. It was all about creating what they called "good television", which was defined as anything that garnered good ratings.

It's important to note that at this point in time, the cost of a full production Betacam Camcorder package was still prohibitive for most companies who stayed afloat by having a constant flow of TV shows in preproduction, production, and post-production. The cable networks doled out the money in stages so the production companies were always paying the costs of the last show with the advance money for the next show.

With the cost of purchasing a production package running over $100,000, plus the cost of maintenance and repair, very few production companies were willing to make that big a financial commitment. Besides, between projects, what would they do with the gear? If it wasn't working, they were losing money. That was a lot of investment to have lying around the office. A few slow months and the gear would start eating away at their profit margins. It made way more sense for them to turn to the freelancers.

In fact, the demand was so great that individual freelance guys with packages bought a second package, then a third, then a fourth and started booking crews for their clients in order to meet the production demands. Eventually, gear rental/crewing companies emerged that became one-stop shops for their clients who required an ENG type camera package and crew.

In 1989 I founded one of those companies along with my soundman/partner at the time, Gar Smith seen here with me in the picture below.

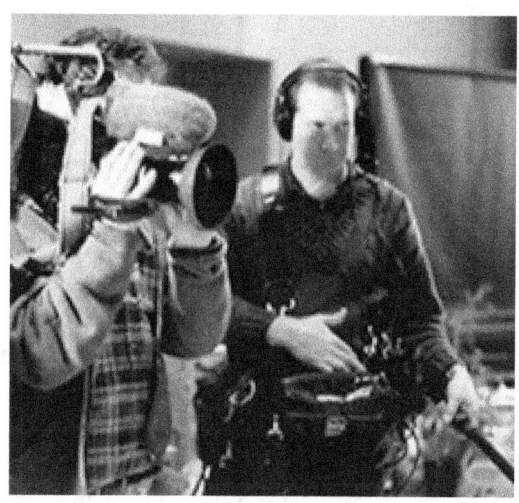

We called our company Imagecraft. Our goal was to facilitate production, by providing everything and everybody our clients needed to shoot their shows. This included two-man ENG style crews, lighting packages, dollies, grip gear, and everything in between. We created what we called the one-stop shop and the production managers loved us. The goal was to keep our clients in the fold, instead of watching them go somewhere else because we were booked.

Gar has since passed on, and I have retired and sold the business to longtime friend and tech genius Jason Been. I am proud to say Imagecraft, under Jason's leadership, is bigger than ever and still going strong today.

Anyway, back to history. The television production industry was in a state of rapid expansion, and the image gathering community was thriving. Everybody was shooting something on Betacam. Everybody was working. Everybody was making money. In fact, we were all so busy that it was difficult to keep track of which show you were working on and what style of shooting was required. It was kind of like going on a five country tour of Europe in seven days where you wake up in the morning on the fifth day and ask, where am I?

Recollections
Who Am I Working for Today?

I had come out to Los Angeles to seek my fortune as a freelance cameraman in 1983. Back then I shot segments for a multitude of magazine shows. There were busy times, and then shows would go on hiatus, so there'd be slim times. It went up and down like a yo-yo. I learned to live like a squirrel, saving up for those cold winters.

By the 1990's though my world changed. There were shows everywhere and year round. When one ended, another began. My pager, no cellphones yet, went off constantly. I became an expert on where all the pay phones were in LA. I was a master at the quick pull off, run to a phone booth, make a call, book the tomorrow's job, and back in my car in two minutes to get to today's job. I was never late to the day's shoot, but it was close sometimes. By the way, I was thrilled when cellphones were invented. Anyway, in a given week I might work for two or three different shows. One day it was *Entertainment Tonight*, shooting behind the scenes on a movie. The next day, I'd be over at *Hard Copy* stalking a celebrity. The third day I would be shooting a sad story about a destitute mother of five for a talk show. Then I'd wrap up the week shooting an exercise segment with a trainer doing arm curls with two cantaloupes in a grocery store for a Cable TV show. Yes, I really did that.

All of the shows used completely different styles of shooting. *ET* was quick, get in and get out news style shooting. You had to be economical with your shots, and fast with your lighting set ups, though you still were dealing with celebs so it had to look good. The talk shows were a little slower paced. They liked pretty looking interviews and dramatic sunsets for their piano music closes. The cable shows were all over the place, but I could always count on a long, hard day. They always required creativity and stamina to get it all shot. *Hard Copy* was a down and dirty type tabloid show, so you just had to be crazy. Hold on, I gotta tell this story.

Back in the Monica Lewinsky/President Clinton days we got a tip at *Hard Copy* that she was on a beach in Malibu doing a photo shoot. We showed up, and sure enough there was a photo shoot going on with a woman who, from a distance, sure looked like her. We shot a bit from about two hundred yards away with a telephoto lens, then made the decision to charge. I of course led the way with my camera rolling. When we got about fifty yards away, everybody but me stopped. I ran on another ten feet, then realized nobody was with me. The crew doing the photo shoot looked at me like I was crazy. I turned around to see what was going on and saw our producer waving me back. Up close, it was clearly not Monica Lewinsky. Oops excuse us we mumbled as we slinked off. Too bad, I had some great shots.

Back to the history, as the above story described, you literally could end up anywhere, shooting anything. You had to close your eyes and charge. The trick was keeping track of whom I was shooting for and applying their style to the shoot. This was no easy feat when your week bounced around like a ping pong ball. I always had to remind myself before I got to location exactly what I was shooting and who I was shooting for in order to mentally prepare myself.

There was one aspect of shooting that I always tried to hold consistent from show to show. I always challenged myself to get at least one spectacular shot. No matter what the show, I had to find a special moment more for myself than anybody else. Maybe it was just the way the light hit someone's face, or a moment at sunset with an orange sky. It could be something I planned or a maybe just a lucky accident. It didn't matter, but one great image made my entire day worthwhile. It is, was, and always will be all about the images I gathered on a given day that determined my true daily success.

PART VI
Chapter Six
Even More Media

In the old days TV networks signed off around two in the morning. By the 1990's, between Network and Cable TV the public had something to watch twenty-four hours a day, three hundred sixty-five days a year. TV sucked people in like a vacuum cleaner.

As has already been mentioned, celebrity based shows were particularly popular. There had always been a certain level of prurient interest in the American royalty of TV, movie, and sport's stars, but as all these new celebrity shows proliferated, access to their lives seemed unlimited. Celebrities translated into ratings so every show tried to find a celebrity angle to play. As a result, major star driven media events became really big deals, especially in Los Angeles.

Movie premiers had always attracted crowds of people hoping to catch a glimpse of their favorite stars. Now the image gatherers flocked to these events like moths to a flame. The term paparazzi was used to describe the still photographers who would line the red carpets and hang out at the hot night spots shooting hundreds of pictures of the stars hoping to sell their images to the many international newspaper and magazine outlets. The video world was not to be outdone. News shows, magazine shows, and every other show imaginable booked stars for guest appearances and sent crews out to line the red carpets hoping to get a brief interview that they could run on their broadcast. In addition, on the dark side, self-employed camera crews roamed the streets at night, cruising by the hot clubs hoping to catch a glimpse of a drunk celebrity doing something that they shouldn't be doing.

The king of all of these celebrity events, the event of events, of course is the Academy Awards. Every imaginable A-list, B-list, or C-list actor is there and media outlets gather accordingly. There are literally hundreds of image gatherers lining the red carpet. However, when I first covered the event, media coverage was but a mere shadow of what it is today. In my thirty years of covering the Oscars I was witness to a tremendous growth as the show went from big, to bigger, to out of control. From my first Oscars to my last one three decades later, things sure did change. In so many ways this growth reflects the overall exponential growth of the passion the public had for gathered images.

Recollections
The Oscars

I was a freelancer for *Entertainment Tonight* for nearly thirty years. Of course Oscar coverage has always been a big day in their yearly schedule, but the first time I covered it for them in 1989, the overall media interest was fairly modest not to mention minimal security.

At my first Oscars, I was given the task of shooting fashion shots of celebrities as they got out of their limos. There was little or no security back then so we just roamed around where the Limos pulled up and dropped people off. Our producer would shout "There's so and so" and we would dash through the traffic to get the tilt up and down and a quick answer to "who designed your dress?" It really was that easy.

This was pretty typical the first few times I covered the Oscars, but then something changed. It became Oscars on steroids. I am not sure why or how it happened but suddenly there were thousands of crews and photographers from all over the world standing at assigned spots on the red carpet that was over one hundred yards long. Even with the live broadcast the public thirst for images seemed insatiable.

Shooting the Oscars became totally insane. We had to arrive hours before the event then literally sit around waiting for things to get going. About an hour or so before the Oscar's began, the celebs started to trickle in. The early arrivals though were mostly the B-list players consisting of yesterday's stars hoping to somehow get their face in front of the public in order to launch their comebacks. Our producers would tell us to grab shots of those poor souls in case they overdosed at some point in the future. They could use the footage for their obits. Hey, I am not making this up.

With about forty-five minutes to go, the big stars began to arrive in all their dazzling glory. They would walk down the carpet posing and giving quick interviews. I just rolled and rolled and rolled and rolled. For a solid hour I shot away amidst great chaos and noise. I did snap zooms, rack focus shots, and tilts up and down to show the gowns. These shots were all known as "*MTV*" type of shots because they had become a popular style in music video production. So I snapped, tilted, and racked away. Every once in a while I'd catch a moment, maybe a look, or a rack focus that just hit perfectly. Man, that made my night.

By fifteen minutes before show-time, the A-list celebs started coming in endless waves. At this point my back started to tighten up. A fully loaded Betacam weighed about twenty-five pounds, even more with a mounted sun gun. After that much time without a break, I started getting a sharp pain mid back. Didn't matter, I just kept shooting. As the tape neared the end, I'd yank it out and slap in another. Of course less than one percent of what I shot in coverage of the Oscars ever got used, but whatever. That was not my concern. My job was to gather the images of the event, so that is what I did. I generally made it a point to not watch the finished pieces that aired. I swear the editors used shots from the first few minutes of the tape to save time. There were so many of my great shots that never got used because the celebrity was not important enough.

After the main event came the after parties. For these we had to load up our gear and drive off to some local hotspots. When we arrived, we were ushered into designated media areas and the celebs would be walked past us for more shots and more interviews. I remember one year waiting forever for a star from a very successful movie that everyone thought for sure would win her an Oscar. Sadly, for her, everybody on the movie won an Oscar, but not her. Nevertheless, we were camped out in front of the studio's party waiting for a shot. She had snuck in a back entrance, when she arrived so we had to wait for her exit.

Finally, after standing around forever on this cold, damp night she emerged and started heading for her limo. Clearly she was not in the mood to talk. Screw that, I thought as I broke past the barricade. We charged over to where she was, as the rest of the press followed me. A near riot ensued. The field producer yelled out a question, and she gave a brief response. She wasn't happy, and her publicist was livid. I guess we had broken some rule. Whatever, I got my shot. Oh and *ET* was ecstatic, thus reaffirming the old maxim- "Better to beg forgiveness than ask for permission."

I still look back at all those red carpet experiences and can recollect the incredible frenzy of activity as the tape literally burned through my camera. I just got lost in the action and pretty much operated on autopilot. Hard to describe, even harder to forget the rush and the pain in my back.

PART VI
Chapter Seven
Rescue 911

Rescue 911 was a prime time program that premiered on CBS in the spring of 1989. It was a reality format show shot entirely on Betacam at locations all over the United States. The show has a place in image gathering history as it introduced the concept of "re-creations" to video productions.

Rescue 911 had a very simple concept. It featured two types of stories. First, there were stories that depicted real life rescues. Crews fanned out all over the country and did ride-alongs with local fire and police departments. When stuff went down, the image gatherers shot it on Betacam, covering it like a news story.

Rescue 911 also presented a second type of story that pulled Betacam into the world of dramatic production. The show took the actual rescue 911 command center audiotape of real life rescues and recreated the action using actors mouthing the words of the dialogue.

The stories also included interviews with the victims and the rescuers. These segments came to be known as "re-creations" and this technique was soon adopted by other shows as a means of visualizing real life stories. Again all of this was made possible by the quality of Betacam. It met all of the network's standards.

For the TV image gatherers shooting re-creations was an entirely new challenge. Using skills they had learned covering real news stories, and applying them to the controlled environment of a semi scripted show, created some very exciting visuals. Everything imaginable was shot. Betacams flew through the air, went underwater, and raced down roads in ambulances in the middle of the night. Most of the shooting was done "hand-held" something the Betacam Camcorder was truly built for. The camera performed brilliantly and was the mainstay of the show for its entire run.

I had the opportunity to work on *Rescue 911*.

Recollections
Shooting Re-creations

Yes, *Rescue 911* used actors and yes there was a director, but the segments were shot as if they were part of a real news story. The director would set up the actors, tell them what he wanted, and then basically let them have at it. I'd shoot the scene hand- held a few times from beginning to end, trying to get different angles and points of view that they could edit together into continuous action.

I did everything imaginable including car chases, helicopter rescues, air to air shots, blowing up homes, wrecking cars and everything in between. One of my favorites? Shooting the point of view of an ambulance racing down the road, by sitting on the front of the vehicle and hanging on for dear life. Yes, that is me.

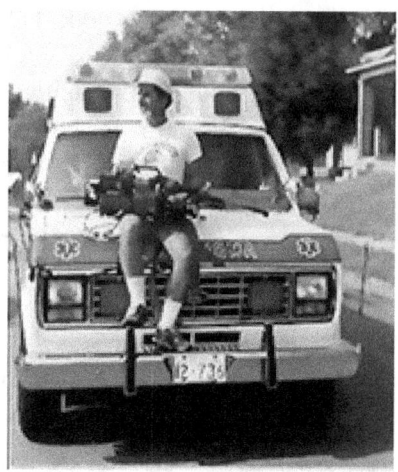

When I finished a day of shooting on *Rescue 911* my brain hurt. My mind was always on overdrive, constantly looking for that great angle that would best visualize the story. *Rescue 911* really defined the term "thinking on your feet".

Looking back on it all I realize that my news background helped me see where the action was flowing and get into position fast. I did a lot of editing in the camera. I was always thinking, establish the action then get the coverage just like I did in my news days. We always shot the scene a few times, which allowed me to take chances and go for creative shots. When it hit, it was magic.

I remember this one shoot about two kids that had been injured in a propane explosion. Because they were children, the director did not want to get too graphic. He was trying to figure out how to shoot the kids immediately after the explosion without getting in their face and freaking the child actors out.

The Art Department had dressed the kitchen to look like an explosion had gone off. There was smoke, over turned furniture, and burned and tattered curtains blowing in the open window. I lit it with HMI's but shot it with the camera balanced for tungsten light. This turned everything blue and after a couple of puffs with a smoke machine, it got real hazy looking. It looked great, but the original problem remained. How can we shoot this dramatic shot without overly exploiting and possibly scaring the kids?

The answer just came to me. I ran outside, set a ladder up by the window, screamed for the director to call action, and shot this amazing footage through the torn curtains of the kids standing in that smoke filled room. It was magic. It was a fantastic image that perfectly told the story of what had just occurred. It was what re-creation were all about.

Then there was the time we were shooting the re-creation of a helicopter rescue in a small town outside of Atlanta, Georgia. In the original story a kid had been hit by a car while riding his bike, or something like that. We had helicopters, police, and firemen all out on location to re-create the story. Then the clouds started rolling in, you know those big black clouds that bring thunder, lightning wind, and torrential rain. It looked like we had at the most half an hour to get it all done before the sky opened up and completely shut down production.

I told the director that I got this, and to his credit, he trusted me. I instructed the rescue people to just go for it like it was real while I went into news mode. I shot it as one continuous shot. I ran around like a maniac covering every element of the rescue. I got wide shots and tight shots. I caught every dramatic moment. I mean everybody was really into it so everywhere I pointed the camera there was stuff going on. In so many ways this was far more realistic and therefore far more dramatic than if we had shot it piece by piece. It allowed all the rescue people, who were not actors but the real deal, to get into a true rescue mode.

The whole thing took less than half an hour to shoot. I remember as the chopper took off in the final shot, big drops of rain started to fall. There were a lot of high fives going around as we shoved our gear into the van to get out of the thunderstorm. Yes, these re-creations were a hybrid of news, reality, and dramatic coverage. They were also a great opportunity for some fantastic image gathering.

My favorite Rescue 911 shoots were the ones that used the real people from the actual event. These were generally low key types of stories with happy endings. I did one like that in Boston. A city gas regulator failed and a sudden rush of gas blue out pilot lights in a neighborhood in South Boston. A couple who had a pet parrot that they had rescued were awakened and saved by this parrot when it reacted to the smell of gas.

We shot a night scene that involved the entire neighborhood dressed in their pajamas running around the streets in the middle of the winter. It was awesome. Again, I relied on my news instincts and covered it all as if it were the real thing. This allowed the entire neighborhood to just go for it.

Looking back on those days and those experiences I cannot even begin to tell you how I did it. Shots would just jump into my head as I was shooting. I would get one, and then somehow know what the next one was, and the one after that. At this point in my career I had been shooting for over twenty years. I had spent a good percentage of that time with a camera on my shoulder getting shots. There were no directors telling me what to do. It was just me and my camera I guess after image gathering for as many years as I did, it just became second nature.

PART VI
Chapter Eight
Re-creations Make a Difference

Re-creations were also a key element of a show called *America Most Wanted* that also premiered during this time period. Hosted by John Walsh, *AMW* was another primetime show that owed its existence to the fact that it could be shot on Betacam primarily in the field at a fraction of the cost of scripted shows and still gather great ratings. It was also the darling of law enforcement. *AMW* was another show that took image gathering into a whole new world.

The unique aspect to *AMW* was the fact that it was not geared toward entertainment, but rather toward the capture of wanted criminals, which turned image gatherers into crime fighters. TV shows had millions of viewers and so by definition, the image of a wanted criminal, broadcast on television, was potentially seen by a huge audience. The hope was always that someone somewhere would recognize a picture, or some other element of the show, and call in that information to the show's hotline. The re-creations were done as a means to detail the heinous nature of the criminals and hopefully inspire the viewers to respond. In fact, *AMW* was very successful and was responsible for the capture of over eleven hundred criminals.

A typical segment of *AMW* consisted of interviews of actual victims or the families and friends of victims, along with investigating officers. Elements of the interviews were then visualized through the use of re-creations. Actors were used to recreate the crimes that were depicted with as much accuracy as possible. The re-creations were shot on location as near as possible to where the crime had occurred.

Shooting for *America's Most Wanted* was very different than any other show you worked on. It never felt like just another day at work. With each segment, you worked closely with law enforcement personnel and were considered a vital part of that team. When a segment you had worked on led to a successful capture, you felt a definite pride that your images had contributed to getting a criminal off the streets. You felt like your work had really made a difference. Your images had made a positive impact.

Recollections
Catching Bad Guys

I worked on *America's Most Wanted* for several years. Among all the many and varied TV shows that I worked on *AMW* was a unique experience. Added to our usual image gatherer's goal of compelling images, was the overriding goal of the show, let's catch bad guys. When I shot for *America's Most Wanted* I always had it in the back of my mind that if there was anything I could contribute that might lead to getting these heinous criminals off of the streets, well I wanted to do it. In other words, I always went the extra mile.

Actually anytime I forgot this fact, I was reminded by the interviews we did with both the victims and the victims' families. Their raw emotions left all of us normally blasé production people burning with rage and determination to get the guy who brought so much pain and misery to these people. It could get very emotional for us witnessing the suffering inflicted on these innocent victims. I would always finish these shoots and immediately call all my family members warning that not to get gas at night, or walk alone anywhere, anytime. There are a lot of bad people in the world that you have to watch out for.

The re-creations were fun to shoot because we had the full cooperation of the police department. We never had any trouble stopping traffic, getting into buildings, and parking our cars at locations. I remember a shoot we did out near Palm Springs, CA. The story was about a serial rapist who in this case had been seen driving a stolen red Cadillac convertible. The police had called the show with hopes that publicity might help find this guy. We came down, did some interviews, and prepared to shoot the re-creation. Our only problem was we could not find a red Cadillac convertible. We searched everywhere and were getting quite desperate when suddenly our luck changed. Sitting in a used car lot across the street from the Police Station was believe it or not, a red Cadillac convertible.

It was amazing. Once we told him what we were doing, the guy who owned the lot was nice enough to let us have it for the day. We shot our re-creation and sure enough someone recognized the car and fingered the bad guy. The police got their man, and a serial rapist was taken off the streets.

We always tried to make the re-creations as real as possible, hoping that one more detail would be the key element that would solicit a vital piece of information and lead to a capture. We had a tiny little budget to work with, which forced us to get quite creative with how we shot the segments. We dug graves in the middle of the night, threw people out of cars, turned our PA's into dead bodies, and interns into crime victims. Everybody was on board to do what needed to be done.

Nothing made me prouder as when a segment I had shot led to a tip to police and an arrest. Afterwards, the police gave us access to a shot of the bad guy as they led them off in handcuffs. The reporter would shout "Did you see yourself on *America's Most Wanted*?" as the criminal glowered at us as they walked by. It gave a tremendous sense of accomplish and strong feeling that our work had made a positive difference in the world.

PART VI
Chapter Nine
The Evolution of Technology

While all these shows were hitting the airwaves, technology was not standing still. Betacam was a great recording format, but the original cameras still had tubes which had all the previously mentioned limitations. Much like the tubed cameras of the three-quarter inch video era these cameras were big and heavy, and with the extra length of the record deck, were a bit unwieldy. Those tubes were also prone to have burn-in and registration issues.

By the late 1980's this was all addressed. Sony got rid of camera tubes and replaced them with solid-state technology. Gone were all the problems of color registration and image burn as the new chip cameras emerged out into the image gatherer's arsenal. They were solid as a rock and better able to withstand the rigors of image gathering. The Betacam decks remained the same. They were built to dock onto the back of the camera head.

During the ensuing years, there were several generations of Sony chip cameras. In time, Sony engineers took the next step with the creation of a "one-piece" camera. Now the camera and deck were one solid piece. In this configuration the camcorder was significantly lighter. It looked like this archival picture below.

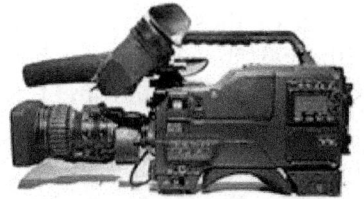

The Sony called the camera the "400". It was a very light and versatile camera that gained immediate popularity. A couple of years later it was followed by the Sony "600" which was a very successful camera model that quickly took over image gathering. These camcorders were lighter, more streamlined, and gave the user access to specific menus that allowed the cameraman to manipulate the image and create a specific look. In fact, it was almost too easy. These menus in the hands of people who did not know what they were doing often led to disasters.

The only downside for the Sony "600" was the fact that since it was a one-piece camera, if anything happened to the deck, the whole thing had to go in for repair, whereas before you could pull the deck off and replace it with a spare. In the end though these cameras were tough as nails. As long as you did your basic maintenance, they were very reliable workhorses.

Recollections
My Camera Buddy

A cameraman's camera is like a soldier's rifle. Over time, it becomes an extension of the body. I have been fortunate, in my career, to own most of the cameras that I shot with, and I got to know them all intimately, and I do mean intimately. There were weeks where I spent more time with my camera than I did my family. Each one was different, but each one became a part of me. I swear the camera knew what I wanted and reacted to situations as if it had they had a mind of their own.

Even though the viewfinder was black and white, I could tell whenever there were any issues with the image. The only thing I didn't like about most of those cameras was their weight. Since it seemed that everything I shot was hand held this issue was a big deal. Even when shooting man on the street, the producer wanted me to dance around as he asked questions. After doing this for an entire day, everything hurt. Then along came the Sony 400.

I have to admit, the first time I saw a Sony 400, I was skeptical. It just didn't look like a real camera. It was small and streamlined looking. Then I picked it up. It weighed about fifteen pounds with a battery on it, but to me it felt like a feather. I'd been hauling around a boat anchor for years, so the weight difference was dramatic, I checked out the picture quality. It was incredible. I was sold.

I could shoot hand-held all day without the back and shoulder pains I always got with the heavier camera. It was kind of like going from driving your Mom's old Buick, to getting behind the wheel of a Corvette. Even shooting those long and arduous red carpet event, where I had to have a camera on my shoulder for hours at a time, was no problem at all for that 400.

That Sony 400 was my buddy for several years. It's lightness and versatility gave me so many more options for shooting. I could swing it up high and shoot down, or hold it low and cruise along inches from the ground. We had many adventures and I never had any major camera issues. In the end the camera never died. Instead, technology pushed it out of the way. It was a sad day indeed when I had to put my buddy down and move on to the next greatest thing. It was like the day when you have to take your old dog to the vet to be put to sleep.

Oh well, technology marches on.

PART VI
Chapter Ten
Shooting Real Life

As the year 2000 rolled around, the Reality Show was king. They came in all colors and shapes. There were human interaction shows like *Survivor,* competition shows like *The Amazing Race,* romance shows like *The Bachelor* and on and on. Images abounded of crying women, cheating husbands, and dysfunctional families. Everything imaginable was fair game. In fact, the more outrageous the images, the better.

Reality shows also took image gathering into the arena of remote cameras with shows like *Big Brother.* Sitting in control rooms and working robotic cameras with joysticks, this new type of cameraman could remotely follow the action of people interacting in the pressure cooker of a real living situation. It was still image gathering albeit once removed.

The "real" aspect of reality was especially powerful on the viewers. Movies and TV Shows could be very exciting, but everyone knew they were only stories with actors. News images were real, but generally gathered after the fact. They could be compelling, but they usually were not live.

Reality TV introduced the idea that you were watching real people screw up in an unscripted setting. You were a witness to a slice of life that was really happening. This fascinated the public much like viewing carnage on the highway after a horrible traffic accident. People viewed these reality type shows the same way. They'd spend hours the next day talking with their friends over what they had witnessed on TV, like they couldn't believe that so and so did such and such. It was yet another testimony to the power of gathered images a power that is magnified significantly when it is watched in what appears to be real time.

Image gathering for these types of shows consisted of bulk recording of everything that moved. It was usually not very creative, but nevertheless, for the image gatherers it offered a different set of challenges. The first challenge was sheer endurance. Shooting Reality TV required a camera equipped with wireless audio receivers and wireless video transmitters strapped on. This added a significant amount of weight to the rig. Oh and by the way, you had all that on your shoulder for hours and hours without a break. The second challenge was subtler. It was learning to be invisible.

Recollections
Shooting Real, Real Life

Generally speaking, reality shoots are multi camera affairs, so we are taught to stay in our zone, and try and stay out of each other's shots. This discipline is important. Without it the shoot just falls into chaos. A good reality show cameraman also is someone that keeps his shot steady and rolls constantly. The producers and editors add the effects later. We just provide the bulk images. Finally, it is imperative that we do not interact with the guests. We are not there to make friends with these people, just shoot what they are doing.

One of the strangest things I discovered shooting reality is that the people we are shooting actually forget that their words and actions are being recorded and that the camera crews in the room are really there. It has to be either that or they just don't care. I would be standing next to someone with a camera on my shoulder, my eye to the eyepiece, the red record light on, a sound guy holding a boom up in the air and the people acted as if we were invisible. They really got into it and just lost themselves in the moment. I'm talking screaming, crying, and once in a while getting physical. I once saw a ten-year old boy haul off and slap his mother in the face while the cameras were rolling. I'm telling you they had completely forgotten that we were there.

Of course, the worse it was the more the producers loved it and encouraged it. I remember the time a cheating wife broke down in tears telling the world that she was a whore, while the control room went crazy with joy at her on air confession. I mean, producers lived for that kind of stuff. They called it "good TV" when people bared it all and went crazy. Good or not, I was just there to record the images.

For the image gatherers, the reality world was not and will never be a creative world. Shooting it has evolved into more of an endurance contest than anything else. The lighting is generally flat. The cameras, with their wide-angle lenses, just need to be able to move anywhere in the room and have enough light to shoot, so the lighting is not shaped or sculpted. It is just ambient. It is still possible to find little gems of shots, but there is always the sense of hurry up, hurry up, then it's on to the next set up.

A great reality show is not necessarily one that looks great, but rather one that has outrageous content. There is even a documented moment where dog poop on the rug propelled a show into the stratosphere. The producers like it gritty. They call it organic. They could care less if the shots are dark or grainy. If someone ran off the set in a fit of anger, we were told to chase after them regardless of the fact that we were off the set and the lighting was bad. A good reality TV shot is not a beautifully composed image, but one where someone displays raw emotion to the world. The reality of Reality TV is that the producers are not looking for any kind of creative shooting. Zoom in when they cry, but stay wide and keep your eyes open for the insane.

Finally, to shoot reality shows you also have to have a humanity filter. You have to be able to insulate yourself from all the craziness that surrounds you. I'm talking people craziness. I often found myself in some very uncomfortable situations. I mean we're talking couples in relationship crisis, drug addicted teens, alcoholics, you name it I did it. It was always tough to stand there and witness those emotionally charged moments. I often felt like an intruder, but whatever, the people agreed to do it, and I was paid to shoot it.

My natural inclination was to want to be helpful, to reach out to these people, but that's not what I was there for. I was there to collect the footage that the show would use to tell their story. Ultimately I hoped that the work I did would in some way be seen by someone else in crisis and would convince them to go get the help they needed. At least I hoped that that was the case. I worked for several years on the *Dr. Phil* show where psychological therapy and support was the main goal. Because of that the number one rule was not to engage with the guests. We were not the psychological experts he was. Our job was, yup, gather the images for the show.

In the end I was the image gatherer. I handed off the tapes at the end of the day and moved on to the next job.

PART VI
Chapter Eleven
Mini Cameras

Incredible technological advancements also created a generation of tiny little cameras that could be mounted and hidden in cars, eyeglasses, baseball caps, really anywhere. They took the concept of hidden cameras to a new level. Whereas shows like *Candid Camera*, hid camera crews in specially designed props and sets, now the cameras were small enough that they could be placed wherever you needed them.

They had names like lipstick cameras, bullet cameras, or mini chip cameras, but whatever you called them, directors loved them. They began figuring out ways to incorporate these camera angles into their shows. They really opened up shots that had previously been impossible and they soon spread from being just for hidden camera shots to being considered as an extra camera for a multi camera shoot.

In addition to all this, advanced surveillance cameras original introduced by a company called Pelco, were adapted for production work. Pelcos sat in clear plastic bubbles, mounted on a remote head. These cameras were remotely operated from a control panel. They could pan, tilt, and zoom.

Needless to say, as has always been the case with new technology, an entire genre of shows was developed that took advantage of these ground breaking capabilities. Among the many was a very bright, innovative man who saw a very interesting possibility and ran with it.

Recollections
The World Poker Tour

In 2002 a TV producer named Steve Lipscomb created a show he called the *World Poker Tour*. His concept was to shoot big poker games in casinos all over the world kind of creating a PGA like season for poker players. There would be preliminary rounds until a final table was reached. This finale would be extensively covered with multiple cameras; hand held, on a jib, and on remote controlled gear heads, plus two commentator poker expert hosts to call the action.

I can still remember sitting at the very first production meeting as Steve explained how the show was going to work. I'm thinking, who wants to watch people playing cards. Steve was right though. The key to it all though was that the TV viewer would know what was in each player's hand via a mini chip camera mounted in the table. The players would also be aware that there was a "card" camera, as Steve called it, and they would be told to periodically lift their hole cards and reveal them to the camera. This way the television audience knew who had what and they could sit back and watch the players bet and bluff according to what they held. It was simple and it was brilliant.

The TV audience loved this and the show became a huge hit. It was mesmerizing to watch the images of poker pros betting and bluffing. The mini camera technology allowed the viewer to follow the cerebral action of the poker game. They knew when a player was bluffing or not, and it made a huge difference. Without it, you would have just been watching some people playing cards. With it though, you had an exciting TV show. You could see the strategy and follow the drama. You'd know in an instant when a bluff got called and see both the exhilaration of the winner and the devastation of the loser. New technology had once again created a new way of gathering images that provided us with a view into yet another new world.

PART VII
Technology's Next Steps

INTRODUCTION

In 1993, Sony introduced Digibeta a higher quality Betacam format. It was designed to replace Beta SP, but it was not a big enough quantum leap for the industry to ditch all their old equipment which by the way included new editing playback and record machines. They just had too much invested, and the improvement was not that dramatic. As we say if it ain't broke don't fix it. However, the emergence of Digibeta resumed technology's march forward.

Digibeta ultimately found a home in higher end TV video production, but the major complaint was that no matter how good it might look, it was not as good as film. 35mm and 16mm film still dominated when you had the money to Then along came hi-def.

Part VII discusses new cameras, new formats and beyond. Remember, once technology made the leap from the manual world of film to the electronic world of videotape, the rules of the game changed. Film stocks might improve but there was only so far you could go with emulsion on plastic. Electronic media did not have any restrictions. It could go as far as research would take it, which essentially is as far as human imagination can travel.

PART VII
Chapter One
Hi-Def

In 2001 Sony introduced the F900, the first field capable hi-def or HD format camera, as seen in this archival photograph. Physically it looked pretty much like all the other cameras, though it was heavier and required higher quality HD lenses. It also still used videotape cassettes, although these were specially formulated HD tape stock.

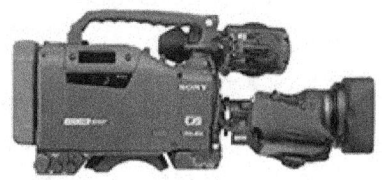

With hi-def came 1080-line video a much sharper and cleaner image than the analogue 480-line video then in use. Hi-def was the first electronic format that approached film in terms of quality of the image. It also brought with it a more filmic aspect ration. Gone was 4:3 in was 16:9 which more closely lined up with cinematic standards.

For the image gatherer this was a significant change. Looking through a viewfinder and framing a 16:9 shot was totally different than 4:3. For the image gatherers it was yet another adjustment that had to be made. They now had to think in wide rectangles. Amazingly, it was a relatively painless adjustment.

Recollections
Oh That 16:9

When the HD cameras came along in theory, it was not a big deal to us camera people. I mean a camera is a camera is a camera, right? I turn it on and shoot. There were lighting issues to deal with, but all that was a fairly simple adjustment. The change of aspect ration presented a bigger challenge. After looking through a viewfinder that was 4:3 for twenty years, suddenly it gets squished and I have this 16:9 image to deal with. I start seeing a whole bunch on the sides and a whole lot less on the top and bottom.

If that wasn't a big enough problem, the TV viewing public did not all run out and buy new wide screen TV monitors. Somehow the old 4:3 screens could squish the image and people were ok with it. So, the producers are screaming at us to be 4:3 safe because there are still people out there with old TV sets. Really? Why is that my problem? Tell them to buy new TV's. I mean it is hard enough to do what we do without having to constantly worry about shooting two formats at the same time.

It's weird though, after a relatively short period of time my brain began to adjust to it. It all became second nature, even the crazy 4:3 safe requirement. Before I was even really aware of it, I was shooting 16:9 like I'd been doing it my whole life. Weird how that works. Our brains adjust to new situations and we move on. Before I knew it, 16:9 was just the natural way to go.

I just wish someone would explain to me how the engineers come up with this stuff?

Part VII
Chapter Two
Non-linear editing

During this same time period, editing also made a quantum leap to a nonlinear format as editing became completely computerized. You never physically touched the field media. It was all ingested into the system via a process called digitizing. This digitized media was what you edited.

Because everything was done on a drive in the computer, the process was non-linear. You still built it shot by shot, but if you needed to make changes you no longer needed to start from the beginning. All you had to do was go to your timeline, and add, subtract or whatever you wanted to add or subtract. It was that easy. You could also add dissolves, wipes and other effects with relative ease just by tapping the right button on your keyboard.

Gone were the tape machines, and the clickety-clackety sound of machines synching up. There were no sounds other than the tick, tick, tick of the editor's fingers on the keyboard. It was eerily quiet in the edit bay, yet there was so much more happening. The editor now had a huge world of possibilities only a finger click away.

The other major advantage of nonlinear editing directly affected the image gatherer's work. As the system became more and more sophisticated, it became easier and easier to manipulate the image. Since all gathered media was now digitized, it could be completely controlled. Color could be added, or changed, grain could be added or removed. Slow motion or fast motion, backwards or forward, you could even flip an image to make an interview subject look the other way. Many mistakes were fixable, and really, anything was possible.

A quick aside here. Another by-product of all this advanced technology was that it moved the image gatherer a few steps further away from the end product. At the beginning of this story everything was hands-on. The image gatherer loaded the film into the camera, shot it by first measuring the light, then assessing the color temperature, and finally rolling the film through the camera. As technology became more and more advanced the image gatherer played less of a role. The term "we can fix it in post" pretty much said it all. Someone still needs to press the roll button, but handcrafting of the picture by the image gatherer became more and more minimized.

Things like color temperature, exposure, and even framing could all be adjusted. Having said all that the someone still needs to shoot and frame the footage, a human still needs to go out and get the image that tells the story. Regardless of technological advances, this will never change.

Anyway, nonlinear editing was pretty amazing for those of us who began their careers sitting at a film edit bay, cutting and hot splicing our footage together. I still remember the first time I saw non-linear editing. Quite honestly, it pretty much blew me away.

Recollections
Editing Video Now and Then

The first time I witnessed nonlinear editing, I could not believe my eyes. I was working on a talk show and was sitting in just to watch as they edited a piece I had shot and suddenly realized that the entire process was controlled by a keyboard. Video was rolled, edit information was entered, and edits were made just by entering data at that keyboard.

The room was eerily quiet save for the sound of his fingers tapping the keys. After all my years of editing video, this was a bit disconcerting to watch. Then he started adding effects with just a tap of a key.

So the editor is ticking away, adding shots, building a piece. You need a slo-mo shot, he dropped that in. Shot too long, he trimmed it. Let's punch up the color on the guy's face, done. Now we need a two second dissolve, done. You want a page turn wipe? No problem, done. Effects that used to require a million-dollar edit bay and hours of rendering were easily accessed and created on this system. When you were done, you hit the play button and there it was.

I flashed back thirty years to the good old days of editing film. I remembered when a dissolve was something you dreamed of in the setting of TV News. I mean, you could set it up by creating an A-roll and a B-roll, but then the best you got from a director on a news show was slam bam thank you ma'am, a dissolve that was so fast if you blinked you'd miss it. He did not have time or patience for artistic stuff like that. Slow motion? You shot that on your Bell & Howell camera by adjusting the film speed in the camera. Color correction? Nope, you got what you got. Now, with non linear editing all these things were possible with the tap of a key. It was amazing.

I remember reflecting at that moment just how far we had come from the time I began my career in 1973 to this point about thirty years later. I also knew that we weren't done yet. A bridge had been built between images and computers. Images were nothing more than digital information that a computer looked at and created an image accordingly. If you wanted to change that image, all you had to do was change that code. Times had changed. It really wasn't photography, "drawn by the light", anymore, it was drawn by a machine.

Sure enough, a shot came up that the producer thought was a little dark. A click later it was fine, another shot was a bit too red, a click later it was fine. A sound bite where they wanted the guy facing the other directions, a click later it was fine. Everything was suddenly possible. I was both thrilled and depressed. It was great to have that much control, but I hated to see the image gatherer move another step further away.

Part VII
Chapter Three
Even More Tech

Technology kept moving forward. HD cameras recorded on tape, which still had issues. The biggest of those was the digitizing process. Tape could only be ingested into the edit system in real time. The tape could not go any faster. A thirty- minute tape took thirty minutes to digitize. It kind of harkened back to waiting around for your film to be processed. Not to worry though, new formats and systems were soon developed that recorded on hard drives, memory cards, or discs that could quickly be ingested into edit systems.

The cameras also got really quiet. A camera recording on a memory card has no moving parts. You turned them on, inserted the disk or card and started shooting. Image gathering was image gathering regardless of the way the images were recorded, but for old timers, it was a bit disconcerting not to hear the old familiar sound of film or tape moving through the camera.

Recollections
Camera Evolution

When I started as an image gatherer in 1973 we shot on film. When I was shooting the camera was right next to my ear. I got used to the sound of film rolling through the gate. It had such a familiar sound that I knew instantly if there was a problem because the sound changed, so I depended on my listening skills. Video cameras provided the same type of comfort, especially the camcorder. Tape had its own sound as it moved around the record head going from one reel to the next in the plastic tape cassette. Again it was a familiar sound that told me all was well.

Then the hard drive cameras and the memory card cameras came along. These cameras were silent. They made no sounds and I had no idea they were even rolling other than a red light flashing and time code numbers spinning. There was no sound confirming that I was recording and let me tell you, when I spend an entire day on a project I sure as hell don't want to get to the end of the day and find out there was a problem.

The other scary part was generally, when I shot on memory cards, once they were filled they were handed them off to someone to be transferred to a hard drive. The card was then erased and given back to me to shoot on again. Now that was really scary. I hoped and prayed that the guy doing this task knew his stuff. Every once in a while there was an oops and it would get really ugly really fast. Two hours of work could disappear in an instant.

On the other hand, there were obvious advantages. The cards were tiny and easily transported. As long as they were backed up on a hard drive, they could be reformatted and used again. They were easily and quickly uploaded for editing. Well the list goes on and on. As with any new technology, needs were met and improvements in the process were made while we adjusted. I was now thirty plus years into the process. For me it was all revolutionary technology. For the newbies, it was just the way it was. No big deal to them.

In the end though, as I have said many times. Image gathering is image gathering. Give me a camera and I can shoot a story regardless of the recording format.

PART VII
Chapter Four
YouTube, iPhones, and Beyond

Camera technology was not the only thing taking a quantum leap forward. The whole ball of wax was about to change. It all started on April 23 2005. A video was posted on a website called YouTube, entitled ME AT THE ZOO. It seemed a minor event at the time, but as things turned out, it ended up creating a revolution in image gathering. Even the growth of TV pales in comparison. The world loved YouTube. Within a few years, millions of videos had been posted, a figure that is now in the billions or even trillions. In addition, literally anybody can post so the number of image gatherers has also exploded.

Right on the heels of YouTube came the introduction of Apple's iPhone. Somebody at Apple decided to include a movie/photo function to these new phones, and added the capability to email or text the videos/photos. As a result, today, everywhere you go you see people holding up their phones, taking movies and stills of each other or themselves then emailing, texting, or uploading these images on Facebook for their friends and families to see. Apple even figured out a way for people to take photos and videos of themselves, as "selfies" were born.

Everybody with a smart phone has become an image gatherer. Go to any kids dance recital and you'll see moms and dads jockeying for position with their phones held high as they record the performance. The second the show ends, they quickly post the golden moments on Facebook for all of their 'friends" to see.

With all these advances in image gathering and distribution, image gathering has become a universal phenomenon. There are even live sites like Skype and Facetime that can visually connect people to one another live from anywhere in the world to anywhere in the world. This is used by grandparents to talk to their grandkids as well as protestors who are marching down the street trying to overthrow a third world dictatorship. Nothing can stop these new image gatherers who have attained an all-powerful role in society. The phrase "the whole world is watching" has never been truer. More than ever before, communication is all about the images.

The journey of image gathering has been incredible. From the camera obscura and pictures drawn by the sun, to electronic images shared around the world on social media sites, well, it has been nothing short of incredible. Driven by an innate need in mankind to leave a permanent record of our life and times, we have taken image gathering to heights never imagined even a few years ago and there is no end in sight. Whereas our ancient ancestors left their images on cave walls, we are now leaving ours splattered all over this thing called the internet for all the world to see. Everyday it seems there is a new device, a new way of doing things that kicks image gathering into yet a new frontier.

Recollections
Final Thoughts

This is where the image gathering history of my generation ends. Our story has been told. The next chapter will be written by a new generation of image gatherers. Their story will be great, to be sure, but there will never be another period like we have just seen where technology went from writing with the sun to the digital age.

My generation of image gatherers is passing the baton to the next generation. Who knows where they will take it? We can only imagine the technological tools they will have at their disposal. This is both exciting and frightening because with all these tools comes a scary possibility.

The new digital world has brought with it the ever increasing capability to manipulate gathered images. They can be altered with such ease that there is a terrible temptation to cheat. With the right tools, color and composition can be easily changed to the point that the original image is not even recognizable. So then, what are we left with? When we look at a great image today the first question we ask is, "Is it real?"

The challenge of true image gathering is to gather real life images that tell the story, not manipulate images to make them fit your story. There is virtually no way to tell the difference, so it is our responsibility to stay true. Remembering the words of Matthew Brady who wanted photography to be a "great and truthful medium of history", I can only hope that in spite of all the technological breakthroughs, the image gatherers will be able resist temptation and hang onto the truth, honesty and integrity in their images.

www.ingramcontent.com/pod-product-compliance
Lightning Source LLC
Chambersburg PA
CBHW070225190526
45169CB00001B/82